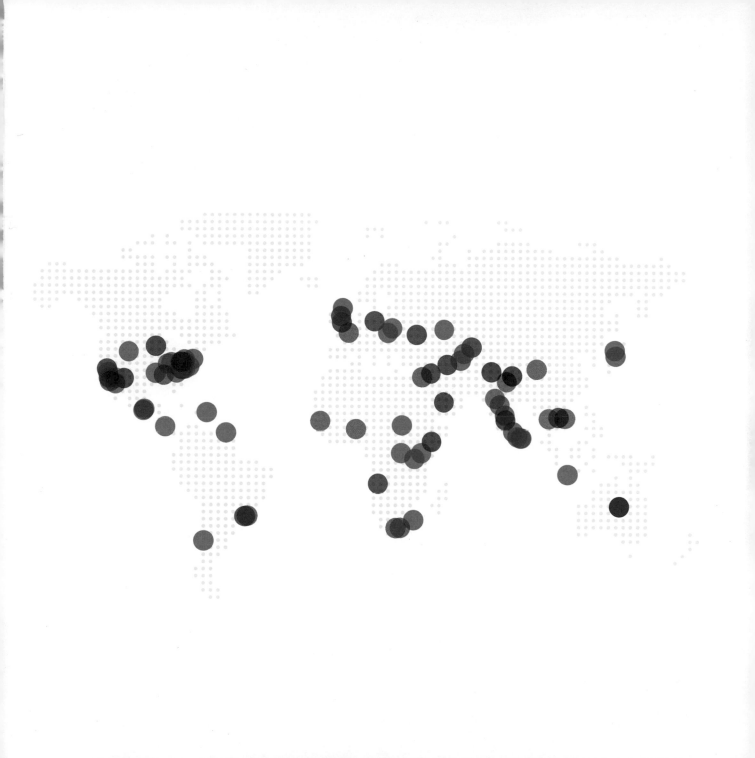

Design Like You Give a Damn

Architectural Responses to Humanitarian Crises

Edited by
Architecture for Humanity

Thames & Hudson

We would like to thank all the architects and designers who, through the power of their creativity, help communities around the world embrace change. This book is dedicated to them.

Acknowledgments

Cameron Sinclair and Kate Stohr

We wish to offer our sincere and heartfelt thanks to all those who graciously contributed to this book. In particular we would like to thank the Graham Foundation and the Lef Foundation for their support, without which this publication would not have been possible.

We apologize for any errors we may have made, whether errors of omission, commission, or, in some cases, conversion of measurements or currencies. They were unintentional. Likewise, we apologize if we have neglected to give credit where credit is due. We have done our best to provide accurate attributions for each project based on the information made available to us. We have also made every attempt to identify accurately the sources and authors of all renderings, sketches, and photographs.

This book was truly a collaborative effort. Many dedicated people lent their time and talents toward making it happen. We would especially like to thank Jason Andersen; Fumihito Ando; Peter Andrews; Paola Antonelli; Allison Arieff; Frith Banbury; Cynthia Barton; Rick Bauer; Rick Bell; Bryan Bell; Robert Bell; Erin Bennett; Paul Berger; Peter Bernstein; Barbara Bloemink; Bryan Burkhart; John Cary; Jonathan Cohen-Litant; Laura Cole; Mary Comerio; Nicholas S. Constantakis; Melanie Cornwall; Nathaniel Corum; Nathan Crane; Ian Davis; Marina Drummer; Tom Dutton; Nevil Eastwood; Shaffiq Essajee; Kathryn Frankel; Ray Gastil; Ric Grefe; Doug Halsey; Rodney Harber; Graham Hill and TreeHugger; Rick Hill; Rebekah Hodgson; Robin Huffman; Timothy Hursley; Satu Jackson; Anne Kellner; Richard Koshalek; Mark Lamster; The Leaf and Bean; Jennifer Lester; Kevin Lippert; Chris Livingston; Hana Loftus; Mike Lorefice; Peter Lynch; Laurie Matthews; Purnima McCutcheon; Steven Meier; Matt Miller; Makoto Mitsumori; Toshiko Mori; Falcon Murty; Robert Neuwirth; Kreg "SuperKreg" Norgaard; Deniz Orhun; Daniel O'Toole; Chee Pearlman; Paul Petrunia and archinect.com; Susi Jane Platt; Michael Rios; Gregory Alan Rutchik; Dave Schiff; Charles Setchell; Samir Shah; Allegra Fuller Snyder and the Buckminster Fuller Institute; Michael Sorkin; Alex Steffen and all the Worldchanging.com writers; Marcia Stohr; Ted Stohr; Susan Surface; Annalyn Swan; Ambassador Richard N. Swett; Susan S. Szenasy; Paul Thompson; Denise Tomasini; Matthew Trumbull; Melissa Vaughn; Raluca Winter; Asia Wright; Nicole Zaray; the faculty and students of Montana State University School of Architecture; Metropolis Books, D.A.P./Distributed Art Publishers, Inc., Pure+Applied, Thames & Hudson, and Beth Orser for working tirelessly under pressure to help us live up to the title of this book...and many others who contributed in thought, spirit, or deed.

Our aim has been to incorporate a broad array of projects from a wide range of regions, but there are many equally deserving projects we did not have room to include, and there are no doubt hundreds more that we have yet to discover. We invite you to tell us about them.

Tree of Life
Basak Altan, Mark Schirmer
Oakland, Calif., USA
Transitional Housing finalist

I hope it's a long list...

Cameron Sinclair

On September 14, 2001, the Architecture for Humanity office phone rang.

I should explain that the "office phone" was actually a cell phone I answered while working as an architectural designer at the firm Gensler in New York City. (A small corner of my cubicle that housed my personal laptop was our "daytime headquarters.") I happened to be working on the relocation of Lehman Brothers after the terrorist attacks on the World Trade Center just a few days before. My colleagues and I were going flat out to help our corporate clients get back on their feet; many of us had watched the towers come down and were committed to doing anything we could.

The woman on the phone said she was calling on behalf of the United Nations High Commissioner for Refugees (UNHCR). She informed me that Architecture for Humanity was on a list of organizations that might be able to help with refugee housing issues if America decided to launch a counterattack against suspected terrorist cells in Afghanistan. I laughed nervously and replied, "I hope it's a long list." Incredibly, the answer was a brief and somber no. It was at that moment I realized that people outside the design profession had developed an interest in our humble undertaking.

Architecture for Humanity is a charitable organization that Kate Stohr, a freelance journalist and documentary producer, and I founded in 1999 to seek architectural solutions to humanitarian crises and bring design services to communities in need. Through competitions, workshops, educational forums, partnerships with aid organizations, and other activities, we have sought to create opportunities for architects and designers from around the world to respond to crises. But at the time of the World Trade Center attack, we had yet to build a single structure. So why would a UN agency reach out to us?

We'd like to think it was because we had already become a voice for humanitarian design—an unexpected touchstone in the movement for socially conscious architecture. The sad truth is that until 1999, when our fledgling organization got started along with a handful of others, there was no easily identifiable design resource for shelter after disaster, and aid groups were often left scrambling for help. Engineers had RedR, an organization now more than 25

years old that connects their profession with frontline humanitarian agencies, but where could agencies and community groups turn when they needed design services? The United States had always had a strong community design movement, but there was no international body engaged in reconstruction and development—for reasons we'd all too soon discover.

Architecture for Humanity began in response to the conflict in Kosovo. I had moved from London to New York and was working at a small design firm as an associate designer, the fancy title for a computer-aided designer, better known inside the profession as a CAD monkey. The firm I worked for was developing international retail stores for American fashion and fragrance firms. After my twentieth project in as many countries, I found myself designing lipstick dispensers for a store in a place where the average weekly salary was equal to the cost of a single lipstick. This experience highlighted the ways in which globalization benefited our profession, enabling designers to work almost anywhere in the world. The real question was whether we now also had an obligation to respond to some of the social concerns in areas where we worked. During informal discussions in the office about the role of the architect, I found myself a lone voice. I also found myself changing firms.

I moved to Lauster & Radu Architects, which turned out to be an incredibly supportive environment. They had an international focus and had taken on a number of socially conscious projects. I was extremely fortunate to work on the restoration of Constantin

Architecture for Humanity Office__1999-2002
[Office Cubicle] New York, NY

Average number of volunteers____1
Maximum number of volunteers___2
Area_____4 sq. ft.
Distance to nearest coffee_____50 ft
Average # coffees per day_____3
Average workday_____10 hours

Useable Workspace

Brancusi's sculptural complex in Tirgu Jiu, Romania, as well as a subsequent 30-year revitalization plan for the town. In New York the firm was working on a number of projects for unions, including a health facility for garment workers of the Union of Needletrades, Industrial and Textile Employees (UNITE). For the first time in my career I also found a mentor in one of the partners: Charles "Chuck" Lauster, whose practice of architecture was as much about ethics as aesthetics.

At about this time I happened to see a film by Dan Reed called *The Valley*, which depicted the ethnic Albanian uprising in Kosovo during the fall of 1998. In villages divided along ethnic lines, Serbs and ethnic Albanians were systematically destroying each other's homes. Over time Serb forces adopted a scorched-earth approach. It became apparent that not only families but also the history of a people was being eradicated. Soon after, the international community intervened to end the conflict. But even as aid organizations focused on the plight of refugees fleeing the country, a second disaster awaited Kosovo's residents when they returned. With their homes in ruins and the region's infrastructure collapsed, these displaced families would need immediate and highly dispersed temporary housing. When I suggested responding to Kosovo's potential housing crisis, Chuck supported the idea and even got involved.

I began researching refugee issues. As the United Nations headquarters was in New York, I phoned them up. To my surprise this led to an invitation to meet with representatives of the UNHCR. Who knew it was that easy! At the meeting Chuck and I were surprised by the UNCHR representatives' positive response. However, they noted that the UNHCR only dealt with refugees located outside their sovereign countries and not people who were internally displaced or returning to damaged or destroyed homes. They suggested we contact a number of nongovernmental organizations (NGOs) that were already working on the Kosovo border and would probably be responding inside the province once the conflict ended. I started making calls and eventually spoke with Heather Harding LaGarde of War Child USA.

She connected us with a number of relief workers in the field, as well as refugees living in some of the camps. It soon became clear that what was needed was not temporary shelter but some sort of medium-term or transitional structure that returning Kosovars could live in while they rebuilt their homes. These conversations left us with a clearer understanding of the needs of those on the ground—and a sense that we were out of our depth.

A phone call with Bob Ivy, the editor-in-chief of *Architectural Record*, brought this point home. Bob, playing devil's advocate, questioned whether one design team (based in New York with little experience in refugee resettlement) could actually make a difference. Maybe one design team couldn't make a difference, I thought, but what if hundreds of architects and designers got involved?

After talking with Bob, we rethought our approach and instead of working on a solution ourselves decided to launch a competition to design transitional housing for the returning refugees. We hoped the competition, which we planned to host online due to our limited budget (i.e., we had no money), would raise awareness and funds for War Child's work. Heather, Chuck, and I rushed to research the problem and create useful criteria, often relying on the help and ideas of complete strangers in far-flung parts of the globe, many of them camped in refugee tents in Montenegro and Albania. We also somehow talked Ray Gastil into lending us gallery space to host the jury and an exhibition. At the time Ray was the executive director of the Van Alen Institute in New York, a nonprofit dedicated to improving design in the public realm.

What happened next was a blur. One day Chuck and I were talking about the impending housing crisis in Kosovo; a few weeks later we were sitting with Heather and Bianca Jagger at the Van Alen Institute about to launch an international design competition in front of a room full of press, having designed the poster for the competition only two hours before. And less than two months later we were sitting in our office surrounded by competition entry boards.

More than 220 design teams from 30 countries responded to our call for entries. Their schemes ranged from the pragmatic to the provocative. Designers proposed structures made from everything from rubble to inflatable hemp (see "Rubble House" and "Low-Tech Balloon System"). Unfortunately, the competition also provoked a negative response. During the entry period we received a number of death threats. One in particular mentioned that we might receive a package from Yugoslavia and that opening it might cause the recipient to lose a few limbs.

A week later a package arrived from Belgrade. (I suggested to Chuck that he open it.)

To our great relief and surprise it turned out to be an entry from three young Serb designers, Katarina Mrkonjic, Uros Radosavljevic, and Dmitrovic Zoran. Inside was a letter stating, "It is not us but our leaders who are doing this. We are not at war with these people, we want to help." We later learned that the team was working on the project at night and volunteering during the day for Otpur, the student-led organization that would later play a key role in overthrowing the Serb president Slobodan Milosevic. The competition had crossed geographical boundaries—and political ones, too.

From the entries the jury selected 10 finalists and 20 honorable mentions to be highlighted in the exhibition. After a successful run at the Van Alen, the show traveled to London and Paris; three of the entries were selected for the 2000 Venice Biennale.

The project, including the exhibition, cost us less than $700 to host. But by charging a small entry fee, we raised more than $5,000. Interest generated by the exhibition and an appeal in the UK's *Guardian* newspaper helped raise another $100,000. Buoyed by the fact that we had not only several feasible designs but also funding, we tried to negotiate building a number of housing units in Kosovo.

It would be our first confrontation with the brutal realities of providing international aid. In order to get building materials through customs, secure a site, get work permits, and facilitate other aspects of a housing program, we needed approval from the interim Kosovo government. However, the interim government, which was seeking aid from the international community, wanted 20,000 homes or none at all. We could build fewer than a dozen. War Child negotiated with local officials to no avail; the project ground to a halt. Short of building the structures in Albania and smuggling them across the border by helicopter—a possibility we briefly considered—we could find no way to get the shelters to those who needed them. In the end War Child used the funds to provide immediate aid to the returning refugees and later to rebuild schools and medical facilities.

We learned a lot during the project. First and foremost, we realized that I wasn't the only disillusioned CAD monkey and that architects and designers really did want to make a difference. Second, it became clear that creating partnerships was essential to implementing a project, as was on-the-ground support for negotiating red tape. We needed more than a great idea to get something built. Most important, we learned that if we wanted to get anything done, we'd not only have to raise funds but also retain control of them.

This is not to say that the competition ended in ideas only. Many designers who entered pursued their projects further on their own initiative and built functioning transitional housing prototypes. Deborah Gans and Matt Jelacic were awarded $100,000 from the Johnnie Walker "Keep Walking" Fund to develop their design (see "Extreme Housing"); a prototype by Sean Godsell was exhibited at the Cooper Hewitt National Design Museum; and Shigeru Ban, who had first designed his Paper Log House to respond to an earthquake in his native Japan, used the improved design he entered into our competition to respond to an earthquake in Turkey in 1999 (see "Paper Log Houses").

In the middle of the Kosovo competition Kate and I got married, and while Tod Williams and Steven Holl were duking it out on the jury, we were in South Africa. Within three days, however, our honeymoon was over. Suddenly we were sitting outside a BP gas station using the pay phone to organize interviews and site visits. Kate had started reporting a story on violence against women in South Africa, which at the time was home to the highest incidence of rape in the world. I had connected with a number of organizations to look at the severe housing needs in the country. Over the course of the next few weeks we darted between settlements, hospitals, rape crisis centers, and new housing projects. Our assumption was that access to clean water and adequate housing would be the residents' highest priority; in fact, their biggest concern was health care and

Architecture for Humanity Transitional Housing competition jury members (left to right): Architect Billie Tsien, Heather Harding LaGarde of War Child USA, architect Tod Williams, Herb Sturz of the Open Society Institute, architect Steven Holl, and, in the foreground, Elise Storck of USAID
Heather Harding LaGarde/War Child USA

the widening AIDS pandemic. Though we didn't know it yet, we had found our next project.

It was apparent that the lack of a widely distributed health system was trapping these communities in poverty. Residents in Kliptown, for example, described how when one family member was ill, another had to stay behind to look after her. In some instances that meant that now two wage earners were not working. In many cases children had to leave school and get a job to put food on the table. One resident, frustrated with the response from the West, said, "We need real care, not awareness. When one sees one's friends and families suffering each day, one is aware of the problem. We don't need pop stars giving concerts, we need doctors giving treatment." Kate and I had one of those "eureka moments"—instead of expecting patients to walk 10 to 15 miles to see a doctor, why not bring doctors to them instead? This was the idea that inspired OUTREACH: Design Ideas for Mobile Health Clinics to Combat HIV/AIDS in Sub-Saharan Africa (2001–3).

It would be a couple of years before we would actually launch the competition. After the bittersweet end to our Kosovo experience,

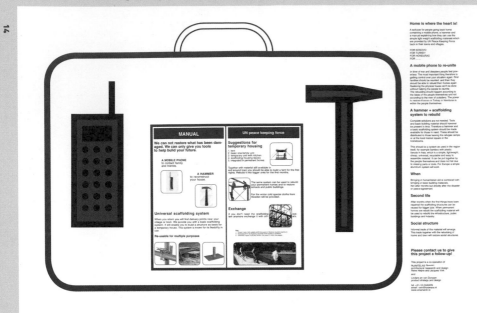

Transitional Housing
Ruimetalab and Linders en van Dorssen
René Heijne and Jacques Vink with Linders en van Dorssen
Rotterdam, the Netherlands
Finalist

Low-Tech Balloon System
TechnoCraft
Masahru Suzuki, Ichiro Katase, Takeshi Chiba, Takashi Kawano, Makoto Tsuchida with Masaharu Suzuki
Tokyo, Japan
Finalist

Extreme Housing
Gans and Jelacic
Deborah Gans, Matt Jelacic
New York, NY, USA
Finalist

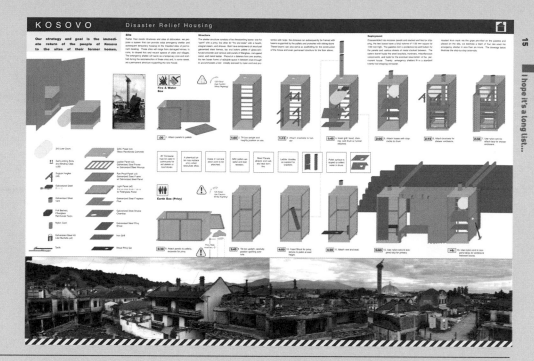

Transitional Housing
Keenen/Riley
John Keenen, Steven Chang,
Jan Greben, Nathan McRae
New York, NY, USA
Honorable mention

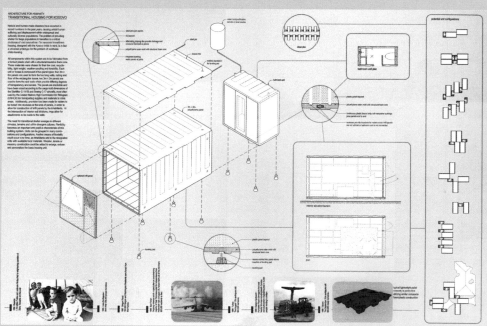

we realized that before taking on a new project we first needed to establish a nonprofit entity. Meanwhile we also needed to earn some money. As neither Kate nor I received a salary, we relied on our day jobs to pay our bills. By now I was working for Gensler and Kate was freelancing. (Many people, especially writers, are amazed to learn that Architecture for Humanity has been partly funded by freelance journalism.) Neither job left much time for extracurricular activities. Still, we managed to enlist the pro bono services of Steve Meier, a lawyer with Morrison and Foerster, who helped us incorporate Architecture for Humanity and apply for 501(c)(3) status. But it took almost two years to get a final determination letter from the Internal Revenue Service.

In the meantime I read a report by Rodney Harber, a South Africa-based architect, who in 1996 wrote the first AIDS brief for architects, highlighting how design could help those affected. It rekindled our idea for the OUTREACH project, and we began researching the issues surrounding mobile health care. Rodney joined the project's advisory board, and we started to enlist the support of dozens of others working in the field of HIV/AIDS awareness and prevention, a number of whom also joined the advisory board.

By late 2001, with the help of the advisory board and this extended network of medical professionals, we had developed criteria for creating dignified and effective mobile care, including ease of deployment and maintenance by a small team of medical professionals, community acceptance, and cost. We were gearing up to launch the project when the World Trade Center was attacked.

When the UNHCR called just a few days later, I felt conflicted: Although we certainly did not have the capacity to take on a project of that scale, it was a great opportunity to get architects and designers involved in a UN initiative. We debated whether to put the Africa project on hold and focus our attention on what seemed to be a more pressing issue. It was an e-mail from one of the doctors in Kenya that made up our minds. He wrote: "You've just experienced a terrible disaster losing 3,000 people in one day; it is truly horrific. Naturally the focus will turn toward bringing those responsible to justice, and projects like ours will be pushed to one side. However, the fact is, Africa loses twice that many people every day to AIDS, and although the loss is not as visible, the pain is just as great."

It seemed obvious that we should let others with more experience respond to the UNHCR call and stay focused on Africa. In the end we simply put out a call to architects in the area interested in working with the United Nations. Although a small gesture, this ability to tap into a network of professionals would become one of the most important functions Architecture for Humanity would perform. Not a month goes by when we don't connect an architect with a nonprofit, government entity, or community group—or vice versa.

In the spring of 2002 we officially launched the Africa competition. Again, we were stunned by the response. During the five-month

call 1,400 designers, medical professionals, and students from over 50 countries responded. A total of 531 designs were submitted, 25 percent more than for the Lower Manhattan Development Corporation's competition for the World Trade Center complex.

Here I should point out that the Architecture for Humanity "office" was now also our one-room, 400-square-foot (37-sq.-m) apartment, dubbed "suite 3A," and we had listed this address on the competition entry form. So on November 1, 2002, all 500-plus entries arrived at our doorstep via three mail trucks, leaving us with little space to work or live in and resulting in one very befuddled building superintendent. Luckily Ray Gastil and the Van Alen Institute came to our rescue again, this time not only providing space in which to store the entries, run the jury, and host an exhibition, but also donating the services of the institute's program director, Jonathan Cohen-Litant, who turned out to be an organizational wunderkind and exhibition miracle worker.

A couple of weeks later an international jury of architects and medical professionals met to go through the entries. The process was rigorous and thorough, with discussions revolving around issues of mobility, storage, security, and community involvement. For example, the jury believed that semiarticulated trucks would not be able to cover the region's difficult terrain, particularly during inclement weather. This brought us to the now-infamous "donkey debate." Many of the jury members shied away from solutions that used animals as a means of transport, but as a number of the Africa-based jurors pointed out, designs dependent on a specific vehicle type could require

above
Competition boards arrive at Architecture for Humanity's "office" on 20th Street in New York.

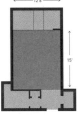

Architecture for Humanity Office__2003-2005 New York, NY

Average number of volunteers	2
Maximum number of volunteers	5
Area	380 sq. ft.
Distance to nearest coffee	150 ft
Average # coffees per day	4
Average workday	14 hours

Useable Workspace

maintenance and spare parts difficult to obtain in many areas. The consensus was that using appropriate technology and a range of transportation modes—even donkeys—offered greater mobility and access. Other significant concerns included adequate and flexible storage; the need to secure equipment and supplies in a lockable space during transport and at night; and creating ownership within the community. Finally, recognizing the diversity of the region in terms of geography and culture, the group favored designs that could be "localized" rather those that were "Africanized." After two days of deliberation the jury selected four finalists and eight notable entries.

Over the course of the jury process we also came across a number of designs that might be considered less than feasible but were, as always, thought-provoking. The giant soccer ball, complete with clinic and strapped-in medical staff, that was to be ejected from a plane into an unsuspecting village completely stumped the jury. Images of bloodied and bruised doctors staggering out of the clinic after it had barreled its way through town came to mind. The other entry that certainly raised eyebrows was the truck with a spherical cab that "extended" on arrival to unveil the clinic in a highly suggestive manner.

Joking aside, a number of the jury members felt that submission boards that incorporated images of Africans afflicted with HIV/AIDS, and in some cases dying of starvation, showed that teams were designing with pity and not pride. The most successful projects were submitted by interdisciplinary teams, which usually included a medical consultant, that approached the issue with dignity and optimism.

The winning designs, along with others that inspired and informed, were exhibited at galleries and museums across the United States and Europe. The show included donkey-powered designs and dirigibles, high-tech and low-tech solutions. One notable entry, by Jeff Alan Gard, was an airship with a fully deployable clinic and detachable motorbikes. Kenya-based juror Reuben Mutiso selected it as a political statement on the inequity of global health care, noting, "If AIDS was at a rate in the United States that it is in Africa, we would not be concerned with cost. We would build these and keep building them until we can put a stop to this pandemic." Numerous projects embraced similar themes: Africa Under Siege proposed a militaristic "pre-emptive strike" approach, whereas the proposal by Soren Barr and Chris French involved converting tanks and military vehicles from Africa's civil wars into clinics. Other designs, some seemingly lighthearted, commented on various other struggles facing the subcontinent. One of our personal favorites was the Kenaf Field Clinic, a grow-your-own-clinic design, which highlighted the important issue of nutrition.

As part of the project we also held a number of workshops for college and high school students to learn about HIV/AIDS and

top **Jury members review competition boards from the OUTREACH competition to design mobile health clinics to combat HIV/AIDS in sub-Saharan Africa.**
Cameron Sinclair/Architecture for Humanity

above **Arup engineers from Botswana and South Africa discuss structural issues of a mobile health clinic with its designers, Heide Schuster and Wilfried Hofmann.**
Cameron Sinclair/Architecture for Humanity

OUTREACH: Design Ideas for Mobile Health Clinics to Combat HIV/AIDS in Sub-Saharan Africa

Mobile Health Clinic
Mikkel Beedholmm, Mads Hansen,
Jan Søndergaard
KHRAS Architects
Virum, Denmark
First-place finalist

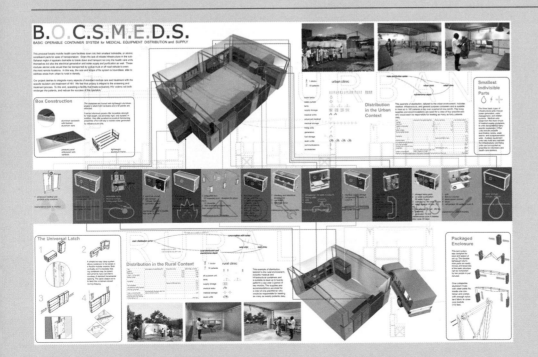

B.O.C.S.M.E.D.S.
Brendan Harnett,
Michelle Myers
Rensselaer Polytechnic Institute
Troy, NY, USA
Second-place finalist

Mobile Intervention
Heide Schuster, Wilfried Hofmann
University of Dortmund
Dortmund, Germany
Third-place finalist

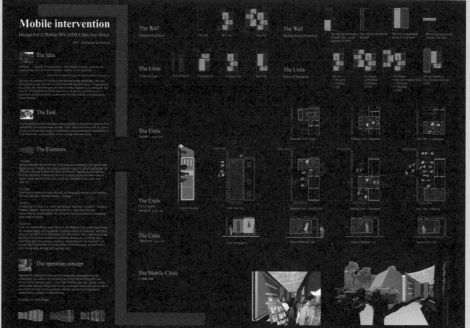

Mobile Health Clinic
Gaston Tolila, Nicholas Gilliland
atelier ⌈gilliland tolila⌉
Paris, France
Founders Award

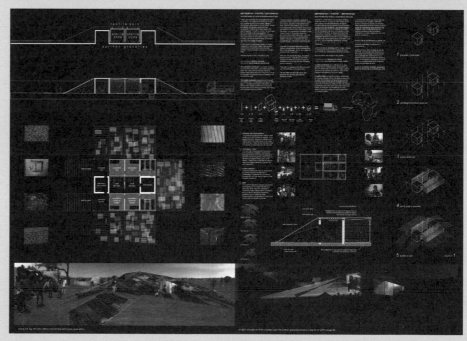

OUTREACH: Design Ideas for Mobile Health Clinics to Combat HIV/AIDS in Sub-Saharan Africa

Africa Under Seige
Craig Coulton, Marcel Botha
London, England, and Cape Town, South Africa

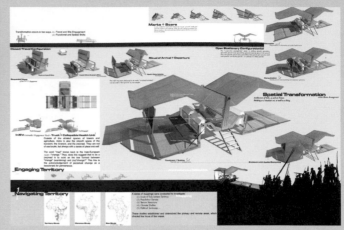

Mobile Health Clinic
Detroit Collaborative Design Center
Dan Pitera, Chris Lee, Christina Heximer, Andrew Sturm
Detroit, Mich., USA

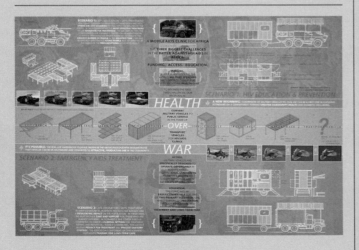
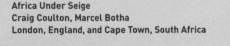

Health Over War
Soren Barr, Chris French
Washington, DC, USA

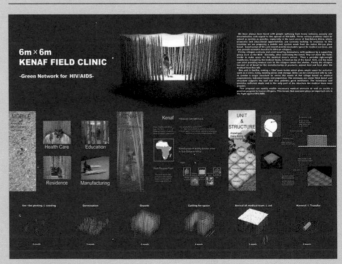

Kenaf Field Clinic
Kyoto University
Hirohide Kobayashi with Takeyuki Okubo, Koichi Shiwaku, Shohei Yokoyama, Ayako Fujieda, Takeyuki Yamada, Yohei Kondo, Toru Fukano
Kyoto, Japan

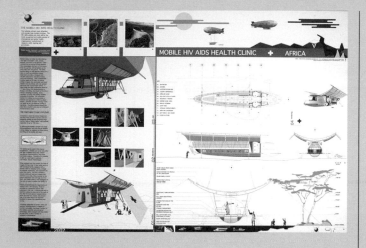

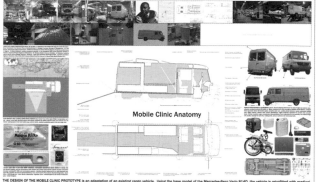

Mobile Health Clinc
JAG Design
Jeff Alan Gard
San Francisco, Calif., USA

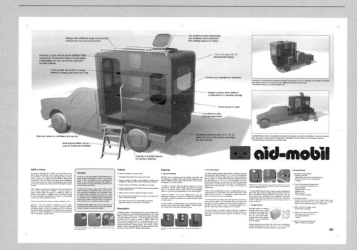

Aid-Mobil
PanicButter
Linus Lam, Denise Lam
Winnipeg, Canada

Mobile Clinic Prototype for Lagos, Nigeria
Pierre Bélanger, MLA; Owens Wiwa, MPH, MD
University of Toronto, Toronto, Canada

Pierre Bélanger, a landscape architect at the University
of Toronto, and Owens Wiwa, a doctor, adapted a
Mercedes-Benz Vario 814D into a mobile health clinic.

top, their entry was selected for exhibition.

above, a prototype of the clinic in production

health care in developing countries. In New York an after-school program organized a group of high schoolers from Harlem to visit the exhibition. (Unfortunately their teacher had written down the address of our "office," not the gallery, and while I was waiting at the Van Alen, Kate found herself with 30 bemused teenagers in our tiny studio, all lining up to use the bathroom after a long subway ride.)

By the end of 2003 the OUTREACH exhibit had been viewed by over 40,000 people and covered in many publications, and it seemed politicians were finally taking the threat of AIDS in Africa seriously. In May 2003 President Bush signed into law a five-year, $15 billion worldwide Emergency Plan for AIDS Relief. A key component called for the development of a layered network of central medical centers that support satellite clinics and mobile units in rural areas. According to the plan these clinics would be staffed by lay technicians, possibly rotating nurses, and local healers, who would be trained in standard clinical evaluation and the distribution of medication. We were taken aback, as the wording mirrored (almost exactly) the criteria we had published on the Web a year earlier. Some have suggested the administration might have been honing its "cut-and-paste" skills during the last rewrite of its plan. Either way, it showed that much of what we had been advocating had broad support and had actually made it into policy.

Yet there was little interest in funding the project. For example, when the *New York Times* ran a two-page story on the project, the writer briefly mentioned that Kate and I had also started something called the Uncoordinated Soccer League, for those among us who are "athletically challenged." The article generated five times as many inquiries about the soccer team as it did offers to support OUTREACH. By the spring of 2004, however, we had raised enough donations, including sponsorship from Virgin Atlantic, to send the top four design teams to Somkhele, South Africa, one of the areas hardest hit by the virus, to participate in a development workshop.

The workshop, cohosted by the Africa Centre for Health and Population Studies, was an opportunity for design teams to collaborate with community members, relief organization representatives, local doctors, engineers, and transportation experts to develop and refine their projects. The teams also visited a range of clinics and clinic types in the area, allowing them to see firsthand the needs of health-care professionals battling the HIV/AIDS pandemic. During the charrette the four teams worked with medical groups and other potential partners. At the end of the two-week trip both the Africa Centre and Dr. Shaffiq Essajee, who directed the AIDS Research and Family Care Clinic in Mombasa, Kenya, and had served on both our advisory board and our jury, expressed interest in partnering with us—if we could find the funding to build a prototype.

When we started pitching the idea to doctors and other health professionals, we had thought that mobile medical care had been around for decades. As it turned out, although the profession had

been discussing it, few programs had been implemented. One of the hard lessons that came out of the project was that even though these designs were contextual and affordable, in some cases costing 80 percent less than a permanent clinic, they could not be implemented without funding to maintain the facility. And while a clinic might cost $30,000 to produce, almost $1.5 million would be needed to run it and provide antiretroviral drugs for the community.

We spent most of 2002 and 2003 applying for grants. At one point we had five people all crammed into the "office," researching and contacting hundreds of foundations. We soon learned that there were very few grants dedicated to building health-care facilities, let alone mobile health-care facilities, and almost no funds dedicated to architecture. More frustrating, the health-oriented foundations that did offer funding for new infrastructure required applications from our medical partners, who were quite rightly too busy with day-to-day operations to take time out to write yet another grant application. At one low point we were turned down for a grant for which we hadn't even applied. We've since focused much of our energy on building a donor base, turning Architecture for Humanity into a fundraising conduit so that architects and community groups looking for funding for community design projects now have a place to turn.

It would be easy to say the project failed for lack of funding, but that wasn't the only reason. We hadn't made the role of the architect—or the commitment required—clear in the development process. Many architects couldn't take time off work to focus on the project. We also hit a snag over intellectual property rights. One of the finalists, Mads Hansen, was caught between a firm that wanted to license his team's idea and *his* desire to implement the project. This situation left the design—and us—in an awkward state of limbo and made it nearly impossible to pursue the project, despite the Africa Centre's enthusiasm for building a prototype of the design.

Nonetheless, the OUTREACH project continues to garner attention. In 2005 we presented the projects at an international conference on mobile health care, where a representative from the National Institutes of Health thanked us for opening their eyes to other ways of delivering mobile care. Moreover, as the cost of antiretroviral drugs has dropped, thanks in part to the Clinton Foundation and countries like Brazil that embraced generic drugs, the concept of mobile care has become even more viable.

Also, as with the Kosovo endeavor, a number of designers pushed forward with developing projects on their own. After the African workshop the team of Nicholas Gilliland and Gaston Tolila formed atelier [gilliland tolila] and built a prototype of their concept to scale for an exhibition at the Pompidou Center in Paris (see "Mobile Health Clinic") and is currently working to design a health center in Tanzania. Pierre Bélanger, who teaches landscape architecture at the University of Toronto and whose design was selected for the exhibition as one of the most pragmatic solutions, teamed

Siyathemba Competition to Design a Soccer "Clinic"

Siyathemba Youth Soccer Pitch
Swee Hong Ng
Pittsburgh, Penn., USA
First-place finalist

Somkhele's Market Square
Tim Denis, David Mathais
Basildon, England
Second-place finalist

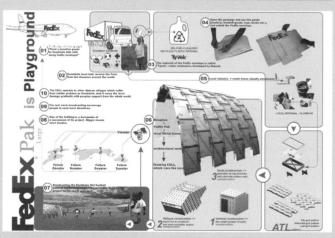

Share the Shelter
Guy Lafranchi, Dietmar Panzenböck
Liebefeld and Bern, Switzerland
Third-place finalist

FedEx Pak Is Playground
Takuya Onishi
REDEK
Bangkok, Thailand
Notable entry

up with Owens Wiwa, a physician from the university's Centre for International Health and a native of Nigeria. Using the university's rapid prototyping lab, Bélanger and Wiwa modified a Mercedes-Benz Vario 814 cargo panel van to create a self-contained, fully operational medical clinic. The clinic is now in use on the A3 highway in southeastern Nigeria. Finally, Geoff Piper, Jamie Fleming, and Matthew Sullivan, a team of former University of Washington students, adapted three motorcycles into mobile medical units for rural areas in Kenya.

Perhaps more important, the project enabled us to develop a relationship with the Africa Centre, which eventually led to our third design competition and a project to develop a soccer club that would double as a health outreach center (see "Siyathemba Soccer 'Clinic'").

As support for Architecture for Humanity grew, we received more and more requests from people and groups wanting to volunteer or get involved in their own communities. Beginning in late 2003 "AFH chapters" began sprouting up around the world, whether we were ready or not. By 2004 hundreds of people were meeting once a month in bars or restaurants to discuss ways of giving back to the community. In New York City, home of the largest local group, designers are providing free services for the rehabilitation and greening of ABC No Rio, a community space in the East Village; a women's shelter redesign; and targeted improvements for The Point CDC, a community center in the South Bronx.

Often we would only find out about the activities of a group when a local representative would contact us. Usually this meant a phone call along the lines of "Hi. This is the head of AFH San Diego, and we want to start a building project on the US/Mexico border. Is that OK?" As far as we know, in the United States there are active groups in around 30 cities including Atlanta, Boston, Minneapolis, New York, San Diego, San Francisco, and Seattle. Internationally there are groups in Dublin, Genoa, London, and Sydney.

Along the way we've worked with a number of remarkable people. Asia Wright introduced herself as our events coordinator, and before long we were traveling the country giving guerilla talks at colleges and community groups. People would randomly show up at our office and start working. Dave Schiff and Susan Surface appeared in the middle of our grant-writing marathon and felt the full brunt of the unsexy side of this work. A number of contributors and researchers on this book, notably Kathryn Frankel and Cynthia Barton, said they wated to get involved and found themselves making calls at all hours to every corner of the globe. Most recently, Matt Miller turned up from Detroit in his Airstream, and Laura Cole showed up in the middle of a road trip with her dog, Ginger, from Memphis. Both announced they had some time to help out—big mistake.

We have also joined forces with universities to host design/build workshops. In our largest to date we collaborated with Miami

Emily Chaffee, Karin Schierhold, and Tiona Martin go over urban planning strategies for Over-the-Rhine in Cincinnati, Ohio.
Cameron Sinclair/Architecture for Humanity

University's Center for Community Engagement in Over-the-Rhine, in Cincinnati, Ohio. The project was held in September 2004 in commemoration of the fortieth anniversary of Freedom Summer and involved over 65 architects, designers, and community members, including an original Freedom Summer civil rights leader. It used design to encourage voter registration, develop urban planning strategies, and inspire community participation in Over-the-Rhine, a disenfranchised neighborhood.

Over time Architecture for Humanity became a conduit, supporting innovative design and creating opportunities for architects to lend their services in times of need. For example, when the city of Bam, Iran, suffered a monumental earthquake on December 26, 2003, we helped raise funds for Relief International, a US-based NGO that had created innovative structures in the region after an earthquake two years earlier, to build innovative earthquake-resistant housing using steel subframes combined with local mud-block construction.

Later in the year we connected Ferrara Design, designers of Global Village Shelters (see "Global Village Shelters"), with the government of Grenada. The father-daughter team behind Global Village Shelters, Daniel and Mia Ferrara, had designed an innovative foldable cardboard shelter, which they believed could be used in postdisaster and other emergency situations. They had partnered with Weyerhaeuser to manufacture prototypes of the design, which cost only $370 each, but they needed help to get the shelters field-tested. At about this time Grenada had just been ravaged by Hurricane Ivan, causing millions of

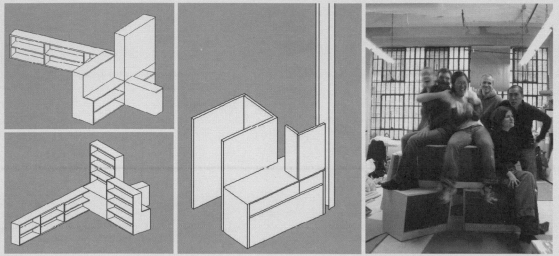

above and right
AFHny worked with The Point CDC to create a phased plan of improvements to their building (identified by letters to the left of the plan). The first project to be realized is a system of shelving and storage, which was funded by The Point and a grant from Architecture for Humanity.

top right
AFHny's Point team atop storage units being built for the building's atrium. Left to right: Jack Heaney, Karen Kubey (coordinator), Pollyanna Rhee, Jason Gibbs, Carrie Bobo, Jon Kan (not pictured: Brad Groff).
AFHny

a **SECOND FLOOR CLASSROOM :** address acoustics and overcrowding issues in this loft-like area

b **MANIDA STREET GATE :** replace existing heavy gate with something equally secure but more usable

c **COURTYARD :** create more usable space by addressing structural issues of buckling brick wall and paving

d **STORAGE :** develop storage space without changing the open feel

e **OUTDOOR DECK :** create a sheltered outdoor deck on top of the music studio

f **MUSIC STUDIO :** develop more functional floor plan while creating storage

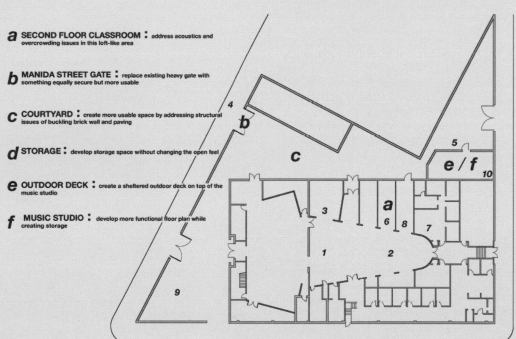

dollars of damage, decimating 85 percent of the housing stock, and wiping out almost all of the island's main cash crop, nutmeg. With no postdisaster relief plan in place and scant media attention, it took many months for recovery efforts to begin. Just as construction was getting under way, Hurricane Emily slammed into the island.

In response to this second disaster, with the help of Laurinda Spear of the Miami-based architecture firm Arquitectonica and volunteer Marisa Fort-Spear, Architecture for Humanity connected Mia and Dan with officials in Grenada and helped fund a collaborative effort between Ferrara Design and Grenada Relief, Recovery, and Reconstruction (GR3). Together we shipped 70 transitional shelters to the island for use as temporary homes and rural clinics. GR3, which is affiliated with St. George's Medical School, helped distribute the units and made sure they got to those most in need.

In another instance, the nonprofit Kids with Cameras asked us to help develop initial schematic plans for a school for children of the brothels in Calcutta, India. We worked with students at Montana State University, where I was teaching at the time, to create seven potential schemes. After a series of reviews the students refined their ideas for final presentation to Kids with Cameras at the end of the semester. The design process helped the organization solidify their plans and launch a fundraising campaign to build the school.

Overall, our projects have inspired planners and others to think creatively about how to solve issues in their community. For example, the Kansas City Economic Development Corporation used our Siyathemba competition to build a soccer club that would double as a health outreach center as a model to persuade city counselors to turn an abandoned lot into a park. We talked them through the process of setting up a design initiative and gave them suggestions on how to plan a design competition of their own.

Then, on December 26, 2004, Architecture for Humanity went from being a small design group to being a design-oriented organization (with an office) seemingly overnight, when a 9.3-magnitude earthquake in the Indian Ocean unleashed the deadliest tsunami in recorded history. Waves traveled thousands of miles, pummeling the coasts of countries as far apart as Indonesia, the Maldives, Sri Lanka, and Somalia. The tsunami took the lives of more than 225,000 people in 13 countries and left over four million displaced. The Indonesian province of Aceh and the coastline of Sri Lanka, both impoverished by years of conflict before the disaster struck, were hardest hit.

This was a key moment, not just for our organization but for the entire movement for socially conscious design. The need was immense, and this was one of the first disasters in recent memory where attention was focused not only on the immediate humanitarian concerns but also on the enormity of the reconstruction task that lay ahead. We partnered with Worldchanging.com to raise funds to bring design services to the area. It would be our largest initiative to date—and the most complex.

In the days following the tsunami we became involved in Kirinda, a small fishing village on the southeast coast of Sri Lanka. Samir Shah, an experienced designer who happened to be in the country as a Fulbright scholar and would soon become our on-the-ground field rep, brought the project to our attention. He had joined forces with a team of local architects, including Pradeep Kodikara, Varuna de Silva, and Sanath Liyanage, to assess the damage in Kirinda, which had been hard hit by the sea surge. Eventually the team volunteered its services to the government as the Urban Development Authority Kirinda Planning Team. For the next two months the architects worked with the community to develop a strategy for a sustainable town plan that would integrate both economic and civic nodes as well as connect with the newer resettled communities. Architecture for Humanity committed to help the team implement the civic and community buildings called for in the plan. However, before the new Kirinda town plan could be approved, a survey would have to be conducted to demarcate what came to be known as the 100-Meter Line.

In the first few weeks after the tsunami the governments of the affected countries started to implement "no-build" zones, areas deemed too close to the shore for safe building. Regulations in Sri Lanka called for a 100-meter buffer zone from the shore, but how the line was measured varied. In some cases surveyors measured from the shoreline, in other cases from the beach, and in still others from the nearest landmark. In Kirinda a line of 100 meters was set; but the team was not too concerned, as this did not affect its plan for rebuilding. However, the line began to move week by week. The most tense day was when a government surveyor started placing

Scale model of a school design for Kids with Cameras by Montana State University students Nicole Bellefeuille, Adam DeJarlais, Marit Lueth, Melanie Boyd, Timothy Sanford, Peter Costanti, and Lauren Anderson
Cameron Sinclair/Architecture for Humanity

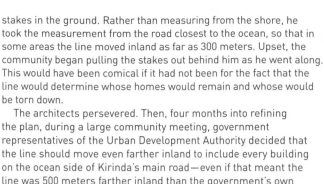

above
Reconstruction plan for Kirinda, Sri Lanka, showing the shifting 100-Meter Line, designed by Samir Shah, Pradeep Kodikara, Varuna de Silva, and Sanath Liyanage

below
Painted pegs in Kirinda, Sri Lanka, mark where it is safe to rebuild. Surveyors would often place pegs such that the 100-Meter Line ran through homes that had been untouched by the tsunami. The extended family pictured here was told that their home would be torn down because it crossed over the 100-Meter Line. They were also told that they were ineligible for housing assistance because their home was still standing and half of it was located on the safe side of the line. At the time there were 17 people living in this structure.
Cameron Sinclair/Architecture for Humanity

stakes in the ground. Rather than measuring from the shore, he took the measurement from the road closest to the ocean, so that in some areas the line moved inland as far as 300 meters. Upset, the community began pulling the stakes out behind him as he went along. This would have been comical if it had not been for the fact that the line would determine whose homes would remain and whose would be torn down.

The architects persevered. Then, four months into refining the plan, during a large community meeting, government representatives of the Urban Development Authority decided that the line should move even farther inland to include every building on the ocean side of Kirinda's main road—even if that meant the line was 500 meters farther inland than the government's own guidelines prescribed. For the team it was the final blow. After receiving approval for their plan three times, the architects were back at the drawing board with no assurances that the line would stay put. Community members lost faith in the process, and reconstruction came to a standstill. In late October—10 months after the tsunami, with no approved plan and residents still sleeping in tents—the line moved again, this time to 50 meters from the shore—in other words, 50 meters farther inland than the government's original zoning regulation.

Sadly, what happened at Kirinda is not an isolated incident; for the most part the relief and reconstruction effort was chaotic and crippled by bureaucracy. Competition for projects between hundreds of groups led to delays, duplication of efforts, and community resentment. (In Sri Lanka alone there are now more than 1,000 NGOs working on tsunami-related projects.) Various decrees from government ministries dictated the minimum standards and funding commitments aid agencies could make in order to receive government support for the construction of housing and schools; in many instances these were in direct conflict with each other, and the ever-changing standards resulted in stagnation. Often multiple aid agencies received official memorandums of understanding for the same project on the same site from different government agencies, further complicating and delaying construction.

Still, before Samir left to return to the United States he helped initiate a number of projects, including partnering with Relief International on a project to design and build transitional schools. The goal was to design a basic cost-effective structure that would enable students to return to school during the two years it would take to rebuild permanent facilities. The resulting plans, designed by Jason Andersen, a student at Montana State University interning in our office, with input from Samir and Relief International, drew from the regional vernacular and included rainwater collection systems. Simple and flexible, the scheme allowed local construction crews, many of them made up largely of parents, to adapt the design to accommodate different materials and building methods. With

above
Nine months after the tsunami classes in Pottivul, Sri Lanka, were being held under plastic tarps provided by UNICEF.
Cameron Sinclair/Architecture for Humanity

right
Three transitional schools were implemented in the Ampara District of Sri Lanka by Relief International and built and adapted by the parents of the children attending. The schools were designed using local materials and are to last from two to four years before permanent facilities are constructed.
Susi Platt/Architecture for Humanity

below
Rendering of a transitional school designed by Jason Andersen with Alan Wright of Relief International. The school incorporates a rainwater collection system and is designed to maximize ventilation.
Jason Andersen/Architecture for Humanity

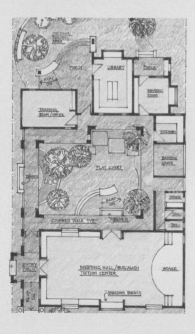

above left
Architect Purnima McCutcheon (seated at center) leads workshops with a Dalit community in Ambedkar Nagar, Tamil Nadu, India, to design a community center.

left and below
The resulting elevations and plans for the community center, which includes a meeting hall, primary school, women's cooperative, kitchen, theater, and playground.
Purnima McCutcheon/Architecture for Humanity

above right
Villagers create an adjacency diagram to establish the site for the new community center.
Purnima McCutcheon/Architecture for Humanity

funding from Architecture for Humanity, five transitional schools were built throughout the Ampara region.

Meanwhile, Susi Jane Platt, a site architect who had worked on large-scale projects in Britain, picked up where Samir left off. She is now working in the same area to implement a number of community-based projects, including women-run bakeries, schools, a medical clinic, and a livelihoods center.

Architecture for Humanity is also funding and providing design services for a number of reconstruction projects In Tamil Nadu, India, which was also badly affected by the tsunami. Here we have partnered with the League of Education and Development (LEAD), an affiliate of the Barefoot Architects (see "Barefoot College"), and AIA-registered, LEED-certified architect Purnima McCutcheon to design and build three community centers and a new pier since the tsunami raised the water level of an estuary, making it impossible for people to wade across it and preventing some 350 students from walking to school.

Rather than build an expensive bridge, the community decided to build a pier that will enable a boat to ferry students across the river. (Parents have joined together to pay a former fisherman to captain the boat.)

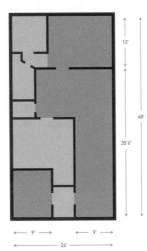

Architecture for Humanity Office __ 2005
Bozeman, MT

Average number of volunteers ____ 4
Maximum number of volunteers ____ 7
Area _____ 1000 sq. ft.
Distance to nearest coffee _____ 10 ft
Average # coffees per day _____ 5
Average workday _____ 17.5 hours

Useable Workspace

We also have supported student-led community rebuilding initiatives, including a joint effort by the Harvard Graduate School of Design and MIT's SENSEable City Laboratory (see "Safe[R] House"), as well as a project to build a women's collaborative near Auroville, India, that was instigated and designed by Travis Eby and Lauren Farquhar, two students from the University of Cincinnati.

Just as our tsunami projects were getting under way there came a new disaster. For years experts had warned of the dangers of a direct hit from a Category 4 or 5 hurricane to the city of New Orleans: "Though protected by levees designed to withstand the most common storms, New Orleans is surrounded by water and is well below sea level at many points. A flood from a powerful hurricane can get trapped for weeks inside the levee system," warned a 2002 exposé in the *Times-Picayune*. On August 29, 2005, Hurricane Katrina gathered speed and force and touched ground near New Orleans as a Category 4 storm. The 145-mile-per-hour (235-km-per-hour) winds cut a path of destruction across the Gulf Coast region. As predicted, the storm surge breached the New Orleans levee system, effectively turning the city into a bowl to be filled with water. Flooding submerged 80 percent of the city under water as high as 20 feet (six m) in some places. The disaster outstripped the capacity of officials at all levels to respond and was compounded when Hurricane Rita hit Texas less than four weeks later. Together, the storms served as a stark reminder of the need to plan for regional emergency shelter before—not after—the inevitable happens. Horrified Americans watched TV footage of bodies floating in the flood waters and thousands of people, stranded in unsafe and unsanitary conditions in the New Orleans convention center, pleading for help.

The storms displaced more than a million people, who found shelter in temporary housing (either with friends and family or through FEMA's rental vouchers) in more than 48 states. The diaspora has complicated the area's recovery and made it difficult for residents to have a voice in reconstruction. FEMA has proposed controversial temporary trailer parks, each to house between 200 and 300 displaced families for the short term. In response many designers have proposed temporary shelter that could be sited on or near families' former residences to help speed the recovery effort. While it is too early to say what shape the rebuilding will take, Architecture for Humanity is working with community centers in the region to create resource centers that will give residents access not only to financial assistance but also to architectural services. We hope the centers will become places where families will come to rebuild their lives and more sustainable communities.

Just five weeks after hurricanes Katrina and Rita struck, a catastrophic earthquake hit the Kashmir region and left the world reeling yet again. On their own each of these disasters was of a scale that overwhelmed the government agencies and NGOs charged with responding. Coming as they did within months of each other, the result was a disaster within a disaster. Kashmir was particularly affected by the lack of capacity to react.

As we write this text, over 87,000 people have died from the quake—many of them children who attended the 6,000 schools that collapsed—and over two million people have been displaced. The real danger is yet to come with the onset of the brutal Himalayan winter. Without aid, officials say, thousands could die of exposure, illness, and infection, potentially multiplying the original death toll several times over. Within weeks agencies ran out of tents, leaving over 500,000 people without shelter. (In one of life's sad ironies, Pakistan has been one of the world's largest producers of emergency tents.)

Since the inception of Architecture for Humanity, we have had varying degrees of success and failure, and with every project we've learned much and progressed a little further. Initially we thought ours would be a small organization focused on small projects. We soon discovered that there *is* no such thing as a small project. And although we have constructed only a dozen buildings, we have managed to create a solid foundation as a conduit for change in the industry.

In the future our goal is to create an open-source network of innovative solutions while still protecting the rights of the designer. Time and again we have come across a building idea that, if allowed to develop, could make a huge impact and possibly help alleviate many global housing crises. Yet the designer has invested

a considerable amount of time and effort and is understandably reluctant to give her design away, for fear someone could "steal" it for profit.

As a result we are currently working with Creative Commons, a nonprofit that offers flexible copyright licenses for creative works, to develop a licensing system for the donation of architectural and design services in areas of great need. This system is to be based on an existing license that allows the holder copyright protection in the developed world while giving her varying degrees of control in developing nations. Using this license we hope to build a database of "some rights protected" designs, including construction documents, so that there can be a wider distribution of innovative ideas.

By supporting innovative design, consulting with NGOs, and connecting professionals with projects in the field, we're creating opportunities for designers to get involved and to bring their services to those in need. We have demonstrated, and hope to continue to do so, that for every "celebrity architect" there are hundreds of designers around the world, working under the ideal that it is not just how we build but what we build that truly matters. This book represents just a sampling of their efforts. In some cases Architecture for Humanity has had the pleasure of collaborating with these designers directly. In other cases designers have pursued their ideas independently and it simply has been a pleasure to learn about their work.

A community meeting facilitated by architect Susi Jane Platt in Pottuvil, Sri Lanka, to design women-run community bakeries as part of a livelihoods initiative. Here, team members talk with the newly formed cooperatives.

Susi Jane Platt/Architecture for Humanity

A refugee camp set up after the great earthquake in San Francisco, 1906
San Francisco History Center,
San Francisco Public Library

A camp for Gulf Coast residents displaced by Hurricane Katrina 100 years later
FEMA

100 Years of
Humanitarian Design

Kate Stohr

At 5:18 in the morning on April 18, 1906, the earth heaved beneath San Francisco, California.

The earthquake lasted for less than a minute, shearing façades off buildings, ripping houses from their foundations, and opening a rift in the ground 270 miles (435 km) long and up to 21 feet (6.4 m) deep. "It was as if the earth was slipping gently from under our feet," wrote one survivor. "Ahead of me a great cornice crushed a man as if he were a maggot."[1]

But if damage from the earthquake was extensive, the fires that followed were catastrophic. With its rows of closely spaced wooden Victorian homes and unreinforced brick buildings, San Francisco at the turn of the century was a tinderbox awaiting a match. The fires raged for three days, charring more than 500 blocks—nearly a quarter of the city. By the time rescuers were able to sift through the cinders, more than a quarter of a million people were left homeless.[2] Although the official death count totaled 700, it is now estimated that the earthquake and fires claimed between 1,500 and 3,000 lives.[3]

San Francisco at the turn of the century was in every sense a modern city: it had telegraph lines and cable cars, a mix of ethnic groups, and a tremendous disparity in wealth. The earthquake marked one of the first major disasters of the industrialized age, and many of the housing strategies employed by nascent relief agencies and the Army Corps of Engineers would later be adopted by today's relief and development agencies—strategies such as micro-credit, appropriate technology, and sweat equity. Yet perhaps the most intriguing outcome of the relief effort was the innovative marriage of policy and design that led to the construction of thousands of small wooden cottages that found their way into nearly every pocket of the city.

In the immediate aftermath of the earthquake and fires, the US Army, a citizens' committee made up of 50 prominent San Franciscans, and the American Red Cross, which had been established only 25 years before, were the first and primary agencies to respond. Survivors who had the means either left the city or roomed with friends or relatives outside of the burned district. Those who remained were those with little alternative, primarily the working poor and the destitute.

Initially the Army, the American Red Cross, and volunteers provided tents. But as aid workers and officials shifted their focus from relief to recovery and reconstruction, a combination of grants and loans were given to middle-class families who owned land (or could afford to purchase land) and who could demonstrate credit-worthiness to support the building of permanent housing in the burned district.[4]

However, more than a month after the disaster some 40,000 "refugees" were still living in makeshift tent camps throughout the city.[5] The camps posed a new worry: How long would survivors live in the city's parks? Concerned by the possibility of permanent squatter settlements, the civilian committee charged with leading the relief efforts debated how to clear the camps. In the midst of this quandary officials noted that many of those remaining in the camps had not lost everything. They still had jobs. With these low-income wage earners in mind, the committee arrived at a novel solution, one that would provide temporary housing for the working poor while guaranteeing an end to the camps. At the center of this strategy was the design for a small wooden cottage.

Between September 1906 and March 1907 San Francisco built more than 5,610 cottages designed by the Army Corps of Engineers. The cottages ranged in size from 140 square feet (13 sq. m) to 400

Timeline of Disasters and Responses

1900s

1906
San Francisco Earthquake and Fires
San Francisco, Calif., USA

1910s

1911
Triangle Shirtwaist Company Fire
New York, NY, USA
A blaze in a garment factory claims the lives of 146 workers, most of them women. Public outcry leads to the creation of fire safety codes.

square feet (37 sq. m) and cost between $100 to $741 to put up. Constructed by union carpenters and painted "Parkbench Green," the cottages consisted of only two or three rooms and were as easy to relocate as they were to build. Families rented the small cottages for $2 a month, which went toward the full purchase price of $50. To free the city's public parks, occupants who could purchase or lease a lot were granted ownership of the cottage and allowed to move it from the park at their own expense. Failure to move the cottages out of the camps by August 1907, a year and a half after the disaster, resulted in forfeiture of ownership.[6]

In this way the cottages provided not only decent temporary shelter but also a path to homeownership for hundreds of San Francisco's low-wage-earning families who might otherwise have never had the means to purchase a home. By the time the last camp closed in 1909, new homeowners had relocated more than 5,343 cottages.[7] Some of them are still in use today.

Until recently, the great earthquake of 1906 was considered the biggest natural disaster in American history. In its aftermath San Francisco implemented safer building codes and designed a more reliable water-supply system.[8] In addition, researchers conducted a thorough survey of the reconstruction effort. The *San Francisco Relief Survey* remains one of best-documented case studies of postdisaster shelter efforts to date. But if the earthquake offered lessons to future relief experts, they were lessons that would have to be relearned and rediscovered.

"Housing in the twentieth century has been one continuing emergency," wrote Charles Abrams, a prominent advocate for housing reform, in 1946. Today these words seem prophetic. For more than a 100 years housing has been gripped by a cycle of war, natural disaster, and poverty. Slums, whether cleared by earthquakes and floods or urban planners with bulldozers, disappear only to regenerate and grow larger. Refugees threatened by ever-more deadly conflicts flee across borders seeking shelter in neighboring territories. And, whether in countries rich or poor, nature has proved that no feat of engineering can completely shield a city from the rumblings of the earth or the rising of its waters.

For decades architects have been called upon to provide solutions to the world's shelter crises. However, as designers embraced the

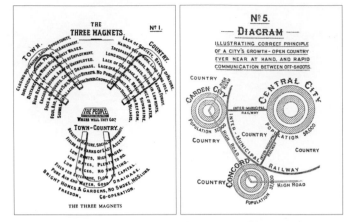

Ebenezer Howard's Three Magnets and No. 5 diagrams illustrate his concept of a planned community that would offer the best of both town and country.

idealism of the machine age, the increasingly technology-driven, often utopian ideas they proposed carried little resonance for aid workers and others wrestling with the day-to-day realities of providing a roof, clean water, and sanitation to families in need. Over time, the worlds of relief and development became divorced from the worlds of architecture and design. What architects considered a design challenge, aid workers considered an issue of planning and policy.

This disconnect would eventually lead to a crisis of faith: What role should design play in providing basic shelter? How could architects best address the needs of the displaced and disenfranchised? And, at the heart of these questions: Should design be considered a luxury or a necessity? This issue would plague not just architects but also planners, policymakers, and aid organizations struggling to balance the logistics of providing shelter with the human longing for a place to call home.

1914–15
Maison Dom-ino
Paris, France
Le Corbusier

1914–18
World War I

1917
Demountable Wooden House
France (various locations)
American Friends Service Committee
Built by volunteers to house World War I refugees, each "demountable" wooden house consisted of two rooms.
American Friends Service Committee

> **"We are dealing with an urgent problem of our epoch, nay more, with the problem of our epoch. The balance of society comes down to a question of building. We conclude with these justifiable alternatives: Architecture or Revolution. Revolution can be avoided."**

Le Corbusier, *Vers une Architecture*, 1923

Utopian Urbanism

The introduction of new building codes was just one of a series of profound changes that would affect the practice of architecture at the start of the twentieth century. The origins of humanitarian, or social, design can be traced at least as far back as the tenant movements of the late 1800s and early 1900s, when social reformers turned their attention to the housing conditions of the poor.

By the nineteenth century increased urbanization brought on by the Industrial Revolution had led to squalid conditions in the working-class neighborhoods of many cities. Photographers such as Thomas Annan in Glasgow and Jacob Riis in New York used their art to document the "insalubrious" living conditions of the "other half." Tenant associations formed, and worker housing initiatives took shape. Many of these housing projects, such as the Familistère in Guise, France, a "working-class palace" founded by the industrialist Jean-Baptiste-André Godin, were undertaken by companies on behalf of their workers.[9] Health, welfare, and productivity became inextricably linked to housing. The reform movement's call for sanitary living conditions led to the introduction of light wells and other design improvements for tenement housing.

Reformers also adopted the concept of town planning as an antidote to the social ills of the day. In 1898 Ebenezer Howard published *To-morrow: A Peaceful Path to Real Reform*. Howard offered a vision of planned communities free of "slums and gin palaces," where clean air, water, and opportunity would abound. In his plan, a central city surrounded by green space was linked by transportation to satellite towns. As illustrated by his famous Three Magnets and No. 5 diagrams, these satellite cities promised the best of both town (opportunity, amusement, high wages) and country (beauty, fresh air, low rents).[10] This concept of town planning combined with modernism would have a profound influence over the construction of low-income housing projects for decades to come.

Modernism

By 1913 the Industrial Revolution had reached a fever pitch. Reinforced concrete, first developed in the 1860s, was by now an accepted building material. Steel-frame construction, water pumps, and the invention of the elevator allowed buildings to soar to unprecedented heights. The devastation of World War I had led to acute housing shortages in much of Europe. At the same time, workers continued to migrate to urban areas, crowding into sprawling slums on the edges of cities such as Paris. This surge in demand called for new thinking about housing design as well as building techniques that not only met the needs of the new machine age but also co-opted its methods.

Today modernism is associated with a minimalist aesthetic of steel and glass, but it began as an attempt by architects and designers to harness the potential of industry to produce low-cost buildings, in particular, housing. The assembly line was revolutionizing the production of everything from toothbrushes to brassieres. Why not housing?

Le Corbusier expressed the new thinking best when he described the house as "a machine for living in." In 1914–15 the Swiss-born architect developed a basic, universal housing unit called the Maison Dom-ino. The unit consisted of little more than floor slabs of reinforced concrete supported by corner columns and lifted off the ground by pilotis, or piers. It could be repeated endlessly or stacked upon itself. Because the walls were not load bearing, the interior spaces could be configured in different ways to meet the varying needs of occupants.[11] Prefabricated walls and uniform door and window heights simplified construction further. Le Corbusier saw his system as a solution for the rapid reconstruction of regions such as Flanders, which had been heavily damaged during World War I. He

---

1919
League of Nations established
Versailles, France
Established after the end of World War I, the League of Nations' goal was to settle disputes between nations and foster peace. After World War II it would be replaced by the United Nations.

1920s

1923
Kanto Earthquake and Fire
Tokyo and Yokohama, Japan
200,000 people die; 370,000 buildings are destroyed. Frank Lloyd Wright's "earthquake-proof" Imperial Hotel (1916–22) is one of the few structures left standing.

1927
Mississippi River Flood
Lower Mississippi region, USA
The lower Mississippi River floods, inundating 27,000 square miles and shattering levee systems from Illinois to the Gulf of Mexico.

1927–32
"The Winona"
Sears Modern Homes
Akron, Oh., USA
Sears, Roebuck and Co.

"Architecture is a process of giving form and pattern to the social life of the community. Architecture is not an individual act performed by an artist-architect and charged with his emotions. Building is a collective action."

Hannes Meyer, director of Bauhaus, 1928 to 1930

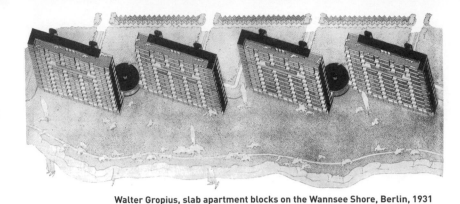

Walter Gropius, slab apartment blocks on the Wannsee Shore, Berlin, 1931

built two prototypes based on his ideas for exhibition: The *immeubles villas* (1922) and the Maison Citrohan (1922), a play on the automobile name Citroën. Throughout the '20s Le Corbusier expounded on his ideas for a new industrialized architecture in a series of manifestos and urban plans.

Another early pioneer of prefabrication and component building systems was the German architect Walter Gropius. Gropius, who founded the Bauhaus and served as its director from 1919 to 1928, personified the architect as public servant and teacher. Throughout the '20s and '30s Gropius experimented with prefabricated wall panels and eventually whole structures. During his tenure and that of his successors, the Bauhaus became a nexus for socially conscious design.

Gropius, along with Marcel Breuer, is also credited with designing the first slab apartment block. This new building type, which would become the model for many future affordable-housing projects, was conceived to overcome the cramped, lightless tenement housing that had resulted from rampant land speculation at the turn of the century. The basic plan consisted of parallel rows of four- to 11-story apartment blocks. Each slab was only one apartment deep with windows front and back. The slabs were sited on a "superblock" at an angle to the street with communal green spaces between them to allow maximum sunlight into each apartment.[12]

Others would also experiment with standardized building components, modular systems, and prefabrication, including the French industrial designer Jean Prouvé and Frank Lloyd Wright, but perhaps none more passionately than the American inventor R. Buckminster Fuller.

Fuller arrived on what he termed "spaceship earth" in 1895. Like Gropius and Le Corbusier, he believed that mass-manufactured dwellings represented the future of housing. His most lasting contribution, however, was his fervent belief in the power of design to improve the human condition. In a sense Fuller, who was known for his eccentric use of language and his marathon lectures (the longest lasted 42 hours and only recently has been fully transcribed), was the first evangelist of humanitarian design.

In 1927, after the death of his elder daughter and the collapse of his first business, he found himself at the edge of Lake Michigan contemplating suicide. He was a failure, "a throw-away." What brought him from the brink, he later recounted, was the simple idea that his experience might ultimately be somehow useful to his fellow human beings. Rather than taking his own life, he decided to embark on a lifelong experiment, using himself as his own best research subject. He became "Guinea Pig B" (for Bucky), the world's first test pilot of a "design-science revolution," the sole purpose of which was to improve "human livingry," and he started with the house.

1929
Dymaxion House
Chicago, Ill., USA
R. Buckminster Fuller

1930s

1930
Housing Act of 1930
England

1930–39
Drought and Dust Storms
Midwestern and southern plains, USA

1931
Prefabricated houses built for the Hirsch Copper and Brass Works
Finow, Germany
Walter Gropius
Arthur Koster

1931
Slab apartment blocks on the Wannsee shore
Berlin, Germany
Walter Gropius

Conventional "handcrafted" homes had undergone "no structural advances in 5,000 years," Fuller argued. They were poorly lit, required much maintenance, and did not make efficient use of raw materials. Most conventional buildings depended on gravity for their strength. But what if a building could be suspended, as a sail from a mast, allowing for greater strength and the use of fewer materials?

Fuller's thinking led to the design of the Dymaxion House, a small-scale model of which was first exhibited at a Marshall Field's department store in Chicago in 1929. His radical scheme embraced the principle of tension and aimed to do "more with less." It was spherical, to make efficient use of materials, and clad in maintenance-free aluminum. It was naturally climate controlled and could be lit by a single light source through a system of mirrors and dimmers. All the mechanicals, wiring, and appliances were built into the walls and mast to allow for easy replacement. The house was also one of the first examples of self-sufficient (or "autonomous," as Fuller put it) green design. Wind turbines produced energy. The roof collected rainwater. Water-saving "fog guns" handled washing (including people), and Fuller's "package toilet" composted waste and recovered methane gas.[13]

While the Dymaxion House was unabashedly ahead of its time (it would be two decades before Fuller could find backing to build a full-scale prototype), the concept of building with tension rather than compression would become central to Fuller's work and would eventually lead to his most lasting contribution to the field of humanitarian design: the geodesic dome. Fuller's principle of tensegrity became a staple of tent design, and by extension, emergency shelter, that endures to this day.

Like the Dymaxion House, few of these early designs for "factory-built" housing achieved widespread commercial viability. For example, Le Corbusier's low-cost housing for workers in Pessac, near Bordeaux, France, went unoccupied for eight years after it was built. However, this concept of mass-produced housing would have a number of lasting implications for low-cost shelter. It prefigured a move away from the craft of building toward the technology of building. It took design out of the realm of the many and put it in the hands of an educated few. Perhaps more important, it negated the need for a dialogue between the architect and the occupant.

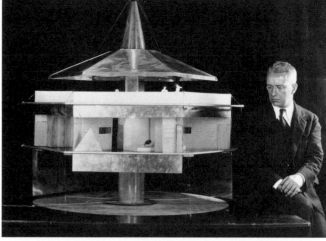

R. Buckminster Fuller with an early model of his Dymaxion House
Buckminster Fuller Institute

Suddenly a house could be designed, detailed, and delivered without the architect ever meeting its owner.

Manufactured Housing

Meanwhile, in the rest of America, the industrialization of architecture took a very different tack. By the early '20s the automobile had become an integral part of American life. Trailers were common and had been adapted by migrant workers and others into dwellings. With the onset of the Depression, the demand for cheap, portable housing grew. A mobile home seemed the next logical step. In 1936 Wally Byam built the first Airstream trailer, a steel-clad, aerodynamic embodiment of home on the road. Although the Airstream would eventually become an American icon, designs such as the Durham Portable House would prove far more influential.[14]

Not only did the Durham, which cost between $1,500 and $3,000, mimic the styling of a conventional home, it also was a precursor

Design Like You Give a Damn

1931
Flood
China
The Yellow River, the second largest river in China, floods. Death toll estimates range from 850,000 to four million. The flooding is followed by famine and outbreaks of disease.

1934
Modern Housing
Catherine Bauer

1934
National Housing Act of 1934
USA

1936
Airstream Clipper
Los Angeles, Calif., USA
Wally Byam

1937
Housing Act of 1937
USA

to the "double-wide" mobile home because it was transported in two parts and assembled on site to form a single dwelling.

Although its architectural merits have been the subject of contentious debate, the mobile home in many ways represents the dream of prefabricated housing come true. According to US census figures, the number of mobile homes has increased from 315,000 in 1950 to nearly 8.8 million today.[15] Approximately 18 million Americans now live in mobile homes. According to research by faculty and students at the Harvard Graduate School of Design, mobile homes have become the most common form of unsubsidized affordable housing in America—despite hostile community boards and zoning laws, higher financing rates for mobile homes than standard mortgages, and the tendency to use shoddy materials and construction. Today mobile homes account for an astonishing 25 percent of all dwellings in North America.[16]

The popularity of mobile homes raises an interesting question: Why have double-wides received such broad acceptance, while other seemingly better designed alternatives have not? The answer may lie in their mobility. With each "box" no wider than a standard highway and production rigidly controlled, the units were cost-effective to make and to transport. For the first time, housing became a product within reach for low-income wage earners and those on fixed incomes. Land could be rented at a nominal fee, and no complicated applications needed to be submitted for government handouts. Manufactured homes filled a growing niche in the housing market and quickly became a part of the American vernacular.

The mobile home was not the only successful attempt to market mass-produced housing in America before World War II. Between 1908 and 1940 the American retailer Sears, Roebuck and Co. sold as many as 100,000 homes from its catalogue.[17] While not truly prefabricated (the homes were delivered in some 30,000 parts by boxcar, complete with assembly instructions and two tree planters for the front yard), for a brief moment these "mail-order" homes offered an affordable alternative to traditional construction in places where materials and expertise were scarce. The homes could be purchased with no money down at prices starting from as little as $650, compared to the average home price of $1,000. What's more, the company guaranteed that "a man of average abilities" could build one of its kit homes in

just 90 days.[18] The Sears approach offered a surprisingly efficient, well-crafted alternative to the concept of delivering fully finished prefabricated homes.

Most Sears homes used wood-frame construction and were conservative in style. However, in 1934 the retailer partnered with the General Houses company to exhibit a truly modern steel-frame home made from prefabricated wall panels at the 1934 World's Fair in Chicago. But by then the stock market had crashed. Homeowners defaulted on their mortgage payments in droves, and in 1940 Sears was forced to shut down its Modern Homes division.[19] The kit-home approach was never revived on a large scale, and mobile homes became the industry standard.

The Social Housing Movement
With the real-estate collapse brought on by the Depression, providing housing for low-income workers took on new urgency. High unemployment and rampant foreclosures sent many onto the street and into cities in search of work. Lending institutions became reluctant to make home loans, and with down-payment requirements as high as 50 percent, few people could afford one anyway. Deteriorating conditions and health concerns in rapidly expanding slums provoked governments to act, spawning a number of urban revitalization and progressive-era housing initiatives.

In England the Housing Act of 1930 tied the construction of government subsidized housing, or "council housing" (which had begun after World War I), to slum-clearance programs in the inner cities. With the Labour Party's ascension to power in 1934, London adopted the slogan, "A Healthy London: Up with the Houses, Down with the Slums."[20] Some 200,000 people were resettled, mostly from inner-city London to surrounding suburbs.

In America many of the programs that would fund the large-scale public housing and Urban Renewal schemes of the postwar era were conceived during the Depression. As foreclosures forced tens of thousands from their homes, a group calling themselves "Housers," which counted the activist Catherine Bauer among its leading members, lobbied Congress to intervene.[21]

Congress responded with the National Housing Act of 1934. The act created the Federal Housing Administration (FHA), which

---

1938
Durham Portable House
USA
M. R. Doberman and John W. Davis

1939
Earthquake
Concepción and Chillán, Chile
50,000 are killed and 700,000 left homeless. 70 percent of Concepción is destroyed and virtually all of Chillán.

1939–45
World War II
Millions are displaced. Emergency housing is still being constructed four years after D-Day.

ca. 1939–45
Transportable Primitive Shelter
Helsinki, Finland
Alvar Aalto
Movable temporary shelters are designed to house war refugees.

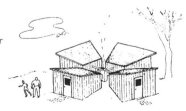

1940s

1940
Dymaxion Deployment Unit
Various overseas US military bases
R. Buckminster Fuller
The units, produced by Butler Manufacturing, provide emergency accommodation for troops in various locations during World War II.
Buckminster Fuller Institute

"Housing in the twentieth century has been one continuing emergency."

Charles Abrams, *The Future of Housing*, 1946
•

guaranteed home-mortgage loans, making it possible for the first time for banks to offer individual home buyers mortgages on terms familiar today, such as 30-year repayment periods and 10 percent down payments. Considered one of the most significant acts ever passed by Congress, the National Housing Act triggered mortgage lending, stimulated a building boom, and opened the door to home ownership for millions of working-class Americans. It is credited with helping to increase the national homeownership rate from under 40 percent during the Depression to almost 67 percent today.[22]

However, the act also gave rise to the practice of "redlining." In order to reduce its financial exposure, the government developed a system in which lenders could refuse to make loans in neighborhoods considered high risk by appraisers. Residential areas were mapped, and neighborhoods that showed signs of decay or "undesirable populations," typically those with ethnic minorities, were marked in red. A single home occupied by a minority family in a distant corner could cause an entire neighborhood to be downgraded for federally backed home mortgages.

In addition, while the Housing Act of 1934 stimulated construction, it did little to shelter those who could not qualify for loans—the nation's poor. As a remedy Congress passed the Housing Act of 1937, which authorized more than $800 million in loans to local housing authorities for the construction of housing for low-income families. The act required that for every dwelling built, the equivalent number of substandard dwellings must be cleared.[23] It was a centralized, top-down approach. Policies were enacted at the national level and carried out locally.

Taken together, this legislation would have a profound effect on the landscape of American cities. By now urban and town planning concepts had gained critical mass in Europe and America. Housing activists extolled the virtues of "garden city" and "new town" planning concepts. Slums were to be cleared to make way for new planned communities. *The City*, a film sponsored by the American Institute of Planners in 1939, perfectly captured the populist, if somewhat paternal, idealism of the time.[24] "Order has come," the film proclaimed. "It's here! The new city, ready to serve a better age."

World War II

The true effects of these housing programs would not be felt for several decades, however. With the outbreak of World War II, the world's attention shifted. The search for a technological solution to the world's housing crisis was put on hold. Factories were retooled as technological advances made in the name of progress during the first few decades of the century were now put to terrifying use. For the first time in the history of warfare, civilian deaths outnumbered those of soldiers. The destruction of towns and cities was also unprecedented. American fighter pilots armed with just two atomic bombs leveled the cities of Hiroshima and Nagasaki in seconds. When the war ended in 1945, millions were left displaced or homeless.

Emergency shelter became a priority. The Finnish architect Alvar Aalto developed a temporary emergency-shelter system that could be trucked to the site and house four families with a shared central-heating unit.[25] Prouvé also developed a number of prefabricated shelters, including a metal-frame tent, demountable barracks, and schools for war refugees that he called *écoles volantes* (flying schools).[26]

The Marshall Plan pumped $12 billion into the reconstruction of Europe and became a model for postconflict humanitarian aid. Military agencies were tasked with providing engineering and technical assistance in the reconstruction of ports, roads, bridges, communication lines, and other infrastructure. It was a role they would play increasingly in postconflict and disaster situations.

The war also marked another major shift: the rise of the NGO, or nongovernmental organization. With the exception of the International Committee of the Red Cross, which was founded by Henri Dunant in the 1860s, most of the large organizations and agencies we've come to associate with humanitarian work today were born amid the suffering and remorse that followed World War II. These include not only the United Nations but also government agencies such as Danida and the United States Agency for

1943
Famine
Bangladesh and West Bengal, India (formerly Bengal)
Crop failures and political complications caused by World War II prompt a sharp rise in the cost of rice and cause widespread famine, malnutrition, and related diseases, killing more than three million people.

1943–48
Packaged House System
Long Island, NY, USA
Walter Gropius and Konrad Wachsmann

1944–47
Wichita Dwelling Machine
Wichita, Kan., USA
R. Buckminster Fuller
The dwelling, shown at right, is based on Fuller's original concept for the Dymaxion House.
Buckminster Fuller Institute

International Development (USAID); humanitarian aid organizations such as the International Rescue Committee, CARE, and Oxfam; and religious organizations such as Catholic Relief Services.

From this point on, NGOs would play an increasingly larger role in providing emergency shelter to refugees as well as responding to natural disasters. After the war the end of colonization ushered in an era of conflict as states struggled for independence. Aid agencies were faced with the need to provide emergency shelter—not just in Europe and America but also throughout the rapidly industrializing "third world."

As their number proliferated in the postwar years, NGOs became more involved in development work, building water and sanitation systems and affordable housing. And the field of housing became more specialized: Disaster relief and development work became two separate fields; slum clearance and urban renewal initiatives were now differentiated from the construction of low-cost housing in rural areas. Increasingly, NGOs cultivated areas of expertise and contracted with governments and other institutions to meet specific humanitarian goals, becoming in a sense specialized service providers. Some employed architects but most depended on engineers to design and oversee the construction of projects.

The Postwar Building Boom

The destruction of World War II, the return of veterans, and the prewar housing shortage combined to create an unprecedented demand for housing. As people tried to put the war behind them and reconstruct their towns and cities, modernism, with its implicit denial of the past and its promise of efficiency and affordability, seemed the perfect vehicle. In West Germany planners embraced the slab apartment block that Gropius and others had first explored in the '20s and '30s. In France Le Corbusier was called upon to put many of his earlier ideas into practice for a project in Marseilles, the Unité d'Habitation. Built between 1946 and 1952, the tower block was composed of 300 residential units stacked between shopping arcades and restaurants to form a sort of neighborhood on stilts. In the postwar years Le Corbusier would also be hired to create urban plans for Izmir, Turkey; Bogotá, Colombia; and Chandigarh, India. The communist states of Eastern Europe also co-opted modernism

> "This is the real news of our century. It is highly feasible to take care of all of humanity at a higher standard of living than anybody has ever experienced or dreamt of. To do so without having anybody profit at the expense of another, so that everybody can enjoy the whole earth. And it can all be done by 1985."
>
> R. Buckminster Fuller, lecture

as part of their ideologies. Shiny "new towns" emerged from the postwar rubble of such disparate places as Poland, Japan, and Israel.

Meanwhile, the war had done little to shake architects' faith in technology. Once again designers returned to the idea of mass production. Governments allocated grants for housing returning veterans, and dwellings such as Fuller's Dymaxion House and the solid-steel Lustron Home (1945–51) found their way onto magazine pages.[27] Gropius, having fled Nazi Germany for the United States, continued to develop prefab systems and partnered with Konrad Wachsmann and the General Panel Corp. in New York to market the Packaged House System (1943–48). The company built some 200 homes in California, but the venture was a financial failure and shut down after five years.[28]

In France a prefab system designed by Prouvé would meet a similar fate. Working from a design he had originally intended to house bureaucrats in French-colonized Congo, the Ministry of Construction in 1949 ordered 25 prefab homes for an experimental low-cost housing scheme. Unfortunately, no delivery instructions were issued and the houses were still waiting at the factory a year later. In the end only 14 were sited in a housing estate in Meudon, outside Paris.[29]

The limited success of these and other prefab projects did not prevent the idea from being exported to the desperate housing ministries of the developing world. For example, according to Charles

---

1945
Houses for Britain
USA
The US Federal Public Housing Authority prepares to ship 30,000 prefabricated temporary emergency family dwellings to Great Britain under lend-lease. Plumbing and fixtures are to be shipped with the structures, but not sinks or closet doors.
Library of Congress

1945
United Nations founded
San Francisco, Calif., USA

1945–51
Lustron Home
Columbus, Oh.,USA
Carl Strandlund
The Lustron Home retails for $7,000. Despite a government pledge of $40 million, only 2,498 homes are produced before the company forecloses in 1951.

Abrams, in the postwar years precast concrete walls poured in Europe were hauled to Ghana by a company that contracted with the government there to build 168 model houses as the start of a larger building program. When the cost of 64 completed houses ran up to $448,000, Ghana quietly abandoned the venture. In Karachi, Pakistan, small aluminum prefabs were constructed, which their owners promptly adapted and expanded with adobe, discarded wood, and other makeshift building components, making them, in Abrams's words, "the first prefabricated slums."[30]

Ultimately, the cost per unit of off-site manufactured housing made most prefabricated dwellings prohibitively expensive for those living on the economic margins. Though examples of postwar prefabricated homes dot America, Europe, and other parts of the world, in the end they could not compete with their more affordable mobile-home counterparts or the new suburban Levittowns that would soon become synonymous with the American dream and postwar prosperity.

The first Levittown, named after its developer, William Levitt, was constructed in Long Island between 1947 and 1951. At the time it was the largest housing development ever constructed by a single builder. But in terms of humanitarian design and construction, the landmark project was significant for another reason: It transferred the concept of assembly-line production from the factory to the building site.

Modeled after one of Henry Ford's wartime plants, the original Levittown consisted of 17,447 homes, each built by construction teams that moved from lot to lot, performing the same task over and over as trucks drove through the area dropping off supplies. The homes, which came in only two styles, were priced at less than $10,000 so that buyers could qualify for federally backed loans. Beginning in the 1950s Levittown-style developments cropped up in places as far-flung as Brazil and the Philippines.[31] Levitt himself went on to build developments in Iran, Venezuela, Nigeria, France, and Israel, and his model remains the dominant construction method for affordable single-family housing developments today.

Urban Renewal

The postwar years also saw the continuation—and expansion—of the slum-clearance programs begun during the Depression. In France the Debré Act of 1964 authorized slum clearance in Paris. In Britain the unemployed and working poor were resettled into council housing built on land leveled by bombs during the war.

In America planning types were given sweeping new powers by the 1949 Housing Act, which financed slum clearance in aid of Urban Renewal programs and authorized the building of 810,000 public-housing units. The act's stated goal was to provide "a decent home and a suitable living environment for every American family." But its passage led to the destruction of more homes than were built, betraying the very families it was intended to help. Whole neighborhoods were bulldozed in the name of progress and replaced by freeways and government complexes. Zoning pushed low-income housing to city peripheries. At the same time, redlining triggered "white flight" in urban areas such as Detroit, increasing the segregation of America's inner cities and creating pools of poverty in once-vibrant neighborhoods. Rather than fulfilling the promise of decent housing, Urban Renewal programs left a legacy of corruption, rioting, poverty, crime, discrimination, despair, and isolation.

In the beginning many of these new developments consisted of low-rise apartment buildings, but over time Le Corbusier–inspired high-rises and slab apartment blocks of the kind designed by students of the Bauhaus became the norm. As a result, in the public eye at least, the modernist tower block became the scapegoat for an era of flawed housing policies. The sight of demolition crews dynamiting projects such as Pruitt-Igoe, a 33-tower public housing project in St. Louis, Missouri—once heralded for its innovative skip-stop elevators, communal laundries, and common spaces—just 20 years after its construction seemed to confirm public opinion. By the 1970s it was clear to many that the postwar approach to public housing had failed. Slums had not been replaced by "new towns" or "radiant cities" but by "vertical ghettos."

Poor siting, cost cutting, and shoddy construction compounded the problems associated with the new housing developments. In 1968 a gas explosion caused the corner of a tower block to collapse in the London docklands, killing two residents and injuring another 260.[32] Two years later in Korea, 32 former slum dwellers who had been relocated into a high-rise housing block were killed when it came crashing down.[33]

1946
The Future of Housing
Charles Abrams

1946–53
New Gourna Village
Near Gourna, Egypt
Hassan Fathy

1947–51
Levittown
Long Island, NY, USA
William Levitt
Levitt pioneers on-site assembly-line construction. The 17,000-home development foreshadows today's "blitz builds."
Library of Congress

1947–52
Marshall Plan
The United States commits $12 billion to the reconstruction of Europe.

Despite these warning signs, the "clean-slate" approach of Urban Renewal continued to shape the policies of overcrowded cities of the developing world, where they were embraced by governments struggling to cope with squatter invasions and exploding populations. Throughout the 1960s and 1970s governments in countries such as India, Zambia, and El Salvador approved wide-reaching slum-clearance programs in the name of economic development. However, housing construction could not keep pace with demand, and ultimately these programs did little to deter informal settlements. The population of Mumbai (formerly Bombay), for example, grew from nearly three million in 1951 to nearly six million in 1976, with 2.8 million people, or just under half the city, living in slums.[34]

Self-Help and Sites-and-Services Programs
Whether or not the design of these buildings led to their demise, the very public failure of modernist public-housing initiatives prompted a general loss of confidence in architecture and its ability to improve lives. As early as the '30s and '40s even some within the profession were beginning to question the role of architects in serving the needs of those who could least afford their services.

"Of all the participants in the business of home building, the architect is the only one qualified to guide the house and its environment toward a civilized form. Well-trained and possessed of practical experience, he should be intellectually constituted to prevent abuses, develop new methods and impart originality to the design. Yet he fails in each of these responsibilities," wrote Abrams in his landmark survey of the housing industry, *The Future of Housing*. Leadership in improving the design of low-cost homes was coming from the materials industry, he argued, not architects. Others felt that architects tripping over their own stylish egos in the pursuit of wealthy clients "had lost sight of the requirements for elementary shelter."[35]

A debate emerged in the profession: Should the work of the architect be limited to design? Or should architects roll up their sleeves and take on the job of the housing activist, working to influence not only implementation but also policy and planning decisions? Could architects play a meaningful role in providing shelter to those who needed it most? And if so, what should that role be?

The self-help housing movement grew out of this disillusionment.

Homeowners had been successfully building their own homes for generations. Moreover, they had been doing it without the aid of government agencies, architects, or outside funding. What were slums but just another form of owner-built housing? Rather than pour money into government-built housing projects, why not use government funding to support and empower families to upgrade and build their own homes? This was the idea at the crux of the self-help movement.[36]

One of the most notable early experiments in self-help-style housing was the work of Hassan Fathy in Egypt. In the 1930s Fathy began experimenting with mud-brick construction. Trained at what is now the University of Cairo, he was inspired partly by the beauty and sustainability of traditional Egyptian architecture and partly by a shortage of timber, steel, and concrete during the war. After building a number of rural homes using traditional vaulted roofs and mud brick, including a demonstration home for the Red Crescent in a village destroyed by a flood, he was asked by the country's Department of Antiquities to design a large resettlement project.

The village of Gourna, Egypt, was situated near, or more accurately above, the Tombs of the Nobles. At the time its residents had a certain renown for finding suspiciously authentic Egyptian relics in their cellars. In an effort to protect the site from tomb-raiders, the government planned to resettle the community in a new village to be built nearby called New Gourna.

For Fathy the project presented an opportunity to test out his ideas of a low-cost architecture based on the sustainable building techniques that had sheltered centuries of Egyptians. To him, "apostles of prefabrication and mass production" did not appreciate or understand the depths of poverty in places like Egypt. "There is no factory on earth that could produce houses these villagers can afford....To talk of prefabrication to people living in such a condition is worse than stupid. It's a cruel mockery of their condition," he wrote. Nor, he felt, could government largesse alone effectively address the problem:

> It is a pity that government authorities think of people as "millions." If you regard people as "millions" to be shoveled into various boxes like loads of gravel...always needing things done to them, you will miss the biggest opportunity to save money ever presented to you. For, of course, a man has a mind of his own, and a pair of hands that do what his

---

1948–49
Geodesic Dome
Asheville, NC, USA
R. Buckminster Fuller
Fuller teaches at Black Mountain College and invents the geodesic dome. Over the course of the next several decades he will refine and expand on the basic design. At right, an early example of a geodesic dome is lifted into place.
Buckminster Fuller Institute

1949
1949 Housing Act
USA

1949
Tsunami
Hawaii, USA
50-foot waves, some moving as fast as 490 mph, kill 96 people in the city of Hilo and destroy 46 homes. The Tsunami Warning System is created, with five seismic stations around the Pacific Rim.

1950s

1953
Storm Floods
North Sea, northern Europe
100-mph winds cause a sea surge to crash into coastal Britain, Holland, and Belgium. In Holland the tidal waves cause dikes to break in 65 places; in Britain sea walls are breached in 1,000 spots. Flooding causes 1,800 deaths. The disaster leads to the creation of the national Storm Tide Forecasting Service and the erection of the Thames Barrier, the world's largest movable flood barrier.

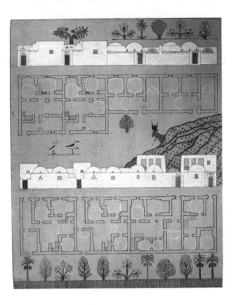

Hassan Fathy, plan of New Gourna Village, Egypt, 1946

Aga Khan Foundation

1946 and continued through 1953. All the buildings were constructed using mud-brick and traditional craftsmanship, down to the doors. But the project did not to live up to Fathy's expectations. From the beginning he found it difficult to develop a true client-architect relationship with the villagers, who resented being resettled and expected their homes to be delivered as finished products. Fathy had envisioned training villagers in the craft of mud-brick building and employing them to build their own homes, but because of their opposition toward the project as a whole, he was forced to hire outside labor. Construction was slowed by "application-in-triplicate" supply procedures, snafus, and a lack of support.

Government ministers viewed the project as a sentimental folly at best and a waste of time and money at worst. The most damning critique came from other architects, who felt that the town failed to fulfill its residents' desires for modern living. The people of Gourna refused to move to the new village. When Fathy went back to the unfinished village some 20 years later, he found it all but abandoned.

Even in failure, however, the New Gourna experiment left a lasting legacy, not the least of which is *Architecture for the Poor*, Fathy's detailed and moving account of the project and its shortcomings.[38] Written 20 years after construction at New Gourna was halted, it offers solace to all architects who find themselves in the soul-destroying task of trying to overcome institutional obstacles beyond their control. Fathy's philosophy of building by the poor for the poor would have a profound influence on a growing cadre of architects working on issues of housing in the developing world.

At the same time that Fathy was building New Gourna, an even more ambitious and far more successful "self-help and mutual aid" project was under way in Puerto Rico. It was initiated as part of a government resettlement and land redistribution program. Some 67,000 farm workers were given small plots of land averaging three acres each. Housing construction began in 1949, and families were organized in groups of 30 to work on each other's homes. Revolving loan funds were set up, and officials traveled to each village to encourage participation. Once families signed on, a construction supervisor and a social worker were assigned to each group. Unlike in New Gourna, families were free to design and build their homes using any method that made sense—whether that involved

mind tells them....Give him half a chance and a man will solve his part of the housing problem—without the help of architects, contractors, or planners—far better than any government authority ever can. Instead of one architect in an office sitting up all night to find out how many houses of each size will best fit the masses to be housed, each family will build its own house to its own requirements, and will inevitably make it into a lively work of art. Here, in each private person's longing for a house, in his eagerness to make one himself, is the alternative to the disastrous mass housing schemes of so many governments.[37]

Fathy saw the role of the architect as that of personal consultant yielding his or her training to the aspirations of the homeowner and to the demands of local construction methods and materials. New Gourna was to be a village built by the villagers themselves. Work on the new community, which was planned to include a mosque, a school, a theater and other amenities as well as housing, began in

---

1955–63
Lafayette Park
Detroit, Mich., USA
Ludwig Mies van der Rohe and Ludwig Hilbersheimer (completed by other developers and architects)
Part of a federally subsidized Urban Renewal project, the development includes town houses and 21-story apartment blocks, grassy expanses, and a system of closed streets.

1958
Earthquake
Arequipa, Peru
10,000 houses destroyed. John F. C. Turner initiates a self-help rebuilding program.

1958
Low-Income Housing
Chandigarh, India
Pierre Jeanneret
James Burke/Time & Life Pictures

traditional construction or not. Between 30,000 and 40,000 small houses were built by the early 1960s.

This program would eventually influence a number of self-help and mutual-aid housing initiatives, including the work of John F. C. Turner, who launched a similar program to rebuild some 10,000 homes destroyed by an earthquake in Peru in 1958. Turner later adapted (and simplified) the model to implement a number of slum-upgrade programs, negotiating one of the first loans from the Inter-American Bank for housing aid in Peru.[39]

Over time a variety of approaches to the basic self-help housing concept emerged. One variant was the roof-loan scheme. In this approach, first developed by Abrams and Otto Koenigsberger as part of a United Nations mission to Ghana in the 1950s, families who had built the foundation and walls of a structure themselves received loans from a revolving fund, repayable over a fixed period, to buy the roof, doors, and windows. Another variant was the "core-housing" scheme, in which agencies provided a number of identical "cores," typically consisting of one room that in some cases included basic services such as water and electricity. The families could then expand these cores as time and money allowed. Many houses erected in the later years of Puerto Rico's self-help program followed this "core" model.

Then in 1968 a young American couple named Millard and Linda Fuller took the basic tenets of self-help and mutual aid in yet a new direction. The idea for Habitat for Humanity was born at Koinonia Farm, a small, interracial Christian farming community founded in 1942 outside Americus, Georgia, by farmer and biblical scholar Clarence Jordan. Working with Jordan the Fullers helped set up a revolving loan fund and orchestrated a program to build 42 homes. Future owners and volunteers worked "in partnership" to construct the homes, which were sold to families in need at no profit with no interest. Jordan died before the first home was completed, but the Fullers carried on his work.

Although Habitat for Humanity is considered an American organization, the first housing project the Fullers undertook on their own was in Zaire (now the Democratic Republic of the Congo). Starting in 1973 they built 100 cement-block houses over three years. On returning to America they officially formed Habitat for Humanity

International in 1976, with its headquarters in Georgia. The mission of the organization, which the Fullers described as a "Christian housing ministry," was to eradicate "poverty housing" by building "simple, decent homes" based on the "economics of Jesus." Within 30 years Habitat for Humanity would claim to be the fifteenth-largest homebuilder in the United States.

The Habitat for Humanity "partnership" model offered a number of advantages over typical self-help and mutual-aid programs. Whereas prior self-help initiatives relied primarily on the labor of families themselves, often forcing wage earners to give up paid work, Habitat for Humanity involved volunteers, speeding the construction process and lessening the burden on already struggling families. Moreover, whereas administrative and organizational costs absorbed as much 25 percent of the funding for a typical self-help and mutual aid program, Habitat for Humanity relied on the built-in organizational skills of local churches to help set up and run its housing initiatives. This not only cut down on costs but also helped overcome local resistance and potential siting hurdles, while guaranteeing a steady supply of volunteers and funding.

Habitat for Humanity published a how-to guide entitled *Community Self-Help Housing Manual* in 1982.[40] It included everything from basic house plans (which have changed little since then) to family selection guidelines to instructions on setting up your own Habitat for Humanity affiliate. Perhaps more than anything else, however, it was Habitat for Humanity's ability to build a grassroots network of zealous housing advocates, including former President Jimmy Carter, that secured its success.

The 1970s also saw a number of significant policy shifts. As the concept of self-help gained momentum, the poor were seen no longer as a burden but as a resource. The United Nations held a number of conferences focusing on urban settlements, at which Turner and others presented their work, and in 1972 the World Bank, drawing on the work of Abrams, Turner, and others, launched an urban lending program that paved the way for slum-improvement initiatives. Rather than investing in housing, the bank advocated investing in land, services, and utilities and, in some cases, granting secure land tenure to residents in existing squatter settlements.

One of the first of these "sites-and-services" projects the bank

funded was in Lusaka, Zambia. Carried out between 1972 and 1975, it provided the construction of roads, installation of piped water to standpipes, security lighting, and garbage removal. The project also offered small loans to residents for housing improvements, including $375 to those forced to relocate to an overspill area to make way for the new services.[41]

Gradually slum redevelopment gave way to "upgrading."[42] The introduction of micro-credit lending helped spur the construction of pit latrines, water delivery, and self-help housing in former squatter settlements. Architects such as Reinhard Goethert and nonprofit groups such as the Cooperative Housing Foundation (CHF) in America and FUNDASAL in El Salvador began to play a significant role in advising governments on housing policy and implementing large-scale self-help and sites-and-services programs.[43]

Unlike previous government-managed programs, the sites-and-services and self-help models promoted self-reliance over institutional support. In terms of sheer numbers, at least, it was difficult to find fault with the approach. For example, between 1969 and 1984 the Kampung Improvement Program, funded by the World Bank, brought essential services to some 15 million people in Indonesia, and by 1996 Habitat for Humanity alone had dedicated some 50,000 homes.

However, in time housing experts recognized a number of shortcomings to the approaches.[44] Because people were unlikely to invest time and money in building or upgrading homes they didn't own, the self-help and sites-and-services models could not be adopted in areas where formal land-tenure was a political impossibility. Others pointed out that both models tended to relocate people who relied on work in the inner city to the city's periphery.

The need to meet financial targets placed an emphasis on quantity above quality. This resulted in homes so basic as to be almost bereft of design, lessening their value over time. Program mandates and policies did little to encourage green building or to mitigate the impact of human settlements on the environment. And whereas public housing—permanent and well serviced—had provided shelter at little to no cost to the tenant, self-help and sites-and-services occupants invariably paid more for less. In most areas, improvements still struggled to keep pace with population growth.

Although architects participated in and in many cases mobilized self-help housing programs, the very concept was a negation of the traditional role of the architect. Design was not perceived as adding value. Architects in the self-help housing model were mere trainers if not unnecessary inconveniences. As Turner, one of the movement's most prominent advocates, put it:

> The certified professional makes a fool of himself, and often does a great deal of harm to other people, by assuming that he knows more than the uneducated by virtue of his schooling. All that second- and third-hand knowledge and intellectual exercising does for him, however, is to reduce his ability to listen and learn about situations significantly different from his own social and economic experience—with consequences that can be tragic when he has the power to impose his solutions on those who are not strong enough to resist.[45]

Once again the relevance of design and of the design professional was called into question. It would require a new generation of architects, policy makers, planners, humanitarian aid workers, and others to bridge the gap between design and policy. In doing so, they would not only reaffirm the essential role of design but demonstrate the importance of building sustainable communities.

The work of two mavericks stands out: Fred Cuny, who made the connection between disaster relief and development work, and Samuel "Sambo" Mockbee, whose thoughtful structures in rural Alabama brought the practice of architecture back to the design of low-cost shelter. In many ways the two led parallel lives. Both men operated on an act-first-and-ask-permission-later basis. Both were shunned by the establishments within which they operated, and both would be outlived by their charismatic, larger-than-life personalities.

When Cuny entered the field of disaster relief in 1970, not much had changed since World War II. Tents were the standard shelter response, and little attention was paid to camp planning. In most countries the military took the lead in responding to emergencies, followed by various housing ministries and other departments or agencies. For example, in the United States no fewer than 100 agencies were tasked with responding to disaster in one form or another. (It was not until 1979, when Carter created the Federal

1970s

ca. 1970
New government-subsidized low-cost housing in the Philippines (above) and Brazil (below).

1972
Freedom to Build
John F. C. Turner and Robert Fichter

1972
Pruitt-Igoe Housing
St. Louis, Mo., USA
Minoru Yamasaki
St. Louis Housing Authority begins demolition of the 33-building public housing complex.
Wide World Photos

Emergency Management Agency, that the many responsibilities for disaster assistance and response were consolidated into a single agency.)[46] This led to duplicated efforts, complexity, and confusion.

What's more, little coordination existed between the nonprofit sector and government agencies. As Cuny would later write: "Most of the agencies operating at the time were oriented toward relief and charity. Development concerns were emerging, but few had yet seen a broader role for the voluntary agency. The favored relief approaches still relied mostly on short-term staff and volunteers. Because of high staff turnover, little accumulated wisdom was incorporated into the basic response pattern of the agencies."[47]

Designers offered up a steady stream of innovative emergency-shelter systems, from inflatable warehouses to polyurethane domes, but most were too costly or too cumbersome to implement. Prototypes for "instant housing" that had failed in one disaster would reappear in slightly altered form in the context of another.

"[Architects] were typically doing these Darth Vader things with helicopters and gee-whiz materials. They came at it with enthusiasm or commercial interest. There was a lot of experimentation going on. The fact that shelter had to come out of local material and processes eluded these people. When you told them that you can build a permanent house in Bangladesh in three days for the same amount of money they were proposing to spend on temporary housing, they ignored you," recalled architect Ian Davis, a shelter consultant with the United Nations and a colleague of Cuny's.[48]

Meanwhile, tents—the solution of choice for most aid agencies—would be shipped over great distances at great cost only to go unused because they arrived too late or were sited in camps away from homes, businesses, and livestock.

At the same time studies began to make a correlation between substandard housing, increased urbanization, and a community's vulnerability to natural disasters. "The study of disasters is almost by definition a study of poverty within the developing world," wrote Davis in his book *Shelter After Disaster* (1978), one of the first analyses of the design, as opposed to the logistics, of emergency shelter.[49] Yet in the reconstruction of housing in disaster-prone areas, aid agencies paid scant attention to disaster mitigation in terms of design, siting, or environmental impact. By the 1970s it had become clear to many

relief experts that the standard modes of shelter provision needed to be drastically overhauled—particularly in handling natural disasters.

Enter Cuny, who, in the words of one biographer, was a "take-charge Texan who spent his life chasing trouble."[50] Cuny's first encounter with the world of disaster relief came when he volunteered as a pilot for the Biafran airlifts in 1969. The tragedy had begun two years earlier, when Nigerian forces cut off supplies to secessionist minorities in the country's southeast. Cuny arrived as aid efforts were coming to an end. Troubled by what he'd seen and seduced by the adrenaline rush of disaster-relief work, at the age of 25 he founded his own for-profit consulting firm, Fred Cuny & Associates, later called Intertect. (It sounded better than "Save the Peasants," he once deadpanned.[51])

Less than a year later, Cuny found himself working as an engineering advisor to Oxfam for the Bengali aid operations in East Pakistan (now Bangladesh), where a cyclone had left 300,000 people dead and millions more homeless. The disaster exacerbated the area's political instability, and the country descended into civil war, causing some 10 million people to flee. Arriving at the refugee camps that had sprouted up along the India-Pakistan border, Cuny was appalled by the disorganized tangle of agencies and NGOs that comprised the international community's response. A *Frontline* documentary described his reaction this way:

> For lack of trucks or road repairs, emergency supplies rotted in warehouses while people starved a few miles away. Refugee camps were constructed with no discernible thought to such basic matters as location or sanitation, with the result that some had scant access to water, others were washed away in the first rains, while still others were turned into death camps by cholera epidemics. Especially galling to Fred—the consummate studier of local conditions—was that many relief groups seemed oblivious to the most basic facts about the region and its cultures. One relief agency had distributed heavy woolen jackets, apparently not realizing that East Pakistan was in the tropics with a median annual temperature in the high 70s. Another handed out cans of pork and beans to the hungry, seemingly unaware that the refugees had no way

1972
Polyurethane Igloo
Masaya, Nicaragua
West German Red Cross and Bayer Company
Experimental dome structures provide emergency housing in Masaya, near Managua, Nicaragua, after three consecutive earthquakes strike the area, killing 20,000 people and rendering 250,000 of Managua's 400,000 residents homeless.
Oxfam

1973–76
Habitat for Humanity builds first project
Zaire
Millard and Linda Fuller in Zaire.
The Fuller Center for Housing

of opening the cans, no way of heating the contents, and that neither Muslims nor Hindus ate pork.[52]

Returning from Bangladesh, Cuny began to develop ideas for refugee-camp planning and design. He recognized the importance of sociology in successful relief operations, and believed that better designed camps, which took into account political realities and cultural mores, could save both money and lives. Whereas most camps at the time were designed in a grid, with multiple families housed in military-style barracks, Cuny's design housed victims in single-family tents clustered around open common spaces. Each cluster had its own latrines, cooking areas, and other basic services. With the tightly knit clusters Cuny hoped to encourage ownership, thereby preventing the camp's infrastructure from being over-burdened, which in turn would help prevent the outbreak of disease and allow for better management.

He first tested his ideas in Managua, Nicaragua, in 1972 following an earthquake in the area that left thousands homeless. The results were dramatic. While nearby camps built by the US military experienced a continual surge of refugees, making any attempt at planning a farce, in the camp Cuny designed for Oxfam the population quickly stabilized. Whereas other camps initiated mass inoculations to curb the outbreak of disease, at Oxfam's camp there was no major outbreak of disease and therefore no need for mass inoculations. Likewise, while security issues plagued other camps, at Oxfam's camp cottage industries and self-help organizations sprouted instead. Moreover, Cuny estimated the camp cost 40 percent less to operate than its counterparts.

Calling on many of the design improvements that had permeated development work, over the course of the next 20-odd years Cuny and his associates at Intertect would rethink virtually every aspect of disaster relief and reconstruction. For example, after an earthquake hit Guatemala in 1976, Cuny adapted the self-help model to train families in seismically safer construction techniques. Rather than bulldozing disaster sites, removing debris, and bringing in imported materials as was typically done, he encouraged aid organizations to pay families to clear sites and salvage materials from the rubble to erect temporary and permanent shelter. And instead of handing out tents, he set up programs to provide families with roofing and other

![Oxfam Emergency House-Making Unit in operation following an earthquake in Lice, Turkey, 1975]

Oxfam Emergency House-Making Unit in operation following an earthquake in Lice, Turkey, 1975
Oxfam

building supplies that could later be used for permanent housing.

It was not that Cuny's design ideas were necessarily trailblazing. Others pioneered cluster-based planning, core-housing, and seismically safer construction techniques. Nor was he the only consultant making the connection between disaster and development. But the force of his personality, his ability to implement new approaches under duress, the emphasis he placed on appropriate design, local materials, and labor, his penchant for publishing his ideas, and his role as an independent consultant working with a wide range of agencies made him an ideal catalyst for change. What's more, his military aspirations as a youth (Cuny was a Marine officer candidate before poor grades and a college prank prematurely ended

Design Like You Give a Damn

1975
Oxfam Emergency House-Making Unit
Lice, Turkey

1976
Earthquake
Hebei and Tangshan, China
Leaves 242,419 dead and 182,000 homeless. China refuses international aid.

1976
Earthquake
Guatemala
Fred Cuny works with Oxfam and World Neighbors to design housing "pictographs" to educate Guatemalans in safer building techniques after an earthquake there kills 23,000 people and injures another 76,000.
Fred Cuny/courtesy InterWorks

1976
United Nations Conference on Human Settlements (Habitat)
Vancouver, Canada
Leads to the formation of UN-HABITAT.

Fred Cuny surveys a UN vehicle that was damaged in an attack by gunmen in Mogadishu, Somalia, 1992. Three years later, at the age of 50, he would disappear in Chechnya.
Judy Walgren/Dallas Morning News

his military career) lent him an easy manner with US and other military personnel, giving him access to influential decision makers.

In time Cuny became more involved with "complex emergencies," often in conflict zones. His work began to focus more on the logistics of providing aid and less on design and engineering. However, others carried on where he left off, including consultants such as Ian Davis and Lisa Dubin and groups like Oxfam, CHF, and shelterproject, to name just a few.

Cuny vanished at the age of 50, on a mission to Chechnya in 1995. His body was never recovered and the mystery of his disappearance remains unsolved. While his frank manner bordered on rudeness and his rule-breaking attitude won him as many enemies as friends, Cuny's influence can still be felt. Today, *Disasters and Development*,

which Cuny published in 1983, is considered the textbook on postdisaster reconstruction—a fact made all the more remarkable when you consider that it is currently, like most of the works cited here, out of print.

Community Design

Meanwhile, a movement toward greater community engagement was taking shape in the worlds of architecture, planning, and design. Influenced by the failure of many of the large-scale public building projects of the '60s and the rise of the environmental movement, some architects began to see themselves not just as professionals bound to meet the needs of their clients but as stewards of the built environment and advocates for more sustainable development.

In Europe the concept of community design can be traced back to the 1969 Skeffington Report "People and Planning," published in Great Britian. The report accepted the need to involve the public in planning and made far-reaching recommendations that influenced subsequent legislation in the early 1970s. Publicity and consultation became required components of the statutory planning system, providing local people with opportunities to comment on and object to development plans and planning applications.[53] Architects such as Lucien Kroll in Belgium and Giancarlo DeCarlo in Italy actively sought community participation in the design process in an effort to make their designs more responsive to community needs.[54] In England Ralph Erskine based his office in a disused funeral parlor in the center of town during the design of the Byker Housing project in Newcastle-upon-Tyne to encourage residents to drop in talk to with the design team and raise concerns that went well beyond architecture.[55]

By contrast, the nature of the community design movement in America was more political, with roots in the civil rights and social justice movements of the late 1960s and 1970s. In 1968 the civil rights leader Whitney M. Young, Jr., then executive director of the Urban League, opened the hundredth Convention of the American Institute of Architects with these words:

> You are not a profession that has distinguished itself by your social and civic contributions to the cause of civil rights, and I am sure this does not come to you as any shock. You are most distinguished by your thunderous silence and your

1984–85
Famine
Ethiopia
Drought and political instability lead to food shortages, killing more than one million people.

1985
Earthquake
Mexico City, Mexico
E. V. Leyendecker, National Bureau of Standards

1985–94
Nemausus I & II
Nîmes, France
Jean Nouvel
The architect adapts an industrial aesthetic for the construction of 114 units of subsidized low-cost housing.
Ateliers Jean Nouvel

complete irrelevance....You are employers, you are key people in the planning of our cities today. You share the responsibility for the mess we are in....It didn't just happen. We didn't just suddenly get this situation. It was carefully planned.[56]

According to Rex Curry, former president of the Association for Community Design, the concept for an alternative design practice emerged from this meeting: The Community Design Center (CDC), where volunteer professionals would provide architecture and planning services to nonprofit neighborhood groups free of charge.[57]

During the 1970s there were eighty CDCs sprinkled throughout the country. The centers brought design professionals, environmental engineers, government agencies, and clients together in the design process, usually through a series of workshops, site visits, and interviews. The approach, called "community design" or "participatory design," combined the aspects of self-reliance and self-determination that made the self-help model so compelling with the same emphasis on design, technical expertise, and sustainability usually provided to private clients.

It was a way of working that came naturally to Samuel Mockbee. Mockbee studied architecture at Auburn University in Alabama and developed his ideas and aesthetic while in private practice in Mississippi, first in partnership with Thomas Goodman in 1977, then with Coleman Coker and Tom Howorth starting in 1983. He became interested in low-income housing in 1982 when he helped a Catholic nun move and renovate condemned houses in Madison County. He built his first "charity house" there for $7,000 using donated and salvaged materials and volunteer labor—a model he would later develop with his students.

In 1993 Mockbee returned to Auburn University and founded the Rural Studio with D. K. Ruth. For Mockbee the studio was a means of combating the entrenched discrimination, substandard housing, and poverty he saw around him, while giving architecture students hands-on experience missing from most curriculums. The homes the Rural Studio built were as exuberant as they were intensely customized. Like Mockbee's earlier work, they were the physical embodiment of a conversation between architect and client. It just so happened that in this case the clients were living on the poverty

"The main difference between success and failure is the degree to which poor people themselves are involved in determining the quality and quantity of the services they receive."

World Development Report, World Bank, 2004

line in rural Alabama—people, as Mockbee described them, "left over from Reconstruction." What made his approach radical was not that Mockbee treated these prospective homeowners with hard-won dignity and respect, though he did, but that he treated them as *clients*. As he wrote:

The professional challenge, whether one is an architect in the rural American South or elsewhere in the world, is how to avoid being so stunned by the power of modern technology and economic affluence that one does not lose sight of the fact that people and place matter....

For me, these small [Rural Studio] projects have in them the architectural essence to enchant us, to inspire us, and ultimately, to elevate our profession. But more importantly, they remind us of what it means to have an American architecture without pretense. They remind us that we can be as awed by the simple as by the complex and that if we pay attention, this will offer us a glimpse into what is essential to the future of American Architecture: Its honesty.

"Love your neighbor as yourself." This is the most important thing because nothing else matters. In doing so, an architect will act on a foundation of decency which can be built upon. Go above and beyond the call of a "smoothly functioning conscience"; help those who aren't likely to help you in return, and do so even if nobody is watching![58]

These were also buildings that one could describe in the highbrow language of architecture. That, too, was a revelation. With its meager

---

1989
Aranya Community Housing
Indore, India
Balkrishna Doshi, Vastu-Shilpa
Foundation
Vastu-Shilpa Foundation

1989
Loma Prieta Earthquake
Wastonville, Calif., USA
One in five victims camps outside his or her home rather than use the officially designated communal shelters.

1990–91
Improved Quincha Earthquake-Resistant Housing
Alto Mayo Region, Peru
ITDG
Developed in response to the earthquake that struck in 1990, the design improves upon traditional Quincha building methods (in which walls are constructed from wooden poles infilled with smaller wooden poles) by adding roof trusses and making them more flexible and

budgets and scavenged materials, the Rural Studio had invented a new palette. Curtain walls were constructed from car windshields, columns from carpet tiles, yet nothing about the structures appeared recycled. There was certain poetry to their form that demanded—and received—critical respect.

Humanitarian Design Today

During the 1980s and 1990s others also worked to bridge the gap between providing basic shelter and building sustainable communities. In 1983 architect Balkrishna Doshi laid the foundations for what would become a vibrant, mixed-income neighborhood in Indore, India, by combining the best of the sites-and-services and self-help housing models with a more heightened design sense.

The project, which was undertaken by the Vastu-Shilpa Foundation (founded by Doshi himself), included 80 demonstration homes and an urban plan for a new mixed-income township in Aranya near Indore, India. With funding from the World Bank, the architect replaced the unsympathetic grid layout of the typical sites-and-service scheme with a cluster-based plan. The demonstration homes, which Doshi designed around a basic service core, included balconies, patios, and other harmonizing details. The project was intended to encourage new owners to expand their homes progressively as time and money allowed and to embellish them according to their tastes. In a testament to the project's success, by 1989 Doshi's original demonstration homes were selling for 10 times their original price.[59] The foundation later pursued an even more participatory approach in the reconstruction of Ludiya, in Gujarat, India after an earthquake hit Gujarat in 2001.

Other projects that incorporated a more sensitive approach to community development included low-income housing designed by Yasmeen Lari in Pakistan; the Alexandra Townships Housing project designed by Jo Noero in South Africa; and the work of Jan Wampler in Puerto Rico.

The 1980s also saw a renewed interest in adapting technology to better meet the needs of communities. In Canada John Todd and the New Alchemists designed ways of treating waste naturally on-site using plant life (see "Living Machine"). In parts of the developing world ITDG (Intermediate Technology Development Group), founded

"Everybody wants the same thing, rich or poor...not only a warm, dry room, but a shelter for the soul."

Samuel Mockbee, architect

Samuel Mockbee (center) with Anderson Harris (right) and family. In 1997 the Rural Studio would build the Harrises a home, affectionately called the Butterfly House, and in return the Harrises would donate land for the Mason's Bend Chapel.

Timothy Hursley

therefore more earthquake resistant. In 1991 another quake destroys 17,000 homes, but the 70 locally built improved structures withstand the tremor, demonstrating the effectiveness of the design and prompting the group to build another 4,000 homes.

1993
Mississippi River Flood
Midwestern USA
American Red Cross spends $44 million to help families recover. FEMA creates initiative to buy or relocate properties to prevent future flood losses.

1993
Rural Studio
Newburn, Ala., USA
Samuel Mockbee founds the Rural Studio at Auburn University.

1994
Rwandan Genocide
Burundi, Rwanda, Tanzania
Interahamwe Hutu extremists kill an estimated 500,000 to 800,000 Rwandans in 100 days. Two million refugees flee the country. The outbreak of disease in refugee camps claims an additional 80,000 lives.

in 1965, worked to improve the everyday life of large numbers of people by investing in small technological improvements, such as more energy-efficient stoves or earthquake-resistant adaptations of vernacular housing. The idea of technology for technology's sake gave way to the concept of "appropriate" technology.

However, for every project that pushed the boundaries of socially responsible design, there were many others that relied on formulaic solutions or excluded the community from the planning and design process. In the 1970s planners had responded to new statutes requiring public participation with enthusiasm, putting time and effort into preparing exhibitions and organizing community workshops. Yet public response was often disappointing, and this led many planning authorities to reassess their commitment and to carry out only the minimum work necessary. Public housing programs experienced drastic funding cuts, and in America many community design centers, which had relied on federal funding, shut down.

Likewise, disaster reconstruction efforts were equally varied. Two catastrophic earthquakes in particular demonstrated the extremes of response: The first was the 1985 Mexico City earthquake, which killed nearly 5,000 people and left 200,000 homeless. The second was the Hanshin earthquake that struck the industrial city of Kobe, Japan, in 1995, killing 6,300 people and leaving 100,000 homeless. Both disasters hit densely populated urban areas. However, Mexico City largely recovered after two to three years, while recovery in Kobe took substantially longer. According to Mary Comerio, who analyzed both disasters in her book *Disaster Hits Home*, the difference had as much to do with design and planning as it did with economic factors and politics.[60]

The Mexico City quake measured 8.1 on the Richter scale and lasted approximately two minutes. It leveled 2.3 square miles (6 sq. km) in the historic center of the city, which also happened to house the city's government buildings. A second quake the next day compounded the loss of life and material damage. More than 600 buildings completely or partially collapsed. Hardest hit were the city's *viviendas*, or low-income neighborhoods, where most occupants were renters rather than owners.

Because these residential buildings earned extremely low rents and almost none was covered by insurance, it was clear from the

After an earthquake struck Gujarat, India, in 2001, the Vastu-Shilpa Foundation facilitated a community-led effort to reconstruct the village of Ludiya. Here, residents outside their newly rebuilt homes.
Vastu-Shilpa Foundation

beginning that property owners would have little incentive to rebuild. Yet residents lobbied aggressively to stay in their neighborhoods. With funding from the World Bank and loans and concessions from the International Monetary Fund, Mexico responded by establishing a number of housing programs, the largest of which, Renovacion Habitacion Popular, was mandated to build or repair more than 48,000 housing units.

This ambitious undertaking combined the best of neighborhood-level community design with a government-administered housing program. Under the program, displaced residents in renewal areas were given a Certificate of Rights, which entitled them to low-interest loans to buy rebuilt units, thus converting them from tenants to owners. Residents lived in temporary metal sheds in public streets, parks, alleys, and other rights-of-way near their damaged homes while they worked with their neighbors to repair their community.

1995
Hanshin Earthquake
Osaka Bay, Japan
Dr. Roger Hutchison/National Geophysical Data Center

2000s

2001
Earthquake Reconstruction
Ludiya, Gujarat, India
Vastu-Shilpa Foundation

2004
Tsunami
Indian Ocean
175,000 people are killed and more than one million people in 13 countries are displaced.

Reconstruction plans were developed by community members aided by technical specialists, including some 280 architectural and engineering firms, and were based on a prototypical two-bedroom apartment unit in a three-story building with a single entrance gate. According to Comerio, by standardizing the building design, the city was able to process as many as 800 building permits a month and a single team of inspectors could monitor construction.[61]

In total the government repaired or built nearly 88,000 housing units over the course of two years. "Neighbors together with their neighbors animated by healthy solidarity, organized spontaneously and efficiently, were able to save lives, put an end to misfortune, rebuild the city and create a promising future," wrote a reporter for the newspaper *Excelsior* in a retrospective published 13 years after the disaster.[62]

By contrast, recovery from the earthquake in Japan took 10 years and exposed large gaps in the social net of one of the world's most developed countries.[63] With a population of 1.5 million, Kobe was Japan's sixth-largest city and the world's sixth-largest port. Although more than 90 percent of the damaged structures were residential, the city's economic importance meant that its commercial infrastructure was the first to come back on line. In the disaster's aftermath the government built 48,000 temporary housing units in parking lots and on undeveloped land and filled them with displaced residents by lottery. Two years later thousands of people still lived in metal crates in temporary camps sited on the city's outskirts.[64]

Kobe's slower recovery can be attributed to a number of factors. Before the quake Japan had no emergency-response system for natural disasters. A reliance on the private market to recover losses also contributed to the slow pace of rebuilding. Also, many blamed the decision by city authorities to place temporary housing outside residents' former neighborhoods, hindering families from returning to work, isolating them from their social networks, and preventing them from tapping local resources to solve their own housing crises.[65] But by far the biggest failure was that of the international aid community and officials in Japan to learn from the mistakes and success of other cities in coping with disaster.

In the years following the Mexico City and Kobe earthquakes, a series of floods, hurricanes, and other disasters did prompt local officials in some cities to take disaster mitigation measures. New codes forced owners to retrofit unreinforced masonry buildings, bolt structures to their foundations, install roof ties, build to higher flood elevations, and take other steps to strengthen buildings in disaster-prone cities throughout the United States, for example. Recognizing the role of environment in mitigating disasters, some cities, most notably Tulsa, Oklahoma, also implemented land-use controls, such as protecting important wetlands and preventing development in areas vulnerable to natural disaster.

Conclusion

A century after the San Francisco earthquake, the solution to housing the world's displaced and disenfranchised remains as stubbornly situation-specific and complex as ever. Even as we compiled this book, a series of tsunamis, hurricanes, and earthquakes reminded the world once again how vulnerable and unprepared we are against the awesome powers of nature—whether we live in the world's poorest country or its wealthiest. The Red Cross estimates that over the past two decades, on average more than 75,000 people have been killed annually by natural and manmade disasters, and another 211 million have been affected by disaster each year—more than 98 percent of them in the developing world. What's more, the agency reports that over the last decade the number of disasters—and the number of people affected by disasters—has climbed.[66]

Likewise, systemic substandard housing conditions continue to plague the world's cities. UN-HABITAT estimates that nearly one billion people, a third of the world's urban population, live in slums. The agency projects that number will double by 2030.[67]

Fortunately, we also live in a time when technology, particularly the ubiquitous Internet, has enabled the rapid exchange of ideas on an unprecedented scale. Groups such as Slum Dwellers International are using the Web to network and exchange models of development between slum dwellers in different countries. CAD software has made professional design services more affordable and enabled architects to volunteer their services in communities near and far. At the same time, computer modeling systems have led to technical advances promoting safer, more disaster-resistant building design.

2005
Operation Restore Order
Zimbabwe
Pres. Robert Mugabe orders a crackdown on "illegal structures," forcing slum dwellers to tear down their own dwellings throughout the country. Nearly 600,000 people are left homeless. UN-HABITAT condemns the slum-clearance program as indiscriminate, unjustified, and conducted with indifference to human suffering.

2005
Green Mobile Home
Mississippi State University, Mississippi State, Miss., USA
Developed by architects at the Carl Small Town Center, part of the College of Architecture, Art, and Design at Mississippi State University, this self-sufficient, solar-powered unit was designed as an alternative to the traditional mobile home.
Jason Pressgrove and Michael Berk

2005
Hurricane Katrina
Louisiana, Mississippi, Alabama, USA
145-mph winds tear a path of destruction through the Gulf Coast. The storm and subsequent flooding of New Orleans kill an estimated 1,325 people; more than one million people are displaced from the Gulf Coast region. Emergency officials respond by bringing more than 50,000 travel

The Engineering Unit of the Thai Army erected temporary housing in Ban Nam Kaem, Takua Pa province, Thailand, following the Indian Ocean tsunami of December 2004.
Roslan Rahman/AFP/Getty Images

A wider appreciation for the importance of design in disaster mitigation and community development has spurred greater collaboration between designers and communities. In addition to the many architects and groups engaged in community design and development profiled in this book, organizations such as the Aga Khan Development Network, Architects Without Frontiers, Architecture + Development, Architectes de l'Urgence, the Buckminster Fuller Institute, Builders Without Borders, Building and Social Housing Foundation, Association for Community Design, Architects/Designers/ Planners for Social Responsibility, the Enterprise Foundation, Design Corps, Design Matters, Public Architecture, Shelter Associates, shelterproject, World Shelters, the Volunteer Architects' Network, and many others have emerged, promising a more innovative and inclusive approach to designing shelter.

Will the start of the twenty-first century be remembered as the golden era of socially conscious design? The answer will likely depend on the willingness of architects and designers to reach beyond the design community and its traditional audience—to humbly venture into the communities in which they live, listen to the needs of their neighbors, and offer their services. As Samuel Mockbee once said: Proceed and be bold.

trailers and mobile homes to the area, but 100 days after the disaster, demand continues to outstrip supply. At right, FEMA tag on the door of a home in New Orleans indicates it has been searched for survivors.
Win Henderson/FEMA

2005
Earthquake
Pakistan-administered Kashmir
A month after the disaster the death toll estimate stands at 87,000; more than two million people are displaced. The United Nations exhausts its stockpile of tents. At right, desperate families in Muzaffarabad, Pakistan, set up a camp using recycled advertising billboards in an attempt to shelter themselves as winter approaches.
David Guttenfelder/AP Photo

1 "The San Francisco Earthquake, 1906," EyeWitness to History, www.eyewitnesstohistory.com.

2 [unidentified director], *Before and After the Great Earthquake and Fire: Early Films of San Francisco*, 1897–1916, Library of Congress, www.loc.gov.

3 Philip L. Fradkin, *The Great Earthquake and Firestorms of 1906*, Berkeley: University of California Press, 2005, 209.

4 Barracks were also erected, but a study later determined they were costly and ineffective. Charles O'Connor et al., *San Francisco Relief Survey: The Organization and Methods of Relief Used After the Earthquake and Fire of April 18, 1906*, New York: Survey Associates, 1913, 239.

5 Ibid., 71.

6 Ibid., 84.

7 Ibid.

8 San Francisco was not the first city to develop new building strategies in the face of disaster. For example, when an earthquake and subsequent tsunami and fires destroyed a third of medieval Lisbon in 1755, reconstruction led to one of the earliest examples of modern earthquake-proof construction, the *gaiola*, a flexible wooden cage formed by diagonal trusses reinforcing a horizontal and vertical wooden frame. According to lore, architectural models were built to test the new construction method by marching troops around them to simulate the effects of an earthquake. The buildings and public squares of the reconstructed city still stand today. Kenneth Maxwell, "Lisbon: The Earthquake of 1755 and Urban Recovery Under the Marques de Pombal," in Joan Ockman, ed., *Ground Zero: Case Studies in Urban Reinvention*, Munich: Prestel Verlag, 2002, 31.

9 Thierry Garrel, dir., *Architectures*, 4-DVD series, Strasbourg: Arte, 2003.

10 American Planning Association, "Individuals Who Influenced Planning Before 1978," http://www.planning.org/25anniversary/influentials.htm.

11 Le Corbusier, *Towards a New Architecture*, Mineola, NY: Dover Books, 1985.

12 Sigfried Giedion, *Walter Gropius*, Mineola, NY: Dover Books, 1992, 79.

13 J. Baldwin, *Bucky Works: Buckminster Fuller's Ideas for Today*, New York: John Wiley & Sons, 1996, 32.

14 Carol Burns et al., "Manufactured Housing: A Double Wide Analysis," http://www.gsd.harvard.edu/studios/s97/burns/index.html.

15 Robert Bennefield and Robert Bonnette, *Structural and Occupancy Characteristics of Housing: 2000*, Washington, DC: US Census Bureau, Nov. 2003, www.census.gov/prod/2003pubs/c2kbr-32.pdf.

16 Carol Burns, "Manufactured Housing: A Double Wide Analysis of Clockwork and Cloudwork," Cambridge, Mass.: Harvard Graduate School of Design, 1997, http://www.gsd.harvard.edu/studios/s97/burns/intro.html.

17 Sears, Roebuck and Co., "Chronology of the Sears Modern Homes Program," http://www.searsarchives.com/homes/chronology.htm.

18 "The Mail-Order House," *CBS News Sunday Morning*, Aug. 24, 2003, http://www.cbsnews.com/stories/2003/05/14/Sunday/main553963.shtml.

19 Sears, "Chronology."

20 Sandra Rihs and Daniel Katell, "The Evolution of Slum Clearance Policies in London and Paris," United Nations Centre for Human Settlements (UN-HABITAT), vol. 7, no. 3, Sept. 2001.

21 Catherine Bauer had been influenced by Walter Gropius and the German school of modernists during trips in the '20s and '30s to Europe, where she was inspired by the power of design to promote social change. When she returned to the United States she was shocked by the conditions she found and became a passionate housing advocate. In 1934 she wrote the book *Modern Housing*, in which she described the European planning and housing strategies she had seen, and applied them to an American context. Modern housing, she argued, needed to be planned, built slowly to reduce speculation, and available to all citizens regardless of income. Peter H. Oberlander and Eva Newbrun, *Houser: The Life and Work of Catherine Bauer*, Vancouver: University of British Columbia Press, 1999.

22 Kerry D. Vandell, "FHA Restructuring Proposals: Alternatives and Implications," *Housing Policy Debate*, Fannie Mae Foundation, vol. 6, issue 2, 1995, 299–394.

23 Charles Abrams, *The Future of Housing*, New York: Harper & Brothers, 1946.

24 Ralph Steiner and Willard Van Dyke, *The City*, New York: American Documentary Film, Inc., 1939.

25 Ian Davis, *Shelter After Disaster*, London: Oxford Polytechnic Press, 1978, 87.

26 Robert Rubin, "Jean Prouvé," Yale School of Architecture, 2005, http://www.architecture.yale.edu/tropical_house/essay.htm.

27 Designed by entrepreneur Carl Strandlund, the Lustron Home was an ingenious but short-lived experiment in low-cost housing. The homes were made from porcelain-coated steel panels mounted on a steel frame. They were advertised as being rodent-proof, fire-proof, lightning-proof, rustproof, and maintenance-free. Each dwelling cost $7,000, but manufacturing glitches led to cost overruns. Despite a government commitment of $40 million, only 2,498 units were ultimately produced, and the government foreclosed on the company in 1951. Although some current owners have compared living in the manufactured dwelling to living in a "lunchbox," the surviving homes have earned a cult following. Douglas Knerr, *Suburban Steel: The Magnificent Failure of the Lustron Corporation, 1945–1951*, Columbus: Ohio State University Press, 2004.

28 Peter Hall, "Living for Tomorrow," *Metropolis Magazine*, Dec. 2002, www.metropolismag.com/html/content_1202/mit/.

29 The estate has since become a well-heeled, upper-middle-class neighborhood, in part due to the caché of Prouvé's designs. Alex Kliment, "Prefab: House as Mass Customized Product," The Architectural League, 2003, http://www.archleague.org/lectures/strategies/prefabsummary.html.

30 Charles Abrams, *Man's Struggle for Shelter in an Urbanizing World*, Cambridge, Mass.: MIT Press, 1966, 166.

31 See http://www.freeenterpriseland.com/BOOK/LITTLEBOXES.html.

32 It was later determined that the building, called Ronan Point, was structurally unsound. Kenny Shaw, *From Here to Modernity*, London: BBC/The Open University, http://www.open2.net/modernity/ http://news.bbc.co.uk/onthisday/hi/dates/stories/may/16/newsid_2514000/2514277.stm.

33 John F. C. Turner and Robert Fichter, *Freedom to Build: Dweller Control for the Housing Process*, New York: MacMillan, 1972, 294.

34 "Slums: The Magnitude of the Problem," Tata Institute of Fundamental Research, http://theory.tifr.res.in/bombay/amenities/housing/slum-stats.html.

35 Abrams, *The Future of Housing*, 129.

36 The first "self-help and mutual aid" project in America took place in the coal-mining areas of Pennsylvania during the Depression. In the wake of mass unemployment at the mines, the program sought to bring unemployed mine workers living in slum conditions "back to the farm" by paying them to build their own housing. Peter M. Ward, *Self-Help Housing: A Critique*, London: Mansell, 1982, 26.

37 Hassan Fathy, *Architecture for the Poor*, Chicago: University of Chicago Press, 1976, 32.

38 Ibid., passim.

39 Roberto Chavez, Julie Viloria, and Melanie Zipperer, "Interview with John F. C. Turner," World Bank forum, Washington, DC, April 2–3, 2002, www.worldbank.org/urban/forum2002/docs/turner-excerpt.pdf; Ward, *Self-Help Housing*, 23.

40 Robert William Stevens and Habitat for Humanity, eds., *Community Self-Help Housing Manual: Partnership in Action*, Croton-on-Hudson, NY: Intermediate Technology Development Group of North America, 1982.

41 It was intended that the squatter community help defray the costs of the new services by paying for water usage and other services and by repaying their loans. Ultimately, though, many residents were slow to pay their loan installments and resented being charged for services. If wealthy Lusakans did not have to pay for them, they argued, why should they, especially when they received much lower levels of service (for example, trash was often not collected at all in the project area). Nonetheless, the program was considered a success and offered an alternative approach for cities struggling with an explosion of squatter settlements. Lusaka Sites and Services Project," Upgrading Urban Communities, The World Bank Group, 1999–2001, http://web.mit.edu/urbanupgrading/upgrading/case-examples/ce-ZA-lus.html.

42 Nabeel Hamdi, *Housing Without Houses: Participation, Flexibility, Enablement*, London: Intermediate Technology Publications, 1995.

43 Ibid., 20.

44 Ward, *Self-Help Housing*.

45 Turner and Fichter, *Freedom to Build*, 147.

46 During the 1920s–30s a series of disasters (including the Mississippi River flood of 1927, which inundated an area almost as large as New England and left 700,000 people homeless, and the Long Beach, California, earthquake of 1933, which caused a number of school buildings to collapse) prompted the United States Congress to pass a number of flood control measures and other legislation aimed at disaster-mitigation and relief. The Reconstruction Finance Corporation gave disaster loans for repair and reconstruction of certain public facilities. The Flood Control Act gave the US Army Corps of Engineers greater authority to build levees and implement other flood control projects, and by 1934 the Bureau of Public Roads was given the authority to provide funding for highways and bridges damaged by natural disasters. Still, as in most countries, disaster recovery was funded on an incident-by-incident basis, and assistance to individuals was considered largely the domain of voluntary agencies and private charity. Congress did not establish a coordinated disaster relief program until the 1950s. "FEMA History," Federal Emergency Management Agency, Oct. 23, 2004, http://www.fema.gov/about/history.shtm.

47 Frederick Cuny, *Disasters and Development*, Dallas: Intertect Press, 2nd ed.,1994, 19.

48 Ian Davis, telephone interview with Kate Stohr, June 13, 2005.

49 Davis, *Shelter After Disaster*, 11.

50 Sherry Jones, dir., "The Lost American," *Frontline*, PBS, Oct. 14, 1997, www.pbs.org.

51 Scott Anderson, *The Man Who Tried to Save the World*, New York: Random House, 2000, 71.

52 Jones, "The Lost American."

53 Barbara Illsley, *Community Planning*, London: Royal Town Planning Institute, Oct. 2002, http://www.rtpi.org.uk/resources/publications/community-planning/01home.html.

54 Mary C. Comerio, "Design and Empowerment: 20 Years of Community Architecture," *Built Environment*, Oxford: Alexandrine Press, vol. 13, no. 1, 1987, 15.

55 Jon Coaffee and Chris Brocklebank, "Byker Urban Design Competition: Developing a Statement of Community Involvement," *Newcastle University Global Urban Research Unit*, Jan. 2005, www.newcastle.gov.uk.

56 President Lyndon B. Johnson later awarded Young the Medal of Freedom for his civil rights work. "1968," Archvoices, July 11, 2003, http://www.archvoices.org.

57 Bryan Bell, ed., *Good Deeds, Good Design: Community Service Through Architecture*, New York: Princeton Architectural Press, 2004, 63.

58 Samuel Mockbee, "Architectural Design: The Everyday and Architecture," 1998, http://www.ruralstudio.com/sambomemorial.htm.

59 Balkrishna Doshi, "Architect's Record of Aranya Community Housing," Geneva: Aga Khan Award for Architecture, 1995.

Doshi designed a master plan and model homes for an innovative mixed-income sites-and-services development. Homes, which include balconies and look onto a shared courtyard, are grouped in clusters of ten along a central spine. Septic tanks are provided for each group of 20 houses, and electricity and water are available throughout. The new development will eventually house a population of 60,000.

60 Mary C. Comerio, *Disaster Hits Home: New Policy for Urban Housing Recovery*, Berkeley: University of California Press, 1998, 128.

61 Ibid., 142.

62 Manuel Magaña Contreras, "The Greatest Catastrophe Ever Suffered by Mexico City," *Excelsior*, Sept. 20, 1998, http://www.tenorissimo.com/domingo/Articles/excel92098.htm.

63 Toshizo Ido (governor of Hyogo Prefecture), "Learning to Live with Risk," World Conference on Disaster Reduction, Kobe, Japan, Jan. 18, 2005.

64 Michael Zielenziger, "Kobe Still Reels from Earthquake; Many are Homeless; Government Lags," *San Jose Mercury News*, Jan. 20, 1997, 1A.

65 Davis, interview with Stohr.

66 Between 2000 and 2004 disasters affected one-third more people than between 1995 and 1999. International Federation of the Red Cross, *World Disasters Report 2005*, table 3, 196.

67 "Millennium Development Goals," 2003, UN-HABITAT, http://www.unhabitat.org/mdg/.

Hou

Emergency

Transitional

Permanent

Homelessness

sing

Of the world's refugees
49% are female and
47% are children (under 18)

"Protracted Refugee Situations," UNHCR, June 2004

The UN High Commissioner for Refugees estimates that there were
9,200,000
refugees in the world in 2004

"2004 Global Refugee Trends," UNHCR, June 2005

In 2003 there were 38 different protracted conflicts in the world, accounting for some
6,200,000 refugees

"Protracted Refugee Situations," UNHCR, June 2004

The average duration of major refugee situations has increased
FROM 9 years (1993)
TO 17 years (2003)

"Protracted Refugee Situations," UNHCR, June 2004

Lightweight Emergency Tent

Location_Various
Date_2002–present
Organization_Office of the United Nations High Commissioner for Refugees (UNHCR)
End client_Refugees, internally displaced populations
Design consultant_Ghassem Fardanesh
Manufacturer_H. Sheikh Noor-ud-Din & Sons (Pvt.) Limited, Lahore, Pakistan
Cost per unit_Approx. $100
Area_178 sq. ft./16.5 sq. m
Occupancy_4–5 people
Dimensions_18 x 9.8 x 6.9 ft./5.5 x 3 x 2.1 m
Weight_91 lb./41.5 kg

In war-torn countries and areas devastated by disaster, the presence of UNHCR tents is one of the first signs of aid.

Designers have tried to rethink this basic tent for decades. Everything from prefabricated structures to shipping containers to polyurethane yurts has been suggested or attempted. But as the agency politely points out in its guide to emergency materials, to date none of these systems has proven effective in refugee situations. Most fail simply because other emergency shelter arrangements will have been made before these systems even arrive. Some tent alternatives are perceived as "too permanent," making them difficult to site in host communities and creating less incentive for a refugee to return home. Others are difficult or costly to replicate.

But in recent years there has been a growing sense within the agency that the design of the standard family tent could and should be radically overhauled. In most emergencies the agency sends out plastic sheeting first. Depending on the size and complexity of the crisis, this sheeting may be the response of first and last resort. However, in cases where local materials are not available to build more permanent structures, where families cannot find shelter within the community or are displaced for longer periods of time, the UNHCR provides more durable alternatives—typically a ridge-style or center-pole-double-fly tent made from canvas. Yet these canvas tents are not only heavy, cumbersome to carry, and costly to ship, but because canvas rots they deteriorate quickly and cannot be stockpiled for long periods. Wear and tear on the weakened material in the field significantly shortens the useful lifespan of the shelter.

In 2002 the UNHCR began testing a new design for the basic family tent it regularly dispatched to areas of crisis. The agency's

Lightweight Emergency Tent

Design Like You Give a Damn

**The UNHCR's new Lightweight Emergency
Tents in use in Meulaboh, West Sumatra,
following the Indian Ocean tsunami of 2004**
T. Pengilley/UNHCR

technical support, supply management, and emergency and security divisions developed specifications over the course of several years. The tent needed to be lightweight, durable, and have a longer shelf life than its canvas precursors. But because tents can cost as much to ship as to make, the primary consideration was one of volume in terms of both weight and size. "We are talking in terms of 50,000 to 100,000 tents," explained Ghassem Fardanesh, a physical planner in the UNHCR Technical Support Section who helped spearhead the project. "Even when we hit the right design, some of the specifications didn't come easily."

The resulting design employs a tunnel shape to maximize headroom and usable space. An inner tent with a "bathtub" liner provides insulation and flooring. Air circulates through vents and window flaps lined with mosquito netting to guard against malaria. Guy ropes at the front and back rather than the sides allow the tent to be spaced closer to other tents. Because it is made from synthetic materials, the tent can be stockpiled in greater quantities, and its smaller volume and weight (91 pounds [41.5 kg] compared with 176 to 242 pounds [80 to 110 kg] for traditional canvas versions) saves on shipping costs and allows for easier handling. It even comes in its own "handbag."

The most innovative aspect of the design is its recognition of the need for privacy. In refugee camps a survival mentality combined

with close quarters can be an explosive combination, often increasing the incidence of the physical abuse of women and children. To mitigate such violence, the designers created a fabric partition to divide the tent, creating a semiprivate space where women can change and parents can sleep away from children. The partition can also be used to create a semipublic workspace to care for the wounded or sell supplies.

The agency made an initial production run of 10,000 units, and the new design has since been field-tested in Chad (in response to the Darfur crisis) and in areas of Indonesia affected by the tsunami of December 2004. But it could be years before the lightweight model replaces the UNHCR's traditional canvas tent. "In our business it's really difficult to say, 'I have something new, and let's replace [the old version].' The tent we have now has been under surveillance for 20 years. This is a newborn baby," said Fardanesh, who considers the tent a work in progress and expects it will undergo a number of manufacturing tweaks and other modifications before it is fully adopted.

Specifications for the Lightweight Emergency Tent for the UNHCR's traditional canvas tents are provided in UN Inter-Agency Procurement Services Office, "Emergency Relief Items Vol. 1: Compendium of Generic Specifications," *United Nations Development Programme, May 2000, http://www.iapso.org.*

above left
Standard UNHCR canvas tents shelter Sudanese refugees in Eastern Chad in 2004. If stockpiled for too long the canvas rots, shortening the useful lifespan of the tent in the field.
H. Caux/UNHCR

above right
The Lightweight Emergency Tent in use in Meulaboh, West Sumatra, after the Indian Ocean tsunami of 2004. The tents are arranged at an angle to prevent those in facing tents from being able to see inside when the flaps are opened.
G. Fardanesh/UNHCR

opposite left
Cumbersome canvas tents required as many as four people to carry. A man transports the new design on the back of a bicycle in Kreung Sabe, Indonesia. The tent packs in a carrying case and can be easily erected.
G. Fardanesh/UNHCR

opposite right
The new tent's partition affords refugees and displaced families a modicum of privacy.
G. Fardanesh/UNHCR

Lightweight Emergency Tent

Design Like You Give a Damn

"In our business it's really difficult to say,
'I have something new, and let's replace
[the old version].' The tent we have now
has been under surveillance for 20 years.
This is a newborn baby."

Ghassem Fardanesh, senior physical planner, UNHCR

Shelter
Frame Kit

Location_Various
Date_1983–present
Organization_World Shelters
End client_Displaced populations,
emergency field operations
Design team_Steven Elias, Bruce LeBel
Project partner_Buckminster Fuller Institute
Cost per unit_$365
Area_269 sq. ft./25 sq. m
Occupancy_6–8 people
Dimensions_24 x 11 x 8 ft./7.4 x 3.4 x 2.6 m
Packed dimensions_15 x 15 x 60 in./
38 x 38 x 152 cm
Weight_66 lb./30 kg

**A health clinic set up by the nonprofit
International Medical Corps
in Uganda using the Shelter Frame Kit**
World Shelters

Bruce LeBel
World Shelters

*Many designers have commented on the
difficulty of breaking into the relief "industry."*

*Underfunded, overworked aid organizations are often unwilling to take
chances with new designs. In their defense not a month goes by that the
major aid organizations aren't besieged by some designer somewhere
offering the latest panacea to the world's housing crisis. As one aid worker
deadpanned, "Sometimes enthusiasm overtakes experience."*

*For Bruce LeBel, however, experience has never been an issue. In this
interview conducted in March 2005, he talks about the inspiration behind
his and his partner Steven Elias's Shelter Frame Kit, their struggle to bring
it to market, and, ultimately, their decision to produce and distribute the
design through their own nonprofit, World Shelters.*

How did you first get involved in providing humanitarian aid?
I started out as a high-school science teacher. I did my first disaster-
relief project in 1976 in Guatemala after the earthquake there. I
was part of a group from the Mohawk Nation that worked in small
villages that hadn't received aid from other sources. The unreinforced
adobe-block walls and tile roofs were what had collapsed and caused
most of the death and injury in the villages. CARE had a program
offering roofing material for anyone who could get up walls. So what

I developed was a combination of Japanese and Mexican traditional building techniques. Instead of thick adobe blocks, we used posts and woven-bamboo lattice with adobe applied as stucco. Then, in 1977, I did a graduate tutorial with Bucky Fuller.

That must have been interesting. What was it like working with Bucky?
He was someone you could spend an hour with and then have a month's worth of work to do. He had an amazing way of asking the salient question. I think that was the key for me. It was just the way he would take the work I was doing and ask the salient question that would take me to the next level. I had a twofold program with him, one part of which was developing design science curriculums for high schools. The other was structural design with an emphasis on tensegrity, tensile structures.

When I finished my program with Fuller, my wife and I moved to Berkeley, and I went to work for The North Face, which was the first company that used Fuller's principles of "tensegrity" in backpacking tents. Bob Gillis, together with Bruce Hamilton of The North Face, developed the first flex-wand backpacking tent. That's the basic technology that we still use for our disaster relief shelter. We still buy clips from Bob [see "GripClips"].

How did the Shelter Frame Kit come into being? Was it something you started while you were at The North Face?
A colleague I had known through work with Fuller, Steven Elias, also had experience doing disaster relief work. He had a little business called Icosa Domes. (Note: Unrelated to Icosa Village, Inc.) The OFDA [Office of Foreign Disaster Assistance, a division of the United States Agency for International Development (USAID)] had used Icosa Domes in Guatemala, Iran, and Beirut before realizing the hard part is the logistics. And doing something that was as heavy and bulky as the cardboard Icosa Dome just didn't work logistically for relief work. The shipping and in-country handling was too difficult.

After Fuller died in '83, Steven and I got together and said, "We really ought to just do something. There's a legacy here. Let's focus on developing a lightweight, human-transportable, flame-retardant, durable shelter." So we started Dymax and began working on product design.

How did you come up with the idea of using standard relief plastic sheeting rather than supplying your own covering?
It was a phone call. We were exploring a range of different sheeting materials and decided that USAID would probably be a good contact, and we should find out what they use. We then found there was a fellow named Roy Limpitlaw, this would have been in 1984, who had done a study and a write-up for USAID on temporary shelters. This was right at the time that Fred Cuny was starting to get going, too. He put us in contact with the supplier [that] developed the specifications for the

"**Then, we had lunch with Fast Eddy. He saw what we were doing and how dialed it was. He said, 'Tomorrow we are going to meet at my office. I am only going to take 20 percent off the top. I've got all the channels worked out, and here is how it's protected.' We looked at each other and said, 'We cannot go to this meeting. Time to get out of the country.'"**

Bruce LeBel, World Shelters

Shelter Frame Kit

Design Like You Give a Damn

USAID sheeting material. When we found out about this material, we brought in samples and started making shelters with it. Then, when we found that USAID was distributing this to disaster sites, we thought, well, this is just real clear. Not only is it an excellent material, but it's already there. What we really need is a design that will operate as a shelter frame kit without the sheeting material and have it made in the field with the sheeting that's there. That's the seed for our work, this extraordinary sheeting material that shows up after every disaster.

We hired Roy as our sales rep, and Roy was able to make the contacts and pull the strings and get an appointment for us with OFDA. We brought in our demo shelter and demonstrated it to the program manager and to the procurement manager and the logistics officer.... And, here we are out on the front lawn of the State Department setting this thing up, and they are sort of gnashing their teeth because here are these young turks from California with this idea. And then the director of OFDA comes down while were just about to set this thing up, and it just went up so fast. It was beautiful the way it went up. And the director says, "We really need to include this shelter in the evaluation that we're doing." So there we were, and all of a sudden we were in OFDA's first national competition for emergency shelter.

What was the competition all about? Were they testing different designs?
They were doing a competition to procure tent supplies for various relief operations. After winnowing down the entries and going through a bidding process, they decided to do a field test in El Salvador and Guam and other areas. So now we're in the national competition for going globally, and after going through various filters, there were two products left: ours and one from an outdoor equipment company.

The first test site was El Salvador, back in 1985, after the earthquake there. They brought in 50 of our shelters to different distribution centers. So we get the call from USAID about this, and we say, "Well, who is going to be the evaluator?" And the fellow who they designated to be the evaluator was the sales rep from the outdoor equipment company. So, we thought, "This is interesting. Tell you what, we are going to go to El Salvador just to watch." It was a huge mistake because we were essentially calling them on their conflict of interest.

We get to El Salvador and it takes a week for the stuff to get through customs. Frankly, I think they were waiting for us to run out of patience and leave. We spend some time with the evaluator, who actually ends up writing some objective reports. And we take some photographs of how the plastic sheeting on its own was being used, which for the most part was nothing more than using it as a lean-to, or draping it over walls or roofs that had holes in it. They'd hang it between trees. It was just draped. There was absolutely no structure to it at all. So it very much reinforced the validity of the concept behind the Shelter Frame Kit.

How did the test go? What was the response to your design?
We learned quite a bit from that experience. During the time we had available while the shelters were clearing customs, we were following the trail of where aid money goes and discovering how little of it gets used for aid and how much of it gets siphoned off. It was really extraordinary to see where so much of the money was going. Basically, the military power structure was siphoning it out and getting the money out of the country.

We met this fellow, Fast Eddy, who was very well connected, very high up. We were given his name by the American Chamber of Commerce, and after we had lunch with this fellow, after being there seven to eight days and having put together a whole scenario for financing redevelopment with low-tech walls and getting the bank and the tractors and the land brokering all ready—I mean, it only took us a week, and we already had this redevelopment scenario worked out—then, we had lunch with Fast Eddy. He saw what we were doing and how dialed it was. He said, "Tomorrow we are going to meet at my office. I am only going to take 20 percent off the top. I've got all the channels worked out, and here is how it's protected." We looked at each other and said, "We cannot go to this meeting. Time to get out of the country." And we left. And that was it. Never did see one of our structures go up. So we learned an extraordinary amount, but it wasn't about what you think.

What about the bid with OFDA?
We followed the test and just kept things on hold for production. We got reports back that they weren't able to perfect the other tent design, and our tent went up like a dream. We won the competition, but unfortunately then the feedback from OFDA was "Our budgets have been cut. We are not going to be buying any of these tents that we thought we were going to be buying thousands of." And the same scenario repeated itself 15 years later.

What happened in the meantime?
They were used in Guam and Mozambique as part of the first OFDA

test, and then we continued working with relief organizations and developing contacts, but we were just never successful breaking in.

Why do you think that is?
The big problem with shelter is that the logistical issues and the cultural issues totally overwhelm the designs. In particular, land is a big problem. Once people are living someplace, they aren't going to move unless they've got somewhere else to go. So, the ideal solution is one that will perform perfectly for six months and the next day turn into dust. Ours lasts two years.

The geometry, the dimensions, the materials are only a small part of the total package. To me, it's really not only having an ability to solve the logistical problems but also being able to maximize the use of locally available materials and labor. You can make World Shelters shipping in nothing more than what I refer to as "user-friendly live ware." All you need is to ship in one of our associates, and as long as there is cord, sheeting, and some kind of pole material, we can produce self-supporting structures.

How did you eventually get the kit into the field? Where was it finally used?
In the end it was back-burnered for seven or eight years, and then we got a call from the group that was doing the next test for OFDA. Once again there was a set of specifications and a test process and a commitment that they would be purchasing X number of units. The upshot was they turned around and said—just as happened in the previous go around—"Thank you very much, wonderful product, our budgets have been cut."

We started getting smart at that point. Even though my partner Steve and I are dyed-in-the-wool entrepreneurs, we realized: You know, we should start looking at this as a nonprofit. Because trying to sell to the government is a 50-year task. It's not a five-year task or a 10-year task. One day it will happen, but we can't bank on it. So we thought, how do we get it to the NGOs, when shelter is nobody's main mission and everybody's scrambling, and we thought, well, we should approach it as a nonprofit ourselves.

In 2002 we started working with the Buckminster Fuller Institute. Through some joint fundraising, we were able to get units out to IMC [International Medical Corps], which used them as temporary clinics, to the Jordanian Red Crescent, which put some units along the border of Iraq, and to the Mexican Red Cross. A German agency also used them in Kosovo for redevelopment activities. They were used as housing for people who were doing construction and as temporary shelters for people until they could move into their new homes.

How much did you raise and how many shelters were you able to produce?
We raised about $20,000 to $25,000, and with that we were able to produce and distribute about 50 25-square-meter [269-sq.-ft.] shelters—including shipping.

That's the thing that so many people don't realize. Shipping can be half the cost of manufacturing the units, if not more.
That's one of the things that we're working on right now. We're trying to put together production facilities and warehouses, managing the logistics from start to finish.

The other really important part of design is not just having a product but having an organization, taking the responsibility to create an organization that is going to make it happen. All of the issues around designing and initiating and coordinating and building are handled by nonprofit organizations, and I've discovered them to be just critical.

Since we spoke with LeBel, World Shelters has gone on to provide emergency shelter to the Red Cross after Hurricane Katrina pounded the Gulf Coast of the United States, to International Medical Corps in Uganda, and in the tsunami-affected areas of Sri Lanka and Banda Aceh, Indonesia. It has also provided shelter in India (including the Andaman Islands), Venezuela, and El Salvador.

After the Indian Ocean tsunami of 2004, World Shelters' structures were used by a monastery in Sri Lanka. The Shelter Frame Kit is intended to "turn sheeting into shelter." The design takes advantage of the plastic sheeting supplied by the United Nations, USAID, and other agencies to disaster areas. The kit includes S-hooks, PVC pipe, cord, guy lines, anchor stakes, clips, connectors, and a pictorial instruction manual.
World Shelters

GripClips

Location_Various
Date_1975–present
Designer_Robert Gillis
Manufacturer_Shelter Systems
Cost_$8–10 (set of 4)

It would be safe to say that few people know the ins and outs of tents better than Robert Gillis.

Not only did he design the first geodesic backpacking tent, based on Buckminster Fuller's ideas, for The North Face in the 1970s, but he also lived in a collection of tents (with his wife and three children) for more than 20 years—all of which he designed himself, including the tent that housed the family washing machine.

Although many of Gillis's tent innovations have stemmed from efforts to improve his own living conditions, from the beginning he saw the potential for translating his ideas to emergency shelter—in particular using the plastic sheeting that has become a standard component of relief projects. However, working with plastic sheeting meant finding a way to "hold on to it." Gillis explains: "It was difficult to join the material without puncturing it. But puncturing it is a bad idea because it weakens it. The material deteriorates less if you don't injure it." The designer went through more than 10 different iterations before arriving at the GripClip, a small plastic fastener that clips onto any type of sheeting and ties it to a frame.

Reducing the shelter to its most fundamental element, the connection between the sheeting and the support, enabled Gillis to design a number of tents, from a basic shelter frame kit to more elaborate dome structures.

The clips also offered another advantage: They allowed for a range of shapes. Whereas most relief agencies distribute tunnel-shaped tents because the structure can be covered

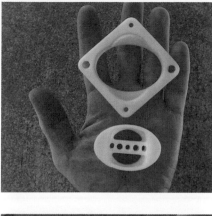 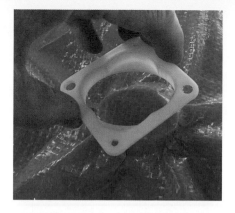 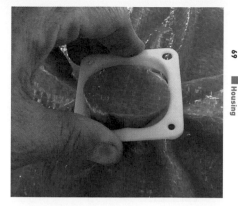

with one large sheet of material, these tents are less stable in the wind than dome-shaped tents. Using GripClips, Gillis found he was able to layer sheeting in shingles to create a more stable structure that would also shed rain. "And I didn't have to sew it or heat-weld it or anything," he recalls. "Here was the perfect thing: It was totally wonderful."

More recently Gillis has focused on creating clips and fasteners to attach plastic sheeting to roofs, frameworks, piping, or plywood, allowing families to turn damaged structures into transitional homes while they rebuild.

opposite
A GripClip, secured to a cross-piece of frame, shown from inside a shelter. The frame pieces are secured with plastic wrap.

above
GripClip's two plastic parts are designed to be twisted together with a piece of sheeting between them. The clip itself can be fastened to a frame structure with plastic ties, rope, or pipe clamps.

right
Robert Gillis inside a tent built with GripClips.
All photographs © www.dometents.com

BOLD
(Building Opportunities
and Livelihoods in Darfur)

Location_Darfur Province, Sudan
Date_2004–5
Organization_CHF International
End client_Displaced populations in Darfur
Design team_Scott Mulrooney, Isaac Boyd
Additional consultant_Richard Hill
Major funding_USAID Office of Foreign Disaster Assistance
Cost per unit_$90
Occupancy_4–5 people
Area_67 sq. ft./6.25 sq. m

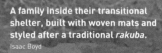

BOLD

Design Like You Give a Damn

A family inside their transitional
shelter, built with woven mats and
styled after a traditional *rakuba*.
Isaac Boyd

One of the difficulties relief organizations often encounter working in areas of conflict is finding a balance between a host community's desire to prevent refugee camps from becoming permanent communities and the needs of refugees for income generation and community building.

BOLD (Building Opportunities and Livelihoods in Darfur), a temporary housing initiative launched in 2004 by CHF International for families displaced by civil war in western Sudan, is one of those rare projects that succeeds in striking a balance between the two.

At the time many people in the camps were living in shelters cobbled together from cardboard and plastic sheeting. "The tents were difficult to get in and out of, dark, hot, and poorly ventilated. It just wasn't a great solution," explains Elin Grimes, a project coordinator. What's more, the plastic sheeting used to construct them, while waterproof, degraded and tore quickly under North Africa's extreme heat. At the same time government restrictions on permanent shelters prevented agencies from working with the displaced population to build more permanent housing. Furthermore, a

lack of work and food in the camps meant that women were traveling outside the camps in search of fuel wood, potentially exposing themselves to physical or sexual attack.

In an effort to provide a source of income generation and improve the makeshift housing of the camps, CHF launched BOLD in 2004. The program employed camp dwellers surrounding the town of Nyala in South Darfur, where grass was plentiful, to weave mats. Those mats were provided to displaced persons in camps in North Darfur, where grass was scarcer, to create temporary shelters modeled on traditional *rakubas*. Constructed from bamboo frames, the shelters were lashed together by cord recycled from rubber tires. The program employed some 3,000 people, 85 percent of them women. Each weaver produced one to two mats a day, providing them with

an income of 250–500 Sudanese dinars ($1–2) per day, enough to buy chickens and eggs and add an important source of protein to their diets.

The shelters are not intended to be permanent. A strong rainstorm caused some to be damaged and repaired. Still, they offered an improvement on the existing shelter. Perhaps more important, by generating income for the weavers, they helped to improve camp life in other ways. "They are a step up," said Grimes of the design. "Everyone would like to see these people living in better homes, but trying to balance what you can do financially, what's immediately available, and what the government will allow you to do doesn't give you a whole lot of flexibility." CHF has since used the same mat-weaving, income-generation program to build community centers in other camps.

above
**The mats were woven in the south, where
grass is plentiful, and were used locally as well
as transported to the arid regions in the north,
where grass does not grow.**
Isaac Boyd

opposite
**Women and men hang woven mats from
a frame to make a shelter.**
Isaac Boyd

Global Village Shelters

Location_Grenada
Date_1995–2005
Design firm_Ferrara Design, Inc.
Design team_Daniel A. Ferrara, Jr.,
Mia Y. Ferrara
Material development_Ferrara Design, Inc.,
Weyerhaeuser, Inc.
Manufacturer_Weyerhaeuser, Inc.
Major funding_Architecture for Humanity;
Weyerhaeuser, Inc.; Ed Plant; and other
individual donations
Cost per unit_$400
Lifespan_8–12 months

It's often said that only from great complexity does simplicity emerge. This was certainly the case with the Global Village Shelter by Ferrara Design, Inc.

The father-daughter design team behind this basic folding refuge experimented with more than 100 different configurations before arriving at an elegant, simple, cost-effective solution to providing temporary shelter. Made from laminated corrugated cardboard, the hut can be erected in less than an hour by two people using only a set of diagrams and common tools. It is designed to house a family of four comfortably. The corrugated cardboard, explains Mia Ferrara, provides strength, privacy, and just enough give to allow the units to be folded for ease of transport.

Daniel Ferrara began developing prototypes of the folding shelter in 1995. Soon afterward, tens of thousands of Tutsis began to flee Rwanda, crowding refugee camps in Burundi, Tanzania, and Zaire. Hoping to provide shelter to these refugees, Ferrara researched manufacturers to produce his design. As it turned out, only three paper companies, one of them Weyerhaeuser, had the capacity to machine corrugate laminate in sheets large enough to meet the firm's needs. The idea simmered on the industrial design company's back burner for several years. In 2002 Mia Ferrara joined the firm, and she and her father turned their attention back to the prototype, which by now had withstood several winters in their backyard in Connecticut. Working with Weyerhaeuser, the pair continued to refine the design and developed a coating that provided material strength and better waterproofing. They infused the corrugate with a fire retardant and added a lock to the unit's door to provide security. The company has also adapted the design to create enclosed pit latrines to be used in emergency situations.

Although the designers believe that, with maintenance, the shelters could last for several years, this is not their intent. "The shelter is designed with a definite limited shelf life," explains Mia Ferrara. In fact, she says, an official at the United Nations expressed concern that the shelters were designed "to last too long." Structures meant to be temporary can often remain in use months and sometimes years after a disaster, leading to problems associated with poverty. "This is often caused by not moving to the next step in the relief efforts," notes Ferrara. "The temporary nature of the Global Village Shelter does not allow for this."

However, as with any portable, temporary structure, the cost and logistics associated with shipping the unit can often be greater than the price of the shelter itself. The company estimates 88 units can fit in a standard shipping container, compared with 500 to 1,000 tents.

Still, Mia Ferrara believes the ease of setup and the sturdiness of the design more than make up for the extra expense. "When the competition is a simple tent, it is difficult to get yourself apart from that and generate interest for something new," she concedes. "People are hesitant to accept change, especially when every penny counts. But this does not mean change should not occur."

In 2005 Ferrara Design partnered with Architecture for Humanity, the Miami-based architecture firm Arquitectonica, and Grenada Relief, Recovery, and Reconstruction (GR3) to field test a prototype of their design in Grenada after more than 85 percent of the island's housing stock was destroyed by powerful hurricanes. Seventy shelters were distributed to rural areas of the country, where they served as transitional homes and health clinics.

Global Village Shelters

Design Like You Give a Damn

left
Global Village Shelters in Connecticut

above
**Global Village Shelters provide much-needed
shelter to a family in hurricane-ravaged Grenada.**
GR3/Architecture for Humanity

Global Village Shelter: Base Assembly Instructions

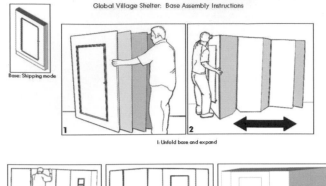

I: Unfold base and expand

II: Once expanded, fold the anchor tabs inward (Step 5). The base is fully secured once the roof is placed on top.

Global Village Shelter: Roof Beam Assembly Instructions

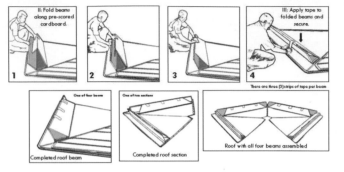

above and opposite above
Instructions for deploying the unit

left
The shelter packs flat for shipping and unfolds to form the walls and roof.

opposite
A variation of the design adapted for use as latrines
All other images Mia Y. Ferrara/Ferrara Design

Global Village Shelter: Roof Assembly (extrusion/ flexible plastic strip insertion) Instructions

The Global Village roof is connected with two flexible plastic strips (extrusions) that are hand-fed through rigid plastic channels. To assemble the roof both flexible strips (extrusions) must be inserted; the second strip (extrusion) will solidify the triangular shape.

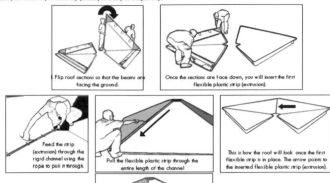

: Flip roof sections so that the beams are facing the ground.

Once the sections are face down, you will insert the first flexible plastic strip (extrusion).

Feed the strip (extrusion) through the rigid channel using the rope to pull it through.

Pull the flexible plastic strip through the entire length of the channel.

This is how the roof will look once the first flexible strip is in place. The arrow points to the inserted flexible plastic strip (extrusion).

Complete Roof

Global Village Shelter: Vent Insertion and Roof/Base Assembly

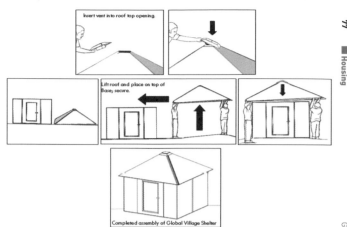

Insert vent into roof top opening.

Lift roof and place on top of Base; secure.

Completed assembly of Global Village Shelter

Housing

Global Village Shelters

Design Like You Give a Damn

Burning Man Shelter Tests

Location_Burning Man Festival,
Black Rock Desert, Nevada, USA
Date_2001–5

In 2001 three distant cousins of the "Bucky Ball" emerged from the desert at Nevada's Burning Man Festival.

Now over a decade old, the annual event draws 30,000 freethinkers to the Black Rock Desert, where temperatures can soar to over 100 °F (38 °C) and dust storms and high winds are the norm. To some, this might seem like the last place on earth one would go voluntarily; for emergency shelter designers, it is the perfect location for testing their latest prototype.

The Icosa Pod instantly became an icon at the event, with its futuristic-looking shell and lightweight material. The shelter was designed by Washington-based Sanford Ponder, a musician-turned-Microsoft-executive-turned-designer. In May 2000 he was watching a TV program on homelessness and decided, "If people are living in a box, we need to build a better box." Sanford went through 200 iterations before settling on the geodesic Icosa. Seventeen months later he was testing his pod under the baking Nevada sun.

He based his design on two main principles: its triangular forms sustain more stress than rectangles and its dome shape provides more usable space. The fire-retardant, waterproofed laminated-cardboard walls create six-inch- (15-cm-) thick cavities providing passive insulation. In more temperate climates the cavities can be filled with insulation. The pod's windows are made from UV-resistant Chloroplast, a white translucent plastic with a five-year lifespan.

Since its appearance at Burning Man, the pod has shed its cardboard skin for a more

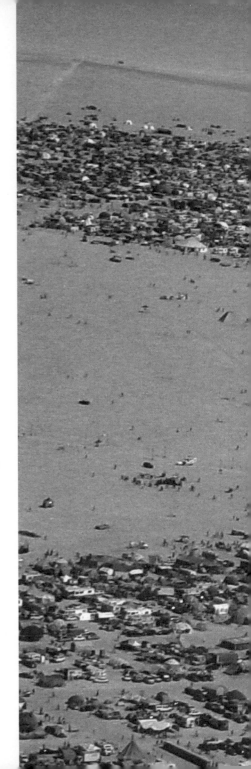

Aerial view of the Burning Man festival in 2003.
(Vinay Gupta's Hexayurt is the 203rd structure in
the fourth row to the right of the main tent.)
Dave Warner /Mindtel

durable laminated-plastic shell and is now being sold at two price points, for retail and humanitarian use. Detractors say that despite the shelter's tool-free assembly, its number of parts make the time of assembly unfeasible for an emergency situation.

On the other end of the Burning Man spectrum lies Vinay Gupta, who tested his small, low-cost refugee shelter, the Hexayurt, at the festival in 2003.

The Hexayurt is designed to create as little waste as possible in its production. Gupta got the idea while hanging around the Rocky Mountain Institute, where he heard about Strong Angel, a project instigated by the US military to test emergency shelter and communication systems (see below). The design can be built using any four-by-eight-foot (1.2-by-2.4-m) sheet material. Construction requires only six straight cuts across the diagonals of the sheets, to make the roof triangles.

Gupta's Burning Man prototype was built from Hexacomb cardboard developed by Pactiv Corporation and connected with fiber tape. It was then wrapped in Heatshield, a reflective vapor barrier for insulation and waterproofing developed by Innovative Energy. Separating the structural and waterproofing elements allows for flexibility in the materials used. To handle the area's extreme heat, Gupta also jimmied an emergency cooling system. A 10-watt solar panel was connected to an improvised swamp cooler, in this instance, a 12-volt computer case fan pulling air through a plastic tub filled with four inches (10 cm) of water. This helped drop the internal temperature even further. In addition to being affordable, the Hexayurt is designed to be lightweight and portable. One adult can carry the hut without difficulty.

However, by far the largest test of relief "ops" carried out during the festival was undertaken by a group of current and former military consultants and personnel. In 2000 US Navy Medical Corps Cmdr. Eric Rasmussen initiated a series of exercises called Strong Angel. The exercises, which are held every few years in Hawaii and involve a wide range of players, including academic, military, and humanitarian

Podville

Location_Burning Man Festival, Black Rock Desert, Nevada, USA
Date_2001
Design firm_Icosa Village Inc.
Inventor_Sanford Ponder
Additional consultant_Markus Robinson
Cost per unit_IcoPod, $1,175; DecaPod, $2,698 (for humanitarian use only)
Area_IcoPod, 108 sq. ft./10 sq. m; DecaPod 472 sq. ft./43 sq. m
Website_www.thepod.net

opposite above
Construction of an Icosa Village DecaPod at the Burning Man Festival in 2001

opposite below
The completed "Podville" at sunset
Both photographs Icosa Village Inc.

Hexayurt

Location_Burning Man Festival,
Black Rock Desert, Nevada, USA
Date_2003
Designer_Vinay Gupta
Additional consultant_Beatrice Aranow
Major funding_Self-funded;
in-kind donations from Pactiv Corporation,
Innovation Energy, 3M, SketchUp
Cost per unit_$80–250
Area_161 sq. ft./15 sq. m

opposite
Designer Vinay Gupta's completed Hexayurt prototype at the Burning Man festival in 2003
Vinay Gupta

left to right, top to bottom
The cardboard shell under construction; application of the reflective heat shield; transporting the shelter; the designer, left, with friend Beatrice Aranow in front of the completed half-scale unit
Vinay Gupta

relief professionals, are intended to improve coordination between military operations and civilian-led relief efforts around the world. Each year in preparation for these exercises a core team of participants gathers in the desert of Nevada before convening at the official event. Burning Man, with its reputation for attracting free spirits, might be the last place you would expect to see a military base camp. For Rasmussen it was the best austere environment for testing new ideas he had ever seen.

His team had been promoting the idea that the restoration of roads, bridges, ports, water, sanitation systems, shelter, and other basic services could be planned for, practiced, and responded to quickly through better communications networks and the intelligent use of cheap technology. (The group has turned Pringles cans into Wi-Fi antennas, for example.) In 2004 the team erected a geodesic dome (designed by World Shelters, see "Shelter Frame Kit") at the Burning Man festivities to test the deployment of shelter and communication infrastructure in relief operations.

After Burning Man the team took the Strong Angel operation to Banda Aceh, Indonesia, to assess and support emergency communications infrastructure in the wake of the 2004 tsunami. They found that aid workers were spending time in helicopters surveying areas of the disaster zone that others had already assessed. Had information been shared through a network such as Strong Angel, they could have used the helicopters to transport food and shelter to those in need, Rasmussen noted. He and his team hope to apply Strong Angel's methodology to future disasters, speeding relief and recovery efforts.

Unofficial Strong Angel Training Exercises

Location_Burning Man Festival, Black Rock desert, Nevada
Date_2001–5
Organization_Strong Angel
Project team_Dave Warner, John Graham, Steve Birch, Cmdr. Eric Rasmussen
Shelter design_World Shelters
Website_www.strongangel.org

opposite (clockwise from top left)
Strong Angel participants erect a geodesic dome designed by World Shelters during unofficial training exercises held at the Burning Man festival in 2004; the shelter is used to create a communications network; a solar-powered GPS bot collects mapping data; a powerful Wi-Fi directional antenna can be made from a Pringles can for less than $10; the Strong Angel participants adapt a similar "cantenna" design to expand the camp's wireless network.
clockwise from top left, photographs 1-4, 6 Dave Warner; 5 Gregory Rehm

Invented by Peter Brewin and William Crawford, engineers at the Royal College of Art, Concrete Canvas is a "building in a bag."

Concrete Canvas

Date_2003–4
Design team_Peter Brewin, William Crawford
Cost per unit_$2,000 (prototype)
Area_172 sq. ft./16 sq. m
Weight_507 lb./230 kg
Website_www.concretecanvas.org.uk

Inflate the bag, and 12 hours later a Quonset-shaped structure is ready for use. Its designers, who both had military backgrounds before pursing their master's degrees in industrial design, believe the structure could be well suited to housing field operations, emergency medical clinics, or storing food and equipment.

Here's how it works: First, position the sack of cement-impregnated fabric and fill it with water. (The size of the sack controls the water-to-cement ratio, eliminating the need for measurement.) Then leave the bag for 15 minutes while the cement hydrates. A clothlike fiber matrix and water-absorbent bonding agents draw water, creating a chemical reaction that mixes the cement. Next, unfold the structure, which then inflates like an air mattress via a chemical pack that releases a controlled volume of gas. Once the structure inflates, leave it to harden and then cut doors and ventilation holes out of the concrete "cloth." Finally, leave the concrete to cure overnight. (To avoid

overdrying, the structure should be deployed at dusk.) The result is a thin concrete structure of 172 square feet (16 sq. m). A plastic inner lining bonds with the concrete to create a sterile waterproof interior.

Although the idea of delivering instant shelter in a bag is intriguing, at 500 pounds (230 kg) the sheer weight of the sack precludes distribution by foot and requires a lightweight truck. Also, water can be scarce in an emergency. Field operations tend to relocate as political and environmental concerns dictate, and the permanent nature of these structures raises questions such as how to dispose of the building or repurpose it once it is no longer needed for emergency use.

That said, Brewin and Crawford have developed a number of small-scale prototypes. Last year Concrete Canvas won the Sustainable Design Award from the British Standards Institute, which allowed the team to conduct field research in Uganda. They have filed a patent on the technology and plan to continue to develop the idea.

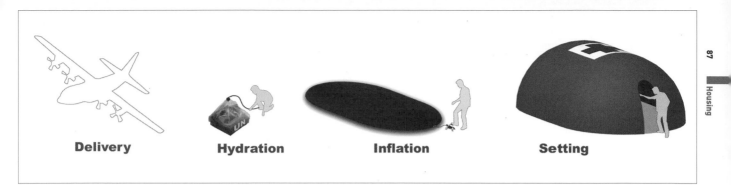

Delivery Hydration Inflation Setting

"If this was available now, we would buy 10 today."

Monica Castellarnau,
Médecins Sans Frontières, Uganda

above
Basic assembly sequence for the "building in a bag"

opposite
A small-scale model of the concrete shell after deployment

All images Peter Brewin, William Crawford

139 Shelter

Location_Ethiopia (unbuilt)
Date_1989
Design firm_Future Systems
Design team_Jan Kaplicky, David Nixon
Structural engineer_Atelier 1
Mechanical engineer_ARUP
(formerly Ove Arup & Partners)
Cost per unit_$30,000
Occupancy_200 people
Area_5,382 sq. ft./500 sq. m
Assembly_12 people/30 minutes

Future Systems is best known for its NASA-inspired conceptual designs and award-winning work, such as the Selfridges department store in Birmingham, England.

But in 1989 the firm conceived of an exceedingly simple and pragmatic approach to providing emergency shelter.

Drought and internal conflict had led to widespread famine throughout Ethiopia. The government responded by withholding food aid to rebel areas and implementing a forced resettlement program to move people from the north to the south. Crop failures, compounded by fighting, hindered the efforts of aid workers to deliver relief supplies. By 1985 as many as 5 million people were dependent on food aid.

The famine dominated news coverage as the international community attempted to pressure officials to distribute aid where it was needed. Every night televisions around the world broadcast images of thousands of hungry families clustered around makeshift food distribution centers—many of the people near death from dehydration and without any protection from the elements.

It was just such an image that prompted Jan Kaplicky and David Nixon to design

139 Shelter, one of the few architectural responses to the famine. "There was no place for people to lie down once they arrived," explains Kaplicky. "You watch television and you see people baked by the sun during the day or dying of cold during the night, and you are inspired, of course."

The shelter, based on the principle of a woman's parasol, was designed to serve as a supply distribution center. The collapsible large-span structure unfolds to provide immediate refuge from the elements for up to 200 people. It can be transported by air or freight cargo, then hooked to the undercarriage of a truck or airlifted to the site. Once on site it can be assembled by 12 people with the turn of a winch. The ribs of the "umbrella" are anchored to the ground or weighed down with sandbags. A canopy of lightweight PVC-coated polyester reflects up to 80 percent of the sun's heat, providing shade during the day and retaining warmth during the night. Ventilation is provided through the central hub.

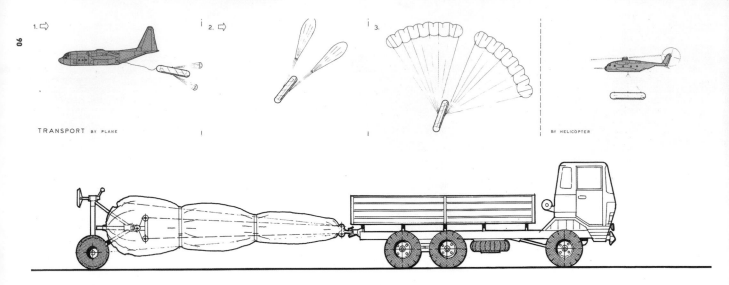

1. ▷ 2. ▷ 3.

TRANSPORT BY PLANE   BY HELICOPTER

Future Systems' emergency shelter, designed in 1989, collapses for easy transport and opens with the turn of a winch. Twelve people can assemble the structure in 30 minutes, according to its designers.
All images Future Systems

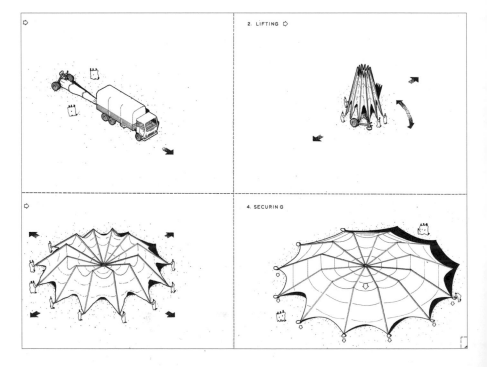

2. LIFTING ▷

4. SECURING

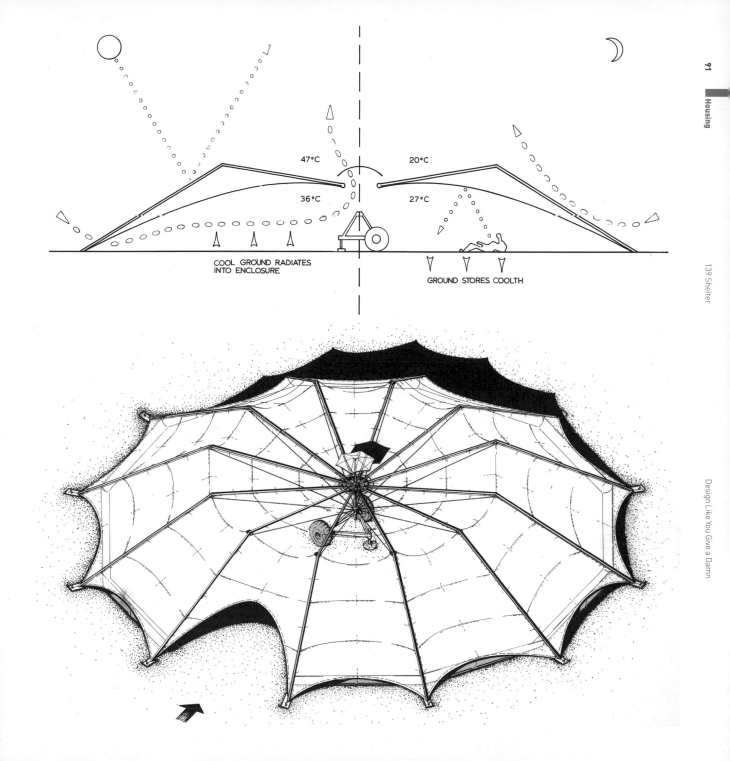

47°C 20°C

36°C 27°C

COOL GROUND RADIATES
INTO ENCLOSURE

GROUND STORES COOLTH

As of 2004 there were

25,000,000

internally displaced persons
[IDPs] in at least **49** countries

"Refugees by Numbers," UNHCR, 2005

The average length of conflicts
that cause displacement and prevent
return is **14 years**

Internal Displacement Monitoring Centre,
Norwegian Refugee Council

70 to 80%

of all IDPs are women and children

MORE THAN HALF of all IDPs live in Africa

Internal Displacement Monitoring Centre, Norwegian Refugee Council

14,000,000

IDPs are estimated to be at risk of death
through violence

Internal Displacement Monitoring Centre, Norwegian Refugee Council

Transitional Community

Location_Tangalle, Hambantota, Sri Lanka
Date_2005
Organization_Oxfam, Great Britain
End client_Displaced families
Shelter and settlement advisor_Sandra D'Urzo
Shelter architect_Elisabeth Babister
Shelter engineer_Zulficar Ali Haider
Water/sanitation engineer_Enamul Hoque
Construction_Volunteer and self-help
Additional support_Local engineering and
construction support
Funding_Disasters Emergency Committee (DEC)
Cost per unit_$580
Total cost_$9,860

Built in a public park, this transitional housing project is meant to be dismantled. The materials can be reused in permanent housing.

Construction of all the units took approximately one month.

An important strategy for speeding reconstruction has been to design and build transitional housing using materials that can be repurposed for the construction of permanent housing.

This achieves two goals: First, it allows humanitarian aid agencies to provide shelter on temporary sites rather than waiting for land-use issues to be resolved. Second, it can help defray families' construction costs for building permanent housing by giving them materials that they can later sell or repurpose. Oxfam's work in Sri Lanka following the tsunami that struck Southeast Asia in 2004 offers an example of this approach.

Over the course of three months Oxfam designed and constructed 17 transitional shelters for families using a mix of wood, corrugated roof sheeting, cement blocks, and other materials. The settlement was located in Tangalle, a coastal village in the Hambantota district of Sri Lanka, near one of five permanent development offices the aid group maintained in the country prior to the disaster.

In the immediate aftermath of the disaster, many people found shelter with friends and relatives. However, community leaders identified a group of 17 families that had lost

everything and had nowhere safe to stay. Through a series of workshops, Oxfam collaborated with these families and the local government to design a safe shelter that would enable them to store their belongings securely and would be spacious and cool enough to carry out everyday tasks, such as mending nets or drying fish. Including officials as well as families in the discussions helped establish an open forum where both felt comfortable asking questions and sharing ideas. The result was a design that met government approval and the displaced families' needs.

But finding a suitable location presented a challenge. People wanted to stay near their community, livelihoods, schools, and families, but there was little land available near Tangalle, and the government was finding it difficult to relocate families out of the "buffer zone," a 100-meter no-build zone along the coast. After discussions, Oxfam agreed with the local government

to build the transitional shelters in a children's playground in the middle of the village, enabling families to maintain community ties and have access to services and support.

Oxfam employed an engineer and a site supervisor to oversee the construction, but skilled and unskilled work was carried out by the families themselves, who were paid a daily wage. In that way the project also helped replace lost earnings. Remarkably, a third of those involved in the pilot scheme were women, giving them access to income and a sense of empowerment.

The shelters were designed so that they could be dismantled after a year. Timber joints were bolted, and the floor was made from cement tiles rather than a solid slab. Latrines also were built for the shelters, including three permanent ones intended to benefit the whole community once the temporary shelters were dismantled and the park returned to normal use.

Transitional Community

Design Like You Give a Damn

> "These are 'transitional' as opposed to 'temporary.' Emergency shelter is temporary and is intended just to provide shelter for survival. Transitional implies something that is longer-term and gives you space to carry out livelihood activities rather than just surviving."

Elizabeth Babister, shelter advisor

opposite
A group of houses ready for inhabitation

right
A covered porch and walkway
All photographs Elizabeth Babister

Paper Church

Location_Nagata-Ku, Kobe, Japan
Date_1995
Client_Catholic Takatori Church
Design firm_Shigeru Ban Architects

**Fifty-eight paper tubes enclosed within
a skin of corrugated polycarbonate sheeting
form the structure of the Paper Church.**
Both photographs Makoto Mitsumori

Paper Log Houses

Location_Nagata-Ku, Kobe, Japan
Date_1995
End client_Displaced families
Design firm_Shigeru Ban Architects
Major funding_Donated materials
and labor
Cost_$2,000
Area_560 sq. ft./52 sq. m

below left
**In Kobe, Japan, Paper Log House
foundations were built from beer
crates, which are durable and not
susceptible to water damage.**
Takanoku Sakuma

bottom left
**In Gujarat, India, the barrel-roof
structure was made from
plastic sandwiched between locally
woven mats.**
Kartikeya Shodhan

below right
Interior of a house in Kobe
Hiroyuki Hirai

bottom right
**In the colder climate of Turkey,
tarp roofs were built without the
side vents that were designed for
the warmer climate of Kobe.**
Shigeru Ban

Paper Tube Emergency Shelter

Location_Rwanda
Date_1998
Client_UNHCR
End client_Rwandan refugees
Design firm_Shigeru Ban Architects
Funding_UNHCR

In 1994 Rwanda's civil war displaced more than two million people.

Following protocol, the UNHCR sent the standard supply of plastic sheeting and aluminum poles to be used as temporary shelters, but the agency failed to foresee the local value of the aluminum. Refugees sold the poles and then cut down trees for structural supports instead, thus contributing to an already pressing deforestation crisis.

Just as the UNHCR was grappling with this problem, the Japanese architect Shigeru Ban, known for his sculptural arbors and galleries made from paper tubes, approached the agency with a proposal to construct emergency shelter using the same material. Commissioned by the United Nations, Ban developed a frame of paper tubes and plastic connectors that could transform standard plastic sheeting into tents. The tubes had no monetary value, thereby ensuring they would be used for shelter. With support from Vitra, Ban designed three prototype shelters, and in 1998 he worked with refugees and relief agencies to build 50 emergency shelters in Rwanda. Ultimately, however, the frame proved too costly and difficult to replicate, according to the UNHCR.

In the meantime the Great Hanshin Earthquake of 1995, the largest quake to hit Japan since 1923, gave Ban the opportunity to channel his ideas toward humanitarian work closer to home. Striking just six months

after Ban first met with UN officials, the earthquake caused unprecedented damage to the city of Kobe. Many of the city's poorest neighborhoods were hardest hit. Temporary housing for displaced families was built on the outskirts of Kobe, but tent camps persisted because many people had jobs in the city center. Working with university students Ban built 21 temporary homes from paper tubes and plastic beer crates donated by Kirin. (Crates by Sapporo, Shigeru often jokes, did not suit the design.) Each home took volunteer and student workers six hours to construct. Indigenous and sustainable, the homes enabled families to remain near their jobs while waiting for permanent housing. His Paper Log House design was adapted for Turkey and India after earthquakes in 1999 and 2001, respectively. But once again the process proved too cumbersome to replicate on a large scale.

Amid the confusion Ban also built a small church in Kobe where a Catholic cathedral had been destroyed by fires resulting from the earthquake. Of all his work this humble, elliptical gathering space would prove to be the most meaningful and lasting. Earthquake survivors used the Takatori Paper Church for meetings, and the building became a symbol of the reconstruction, offering an oasis of healing in a time and place where little comfort could be found. Construction of the church was completed in five weeks by 160 volunteers. Ten years after the disaster the church was finally removed to make way for a new cathedral. Plans were made to reconstruct it in Taomi, Taiwan, which had recently been hard hit by an earthquake.

In Rwanda, frames for shelters were assembled from paper tubes and plastic connectors.
Shigeru Ban

Super Adobe

Location_Baninajar Refugee Camp,
Khuzestan, Iran
Date_1995
End client_Iraqi refugees
Sponsoring organizations_UNDP, UNHCR
Design firm_California Institute of Earth Art
and Architecture (Cal-Earth)
Design team_Nader Khalili, Hamid
(supervising UNDP architect)
Structural engineer_P. J. Vittore, Ltd.
Major funding_UNDP, UNHCR
Cost_$625
Area_150 sq. ft./14.6 sq. m
Website_www.calearth.org

Super Adobe

Design Like You Give a Damn

Baninajar Camp in Khuzestan province, Iran.
Refugees of the Persian Gulf war built 15 domed
shelters using architect Khalili's sandbag-and-
barbed-wire method. The project was funded and
supervised by UN agencies.
Hamid/UNDP

Nader Khalili
Cal-Earth

In 1984 Iranian-American architect
Nader Khalili responded to a NASA call
for housing designs for future human
settlements on the moon and Mars.

The assignment presented a number of challenges, chiefly a dearth
of building supplies and materials. In response Khalili created a system
of tiny plastic bags that could be filled with lunar dust and affixed to each
other by Velcro, which he later adapted and dubbed "Super Adobe." It was
a purely theoretical project and might have remained that way had the
Persian Gulf war not sent refugees streaming into his native Iran.

In 1995 Khalili partnered with the UNDP and the UNHCR to apply his
Mars research to providing emergency shelter for Iraqi refugees seeking
safe harbor at the Baninajar camp in Khuzestan, Iran. Using only "the
tools of war"—barbed wire and sandbags—refugees built 15 domed
shelters using his Super Adobe system.

In this interview, conducted in February 2005, Khalili talks about
designing lunar housing, working with the UN, and his decision to
abandon conventional wisdom and run his own race.

How did you start doing work with emergency and transitional
shelters?
I really had a dream in my mind. I acted upon it and in time I was
successful. But in order to pursue that dream I had to leave everything
else behind. My dream then was pretty simple. I was raised in Iran,
and I was very interested in the traditional earth architecture of my
country. One-third of the buildings in the world are earth architecture,
and at the time I was looking for a solution [a way of building better
housing for everyone].

I said, "What if I set fire to earth buildings? Why wouldn't they turn
into a ceramic pot?' And the more I went forward with it, the stronger
the idea became to the point where I closed the office and set out on
a motorcycle.

When I closed my business I already had ten years of experience.
I was in the rat race. There were 30,000 Americans in Iran and some
huge companies. I had my own very successful business building
skyscrapers in Iran and Los Angeles, but I was in the middle of this

rivalry to get big jobs. Then one day I took my boy to a park, and he
started playing with the other kids and racing with them. The fourth
time around my son, the youngest and the slowest, said, "Baba, baba,
I want to race alone."

I thought, why can't he race alone? To race alone doesn't mean to stop
racing. If I race with you and win, I only reach your capacity but a little
better. But I will never reach my own capacity. I will never know my own
potential. Sometimes it is better to race against yourself. This moment
affected me so much that less than a year later, I closed my office.

Ceramic houses were what I went after. It was three years before
the Iranian revolution [which transformed Iran from a monarchy led by
Shah Mohammad Reza Pahlavi to an Islamic republic under the rule of
Ayatollah Ruhollah Khomeini]. I missed the whole revolution because
I was so passionately involved in ideas.

The revolution helped my work a lot because it created a crack in the
system. When that happened it became paradise for my work. There
were no ministries, no building department, and there were hundreds of
students wanting to help. Many of the architects who had worked under
the Shah were exiled or put in jail; but I was doing this work and I stayed
in the villages.

When Iraq was bombing Iran, I was firing a school, and we were
not supposed to have any light at night because of air raids. But I had
absolutely no fear. At the time I understood what passionate means.
Everyone said "choke the fire, let's go home." But I had no fear at all.
When you are burning inside, outside fire means nothing. The heart
becomes a kiln.

Two years later religious people took over and I wasn't going
that way at all. So I eventually left the country. That is when I came
to America.

It's interesting that you had to leave the city and go out into the
country to find a new path. How important was it to be in a place that
was free of expectations, free of precedent, in a sense?
It's not the time that arrives with an idea. It's a place that arrives with an
idea. Somewhere in this world the time is always right. And to the young
architects I would say, if you want to have a lot of clients just reduce your
fees. Then you will have millions of clients.

There are two ways of carrying out ideas and dreams. One is to really
go after making a lot of money and then carry out your ideas. But for me,

**Interior view of Super Adobe structure
at Baninajar Refugee Camp in Iran**

I decided I had ha
the office, bough
and went into the
five years to worl
on their ideas and

Nader Khalili

enough. I closed
 motorcycle,
lesert for
with the people
dreams.

by the time you have made a lot of money you have forgotten about your ideas. The second is to reduce your need and want—the mortgage, the cars, the other things we want. And that is a powerful way of going after ideas. When you are dealing with housing for the poor and dealing with poor people directly, you have to really be part of it.

Tell me more about your early "ceramic" or Geltaftan architecture. Explain the building process.

First I set fire to buildings. I take out the windows and the doors, and I close [the structure] with bricks, adobe. The building becomes a kiln. I fire the whole kiln from inside out. Once it becomes a kiln, you keep the fire on for three to four days, then naturally adobe starts becoming fired brick, and if you continue it becomes rock. That was the idea I was constantly looking for.

We went to one village. Half of the houses in the village had deteriorated from the rain and snow. That's the biggest problem building with adobe—it just melts. We got houses, cleaned them up and fired them, and they became strong and water resistant.

And then the revolution came. The top officials came and saw what I was doing and they asked, "Why don't you do a school?" They took

One of Khalili's buildings being fired

me to an office that deals with housing for the poor. A deputy came into the office one day and said, "If you want to wait for a contract, it's going to take a long time." He came with a suitcase and put it on table. Then he went out to talk with the governor. I thought, "There's a bomb in there, that's the end of me." But he came back and said, "Just open the suitcase." He opened the suitcase and inside there were thousands of dollars in cash. He said, "Take what you need, leave an IOU, and when the contract comes pay us back. Just go and do the work." That's dream work for architects, to just go and do a project that you think is right.

You went from designing for rural Iranian villages to designing for NASA. How did you start working with NASA?

In 1984 NASA issued a call for papers dealing with what they called "lunar bases and space activities in the 21st century." I answered that call and spent 90 days and nights writing one page. Amazingly, I was invited to the conference, and there were hardly any architects in attendance. Six years earlier I had been setting mud on fire in small, poor villages, and now I had no problem presenting these ideas for the moon. It was very obvious to me how to think about building in the

moon's harsh climate. If I go to the moon and get the energy of the sun concentrated on lunar soil, I will get molten lava, which is a ceramic concrete. The idea was to build up these structures using just the sun and the moon dust.

You called it Super Adobe, and it used Velcro. You adapted the system to use barbed wire, and eventually you worked with the UN to build a refugee camp for Iraqis just over the border in Iran. How did you connect with the UN?

I was pursuing this issue of tree-free building—no use of forest products. This is how we can fight the destruction of forests. Because up to 65 percent of the trees cut down are used to construct houses and other buildings. Super Adobe is made from soil as is or stabilized with cement or lime.

Then in 1993 an American journalist in Iran wrote an article in English about my work. This journalist was a friend of a UN representative, who became very interested in it because after Desert Storm there were all these refugees from Iraqi Kuwait fleeing into Iran, and the UN needed to build camps. [The UNDP representative] invited the UNHCR to partner with them to carry out a prototype cluster of these houses in the camps. The UN got behind this and the local government and immediately noticed that this may be good. The UN had to construct a prototype in the building research center of the ministry of housing in Iran, to approve and test it before building it in the camp.

So were you working on-site with the refugees?

I went back and forth, but not many times. The UNHCR and UNDP hired a local architect. We trained him and were in constant communication. He was very experienced with refugees. He was also very committed, like ourselves, to breaking through the system and coming up with a solution. The whole philosophy was that the refugees would build their own homes and he was just supervising. Six refugees built homes in six to 11 days. Each structure cost $625.

We built 15 domes as a cluster that could be repeated by the thousands. Some people moved in even before they had finished and plastered inside and out. UNDP and UNHCR together put $20,000 toward the project, and still at the end they had $3,000 left. And that was one of the main problems later. The local officials didn't like this whole idea at all. There was a lot of aid coming into the place and usually officials took 10 percent and by the time it trickled down to building there was very little left. But this project had its own factor of failure in it because they wouldn't make any money in it. The basic philosophy was that it was low cost. People could do it themselves. Women can build it— that's very important. And this was the greatest dichotomy we had to deal with.

The government needs to hire people to create jobs but this wouldn't create contractor profit. It's a single-trade job. It doesn't need a concrete worker or foundation workers. You can build it with just earth and sandbags. In the end there were ten rows of barbed wire and bags,

right
A woman fills a polypropylene tube with sand.

far right
The tubes are laid in courses to form structures in a range of shapes.

below
The domes are finished with lime-stabilized earth.
All other photographs Cal-Earth

and the local officials told the people to take it away. What they wanted us to understand was that there was no money in this for anyone there. And then, of course, Desert Storm ended.

They say the major problem when every disaster happens is that a lot of funds pour in and depending on who is closest to the government they get the contract. But the character of the architect is not conducive to taking that sort of money from people, and that's one of the hurdles—they need nonprofit or government support.

But the UN was very encouraged. A year later the UNHCR and UNDP sent one architect and an engineer to evaluate the project and they wrote a very positive report. The potential was great because it needs minimum skill, it is self-help, uses only local materials, and creates jobs for the refugees, which helps restore their dignity. We took those recommendations and continued to develop the building system at Cal-Earth.

What were some of the recommendations they made?
They recommended that we work with more prototypes, more space division: instead of one big dome, a number of smaller ones. Instead of a standard sandbag, I discovered long tubular bags. So then we started using all of that.

What happened to the camp? Is it still there today?
As far as we know the whole camp is gone, and the UN says the government dismantled it. That is a little bit of a question mark for us because we know it was inhabited for several years and was part of a larger camp.

But this was designed to be temporary structure. Host countries never like to have permanent architecture for refugee camps. They always want it to be temporary. So this is meant to be temporary. If they don't waterproof and plaster it, they could just bullldoze everything back to earth. It's not making a statement; it's providing a means for the refugees to find a way to live.

A few years ago we had a wonderful visit from the UNDP's head of emergency response [to our center in Hesperia, California]. He and his colleagues were going to stay in the penthouse of the Ramada Inn. The minute they got here they started doing construction—filling sandbags—and the next night they stayed in the niches and domes. The UNDP official invited me to go to Iran to a regional conference. It was very serious. Unfortunately, he was transferred to another division. He promised [to pursue it], but finally he couldn't do anything. So even though we were excited by the first project in Iran, it's been a decade...

Many designers have difficulty getting past the prototyping/testing phase. What do you think is the main obstacle to seeing new concepts for emergency housing replicated?
The bureaucracy. People are constantly changing positions and they don't know about each other's work. But the UN is limited in what it can build, and ultimately the request has to come from the country. We can't tell them what to build.

During the American bombing of Afghanistan [in 2001], the UNDP in Iran wanted to build 60,000 of these units on the border. So they asked us for a proposal, but as the war began everything shifted and everything went to Pakistan. And then they had to follow the recommendations of the local government. That is how it works. We had another connection at the UN who wanted to build some domes after a flood in Honduras. They were very close to letting us use our system, but the project got bogged down in the local government.

After ten years, at some point do you say to yourself, maybe I should give up? Maybe this idea is not going to work?
We've thought of giving up and then something happens. For example, I wanted to go through the permitting system in California because here in this country [this building method hasn't been used]. There isn't a building that's constructed with earth and has permits unless it was erected before 1956. If you can get a permit in California, everyone in the world will accept the idea because California has the toughest code. To meet it you need to test your structures physically for earthquake resistance. That's big money. We couldn't afford it. We received a grant from the Grateful Dead and the Ted Turner Foundation. So we tested the structure, and it passed.

It is these people who join in what you are doing who keep the dream happening. As the Persian mystic Rumi said, you have two duties in life: to sharpen your pencil and scratch your paper. If you keep doing your work, the rest will happen. The only way you can really survive with idealism is to be in constant touch with poetry, and that poetry should not be brushed aside by practicalities or viabilities or economics. This is what the juice of survival is—always being in touch with poetry.

Khalili now runs Cal-Earth in Hisperia, California, where he teaches earth architecture and continues to refine his design. For example, rather than using small sacks, Khalili now fills long tubes with earth. Tubes made from burlap or polypropylene are then laid in courses to form a dome. Barbed wire placed between each course holds the bags in place and stabilizes the structure against seismic activity. According to Khalili, a basic dome measuring eight feet (2.43 m) in diameter can cost as little as $100 to $200 in materials to construct using this improved method. Khalili has since employed the system to build emergency shelter near Islamabad, Pakistan, for people displaced by the 2005 earthquake in Pakistan-administered Kashmir.

Iraqi refugees inside a completed structure in the Baninajar camp in Iran, 1995
Hamid/UNDP

Pallet House

Location_Bronx, New York, USA; Ball State University, Muncie, Indiana, USA; Sri Lanka
Date_1999–present
Design firm_I-Beam Design
Design team_Azin Valy, Suzan Wines
Additional support_Chris Teeter, Dr. Wes Janz, Ball State University students and faculty
Construction_Volunteer labor
Major funding_LEF Foundation, New York State Council on the Arts
Cost per unit_Approx. $200 (donated pallets); $1,700 (purchased pallets)
Area_1,200 sq. ft./110 sq. m

Suzan Wines and Azin Valy's firm, I-Beam Design, was only a year old when the team first experimented with the Pallet House.

In 1999 they entered the design in Architecture for Humanity's Transitional Housing competition for returning Kosovar refugees. Since then I-Beam has made significant progress toward realizing its vision of a viable disaster-relief architecture using standard shipping pallets—which are often in great supply in disaster situations because of the influx of aid—as the base component of a modular building system.

After winning an honorable mention in the competition, the team developed the project further, and with funding from the New York State Council on the Arts and the LEF Foundation it has been testing the Pallet House system at increasingly ambitious scales. The team's first dwelling-size prototype was assembled on a vacant lot in New York's South Bronx. Although the Bronx project was short-lived—bulldozed by the city soon after it was finished—in the brief period it was standing the structure became a temporary home to one of the city's homeless.

In fall 2004, at the invitation of architect Dr. Wes Janz, I-Beam led a four-day building workshop that challenged students at Ball State University, in Muncie, Indiana, to develop housing types using the pallet system. The 35 students and four faculty members collected 500 pallets and built six pallet structures in three days, using only basic carpenter's tools. The

workshop resulted in a variety of dwelling structures accommodating a range of living arrangements and including the construction of integral furniture. The students also experimented with creating different types of public spaces between the structures. The school kept the prototypes in place for a number of weeks. According to Janz, during that time they became well-used classrooms and lounges, turning an ordinary lawn into a lively communal space—and encouraging participants that a similar transformation could be achieved elsewhere.

In response to the tsunami that struck Southeast Asia in 2004, the architects adapted the Pallet House system again—this time designing a basic 1,200-square-foot (111-sq.-m) dwelling, using 300 pallets, for use in Sri Lanka. The Sri Lankan scheme also provided an opportunity to think about how the Pallet House concept could respond to various climates. For example, to manage Sri Lanka's heat and humidity, I-Beam adopted the local building practice of leaving space between the top of the walls and the roof for air circulation. In other climates the pallets could also be filled in with wattle-and-daub or other locally appropriate insulation.

I-Beam has always thought of the Pallet House as transitional housing, an immediately constructible and sturdy alternative to a tent in a disaster situation. Drawbacks include the labor-intensive nature of the design and the fact that pallets come in various sizes and materials, which can hamper construction. That said, shipping pallets are widely available. Reusing them offers the potential to lessen deforestation. And perhaps more significant, pallets are prefabricated, which makes them a natural building material.

above
The first prototype of the design, in the Bronx

left
The shipping pallets used to build the structure
Both photographs I-Beam Design

left
The design adapted for use in Sri Lanka after the Indian Ocean tsunami
Chris Teeter

below
The pallets can be plastered in wattle and daub or filled with straw, rubble, or other material for insulation.
I-Beam Design

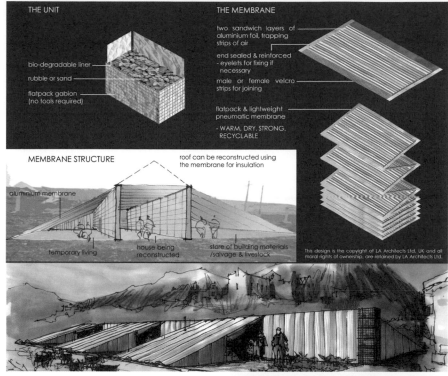

THE UNIT

bio-degradable liner

rubble or sand

flatpack gabion
(no tools required)

THE MEMBRANE

two sandwich layers of
aluminium foil, trapping
strips of air

end sealed & reinforced
- eyelets for fixing if
necessary

male or female velcro
strips for joining

flatpack & lightweight
pneumatic membrane

- WARM, DRY, STRONG,
RECYCLABLE

MEMBRANE STRUCTURE

aluminium membrane

temporary living

roof can be reconstructed using
the membrane for insulation

house being
reconstructed

store of building materials
/salvage & livestock

This design is the copyright of LA Architects Ltd, UK and all
moral rights of ownership, are retained by LA Architects Ltd.

Rubble House

Location_Essex, England (prototype)
Date_1999–present
Design firm_LA Architects
Designer_Mike Lawless
Engineer_Mark Whitby, Whitby Bird
Engineeers
Funding_Self-funded

Many crises leave behind large quantities of rubble, usually from homes and buildings destroyed by natural disaster or war.

A number of designers have tried to tackle the challenge of how to repurpose rubble to create structurally sound housing and in the process clear the land while providing a sustainable, low-cost shelter alternative. More often than not the answer is gabion wall construction.

Gabions are walls built by filling large baskets with broken stone. Typically the baskets are made from galvanized steel mesh, woven aluminum strips, or plastic mesh, but they have also been made from wickerwork or bamboo slats. The strength of these walls comes from the combination of the weight of the stones and the interlocking and frictional support of the mesh.

For Architecture for Humanity's 1999 Transitional Housing Competition for Refugees Returning from Kosovo, a number

of designers employed gabions. One of the most successful proposals was by Mike Lawless of LA Architects and Mark Whitby of Whitby Bird Engineers.

Their system arrives to the site packed flat. A team assembles the wire gabions with rods for structural integrity, then forms walls with the gabions and fills them with rubble. A lightweight aluminum membrane forms a roof, which is then clad with quilted, nylon-reinforced aluminum foil. "It's not just a saggy, aluminum fabric but quite a rigid, well-waterproofed and -insulated building material," says Lawless. Velcro connects the roof's edges to create a fully weathered seal. The entire system snaps together and requires no tools to assemble.

In 2000 the designers constructed a full-scale prototype in Essex, England, as part of an exhibition at the Spacex Gallery. The unit took a team of 10 people less than six hours to build.

top
Proposed transitional shelter. Flatpack gabion mesh frames are filled with rubble to form the walls. Panels made from two sandwiched layers of aluminum foil are joined by Velcro to form the roof. Lawless and Whitby conceived of the design in response to the 1999 conflict in Kosovo but have since adapted it for use in other areas.
LA Architects

above
Details of the gabion wall structure (top row) and the aluminum membrane (bottom row)
LA Architects

Low-Tech Balloon System

Location_Japan
Date_1999–present
Design firm_TechnoCraft
Design team_Ichiro Katase, Takashi Kawano, Takeshi Chiba, Ken Takeyama
Additional consultants_Japanese government, Peace Winds Japan, UNHCR
Major funding_Self-funded
Cost per unit_$1,800 (prototype)

For years the architecture group TechnoCraft has explored the role designers can play in responding to crises by using innovative materials and low-tech construction.

When the team entered its Low-Tech Balloon System into Architecture for Humanity's 1999 Transitional Housing competition, the quirky yet feasible design generated delight and surprise. Jurors dubbed it the inflatable hemp house.

Hemp is one of those materials that tend not to be taken seriously. (Indeed, during the jury process one of the panel members joked, "If there was a fire, would anyone leave?") Still, in many parts of the world hemp is an abundant natural resource that if used correctly is an inexpensive, strong, long-lasting option.

The scheme is by far one of the most unusual transitional structures Architecture for Humanity has come across. But while it might be tempting to dismiss the system as yet another fanciful architectural detour, the team was able to erect its first prototype in a single day. With input and advice from the UNHCR in Japan and the NGO Peace Winds Japan, the architects went on to make four more prototypes with modifications, including a mobile health clinic version for the 2002 Architecture for Humanity OUTREACH design competition.

The idea is to take used hemp sacks, in this case animal feedbags, and sew them together to form a dome-shaped structure. The construction is separated into prefabricated elements that can be assembled off-site or by a local cottage industry "build-up process" at the site. Separating the production process allows for faster production and eliminates the need for electricity.

At the site the sewn hemp "skins" are connected by plastic ties and attached to "Life Elements" (doors, windows, and facilities for cooking, sanitation, and storage) with a maximum of eight per structure. Workers stuff the hemp structure with inflated airbags or balloons, tighten the plastic ties to increase the air pressure, and dampen the entire structure. They then spray or apply mortar over the dome to create a thin concrete shell, much like a papier-mâché model. Inner pressure from the airbags supports the structure during the mortar application, making additional construction devices such as an air-compressor or wooden supports unnecessary.

Once the mortar has dried, teams cut out excess hemp from the openings of the doors, windows, and other elements and deflate the airbags, which can be reused. Then workers mortar and plaster the interior walls, creating a waterproof, thermal-insulated shell. Individual units can be easily combined to create larger living spaces.

Low-Tech Balloon System

Design Like You Give a Damn

Extreme Housing

Location_Philadelphia, Pennsylvania, USA
(prototype for exhibition)
Date_1999–present
Design team_Deborah Gans, Matt Jelacic
Funding_Johnnie Walker "Keep Walking" Fund
Area_24 sq. ft./2.2 sq. m

The basic elements for life include access to water, sanitation, and shelter. All are encompassed in the Extreme Housing unit by Deborah Gans and Matt Jelacic.

The structure is a core system made of two freestanding boxes: One encloses a toilet, the other a hearth, internal cistern, and shower. Beams connect the two boxes, creating enough space for a bed. This easily assembled transitional structure can eventually become the core of a permanent structure or plug into a semidestroyed home. In a refugee situation the prefabricated core could be disassembled and transferred with the occupant back to a permanent dwelling.

Approximately 20 units fit in a shipping container, and a team of four people using a wrench can assemble a unit in about six hours. Developed in response to the Architecture for Humanity 1999 Transitional Housing competition, the Extreme Housing unit was one of 10 finalists; it also won a $100,000 grant from the Johnnie Walker "Keep Walking" Fund.

The grant enabled the designers to refine their idea, primarily by traveling to the area and spending time with NGOs and relief experts. While the team received positive firsthand feedback from people in the field, the design needed a number of improvements, most dealing with cultural specificity. "There is always a great tension between the single universal solution and this cultural differentiation," Gans notes.

Ease of assembly inspired the switch from an array of panels and parts to an unfolding unit. What emerged was a structurally stable three-sided configuration that could be built from a variety of materials in response to regional ecologies. The designers have since built different prototypes out of bamboo, cardboard, and microthin aluminum sheeting over a synthetic core.

Rendering of core unit in relation
to a ruined wall that will form part
of the reconstituted house

Both images Gans and Jelacic

"I count my biggest accomplishment
to date as having helped lawyers, doctors,
and aid workers to make the connection
between good design and human
dignity—dignity being a very important
legal term in human rights law."

Deborah Gans, designer

Prefabricated Core Housing

Location_Chechnya
Date_1995
Sponsoring organization_Relief International
End client_Displaced populations of Chechnya
Funding_UNHCR
Cost per unit_$3,500–5,500
Units_120 prefabricated core-housing units

Because roofs and foundations tend to be the most difficult and expensive components of a house, many NGOs have adopted a strategy of building "core housing" as a staple of reconstruction and development work.

As its name implies, the strategy calls for a foundation and roof to be built around a structural core that often, but not always, includes plumbing and electricity and usually consists of one or two rooms, leaving families to build the rest of the house as time and funds permit.

Relief International, a US-based humanitarian aid agency, is one of many groups that have used core housing, not only to rebuild communities but also to promote self-reliance and strengthen the link between reconstruction and job creation.

In 1994 a ceasefire was brokered over a long-standing conflict with Armenia over the Azerbaijani Nagorno-Karabakh enclave. As a result Azerbaijan lost 16 percent of its

Prefabricated Core Housing

Design Like You Give a Damn

A prefabricated core house
provided by Relief International to
displaced residents in Chechnya

Core Housing

Location_Various sites in Azerbaijan
Date_1995–2001
Sponsoring organization_Relief International
End client_Displaced people
Design team_Trevor Sunderland,
Massimo Marafatto, Tom Merrills
Structural engineers_Garry Govan, Trevor
Sunderland, William (Buzz) Iacovelli, Eamonn
Kilmartin, Massimo Marafatto, Tom Merrills
Electrical/mechanical engineer_Local Azeri
engineers
Contractors_Local Azeri contractors
Additional consultants_Richard Price
and Wolfgang Neumann, UNHCR shelter
consultants
Funding_UNHCR
Cost per unit_$2,100
Units_2,105
Area_258 sq. ft./24 sq. m

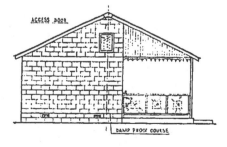

ACCESS DOOR

DAMP PROOF COURSE

A-A
2050

PLAN VIEW

6400   PLASTER

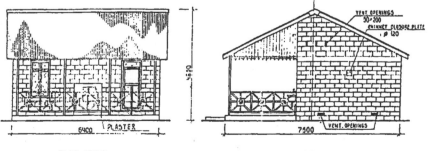

VENT OPENINGS
50×200
CHIMNEY CLOSURE PLATE
∅ 120

4520

7500   VENT. OPENINGS

B-B

opposite and above
**Core housing in Azerbaijan designed
by Relief International**
All images Relief International

territory, prompting some 571, 000 people
to retreat inside the country's new borders.
In response Relief International launched a
shelter initiative to house Azerbaijan's
newly displaced. Over a six-year period the
agency worked with partners in the field
and local laborers to build 2,105 core homes.
Each humble one-room house included a
porch, which could be enclosed to create
a second room.

A year later Relief International also
provided core houses for a transitional-
shelter project in Chechnya. Using a

prefabricated design the aid agency built
40 one-bedroom and 80 two-bedroom units
to house families displaced by conflict in the
disputed territory's Ingushetia, Daghestan,
and North Ossetia provinces. The design
of the home, which consisted of one room
(often divided in two), a foundation, and
a roof, allowed the occupants to extend
the walls to create an additional room.
Relief International has employed similar
housing concepts in war-ravaged Kosovo
and in a number of other disaster-
affected areas.

Safe(R) House

Location_Sri Lanka
Date_2005
Client_Prajnopaya Foundation
End client_Displaced residents of Dodanduwa, Sri Lanka
Design centers_Harvard Graduate School of Design; SENSEable City Laboratory, Massachusetts Institute of Technology (MIT)
Design team_Luis Berrios, Ellen Chen, Eric Ho, Nour Jallad, Rick Lam, Justin Lee, Walter Nicolina, Carlo Ratti, Ying Zhou
Project coordinator_Carlo Ratti, SENSEable City Laboratory, MIT
Project advisors_Tenzin Priyadarshi, MIT, Prajnopaya Foundation
Engineer_Domenico Del Re, Buro Happold, London
Major funding_Architecture for Humanity, Prajnopaya Foundation
Cost per unit_$1,500
Area_400 sq. ft./37 sq. m

The destruction wrought upon Southeast Asia by the tsunami of December 26, 2004, warranted innovative and safe reconstruction of homes for the more than one million displaced people and the overhaul of coastal communities throughout the region.

On January 17, 2005, the Sri Lanka Public Security Ministry announced new building restrictions that prohibited construction within 100 yards/meters from the sea in the southwest or 200 yards/meters in the northwest. The policy, known as the 100-Meter Rule, not only was vulnerable to various interpretations leading to confusion but also came at a high social, cultural, environmental, and economic cost.

The Harvard Graduate School of Design in collaboration with the SENSEable City Laboratory at MIT began a project to investigate the development of technological strategies that could allow families to return and guarantee future safety at lower cost. Guided by high-tech modeling systems, the team developed Safe(R) House, a dwelling designed to resist the force of a tsunami as well as flooding. The designers emphasized the use of locally available materials and building methods to make the house both cost effective and easy to replicate.

Traditional homes in Sri Lanka are constructed from concrete blocks, with two windows, one door, and a tiled or tin roof. By contrast, the Safe(R) House replaces this core with four C-shaped concrete structures that provide higher resistance without blocking the flow of water. Bamboo or traditional woven partitions create a porous,

ventilated skin for the structure, which rests on a raised platform to prevent flooding. This C-shaped core becomes a modular system allowing variation and expansion; families can adapt different parts of the home and add bedrooms or other facilities as necessary. The team also used this system to create a series of options for community buildings.

London-based engineers Buro Happold tested the housing design using structural modeling and analysis, checking mostly for deformations caused by pressure on the walls. Unlike the traditional four solid walls, the Safe(R) House's core columns increase porosity, making the house five times more resistant to the force of a wave than traditional structures, according to the designers.

The Prajnopaya Foundation is currently implementing the design and hopes to build 1,000 Safe(R) Houses along Sri Lanka's southern and eastern coastlines, where officials have not been able to enforce the 100-Meter Rule. Each house will be 400 square feet (37 sq. m), containing one or two bedrooms, a bathroom, and an open kitchen/living space. The designers estimate the Safe(R)House will cost about $1,500, which is comparable to the price of a typical Sri Lankan home.

above and left
The home constructed in Dodanduwa, Sri Lanka, after the 2004 Indian Ocean tsunami
Ellen Chen

opposite
A rendering of the team's design

/traditional design
pressure on facade (not governed by direction)

/proposed safe(r) house
pressure on sea-ward facade

/proposed safe(r) house
pressure on facade normal to sea

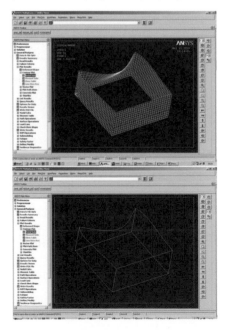

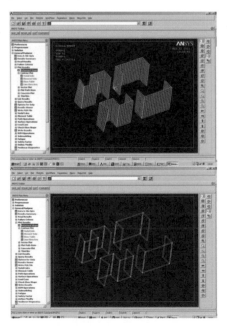

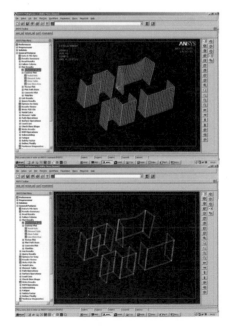

/concepts
for the tsunami safe(r) house

/porosity
in order to maximize the resistance to an incoming tsunami, four independent linear supports, perpendicular to the coast, are created. they replace the uniform skin of the existing design. also, a raised platform guarantees better water flow and health

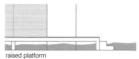

coast line
water flow
raised platform

/upgradability
bamboo partitions are initially provided in between the core elements; with time they can be transformed and customized, engaging residents and promoting the reuse of elements from collapsed buildings

A - bamboo
B - net
C - ...

/economy
the total built surface of walls and roof is approximately the same as the existing house; the total cost will be equal or less

existing house
safe(r) house

/expandability
a modular system allows inhabitants to expand the unit size to accommodate different household sizes

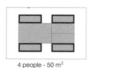

4 people - 50 m^2
6 people - 50 + 25 = 75 m^2

right
A number of factors influenced the design, including porosity, cost, and air circulation.

opposite above left
Wooden latticework allows water to flow between the cores.

opposite above right
C-shaped cement cores form the interior walls of the home.
All photographs Ellen Chen

opposite below
Modeling shows how the design maintains structural integrity when the walls are subjected to water pressure.

/flexibility
different internal configurations within the core elements

kitchen-storage
kitchen
storage-toilet 1
storage-toilet 2

/low tech
walls are made of concrete blocks strengthened with rebars; the roof is made of traditional wooden elements, covered with tiles or tin; partitions are made of recycled elements

/comfort
the porous structure promotes natural ventilation and overshadowing, improving internal comfort

Wooden ring beams were installed to make the homes more earthquake resistant, as seen in this shelter under construction in Herat Province.

Housing in Northern Afghanistan

Location_ Baghlan, Herat Province
Date_1998–2002
Client_USAID Office of Foreign Disaster
Assistance (OFDA)
End client_5,000 homeowners in 76 villages
Organization_ Shelter For Life
Design team_ Robert Bjerre, Harry van Burik,
LeGrand Malany, Baghlan community members
Structural engineers_ Joe Settle, Mark Baltzer
Additional consultants_ Robert S. Yeats,
Christopher Madden (Earth Consultants
International); Charles Setchell, James Smith
(OFDA)
Major funding_USAID Office of Foreign
Disaster Assistance
Cost per unit_$610
Area_370 sq. ft./34.6 sq. m

Shelter For Life, a nonprofit based in Oshkosh, Wisconsin, was founded in response to the Soviet Union's invasion of Afghanistan in 1979.

When millions of Afghan refugees flooded into Pakistan and Iran, a small team of volunteers responded by building multipurpose geodesic domes to provide housing for widows and refugees.

The project established what would be a long-standing commitment to providing shelter to the displaced and disadvantaged in Afghanistan, and the organization's subsequent projects would serve as a case study on the importance of developing local relationships.

For example, when an earthquake devastated a remote, mountainous area of the country in 1998, local ties enabled the group to respond effectively. "It was extremely hard to get to," architect Harry van Burik, director of international programs for Shelter For Life said of the quake zone. "After our vehicle overturned during an assessment, we realized we had to use what I call appropriate transportation." The group hired more than 1,000 donkeys to cart enough material across the Tajikistan border to build 500 homes with seismic-mitigation measures.

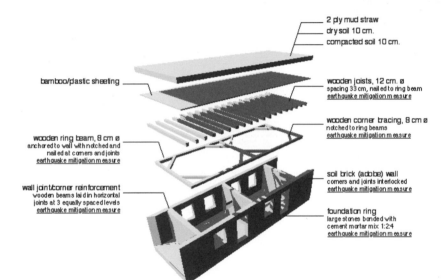

2 ply mud straw
dry soil 10 cm.
compacted soil 10 cm.

bamboo/plastic sheeting

wooden joists, 12 cm. ø
spacing 33 cm, nailed to ring beam
earthquake mitigation measure

wooden corner bracing, 8 cm ø
notched to ring beams
earthquake mitigation measure

wooden ring beam, 8 cm ø
anchored to wall with notched and
nailed at corners and joints
earthquake mitigation measure

soil brick (adobe) wall
corners and joints interlocked
earthquake mitigation measure

wall joint/corner reinforcement
wooden beams laid in horizontal
joints at 3 equally spaced levels
earthquake mitigation measure

foundation ring
large stones bonded with
cement mortar mix 1:2:4
earthquake mitigation measure

top left
**More than 1000 donkeys were hired
to transport materials.**

top right
**Future homeowners make
interlocking adobe blocks.**

Shelter For Life adopted the local vernacular to speed construction.
All images Shelter For Life

When another earthquake rocked the region in spring 2002, the group was called on to supply emergency shelter to some 30,000 people. Instead of providing winterized tents, Shelter For Life used its experience in the area to build permanent housing. For $610 per house, about the cost of a winterized canvas tent, the group enlisted the help of local residents to construct 5,000 adobe shelters in 76 villages over the course of a four-month period.

As many of the beneficiaries were also working to construct homes, the project offered an opportunity to provide training on seismic awareness and preparedness in the earthquake-affected communities. The group conducted more than 100 community workshops at local schools and mosques. Construction laborers and beneficiaries received on-the-job training in how to incorporate seismic-mitigation features, such as wooden ring beams anchored to the walls and reinforced corners, into shelter design and construction to help prevent damage in future disasters.

Mobile Migrant
Worker Housing

Location_Adams County, Pennsylvania, USA
Date_1997
Client_Rural Opportunities
End client_Single male migrant workers
Design center_Design Corps
Design team_Bryan Bell, Kindra Welch,
Lesli Stinger, Melissa Tello
Additional consultant_Gary Shaffer
Major funding_American Institute of
Architects, American Architectural Foundation,
National Endowment for the Arts,
Pennsylvania Department of Community
and Economic Development
Cost per unit_$43,000
Area_740 sq. ft./69 sq. m

A sign hanging above Bryan Bell's desk reads, "The benefits of architecture are for everyone."

It's a motto that has defined his career. After earning his master's in architecture from Yale, he landed a job in the offices of Steven Holl, but he soon felt restless. "I felt like I was doing plastic surgery when I wanted to be in the emergency room," Bell said during a presentation in Austin, Texas.

During this time his sister, who worked with a nonprofit in Pennsylvania, told him about the appalling housing conditions in the area. Before long Bell found himself with Rural Opportunities, a community development nonprofit that had been serving the needs of farm workers and the rural poor since 1969. He struck a deal with them: If he could find funding for his services, they would hire him.

In 1997 Bell established Design Corps with the idea of bringing design services to people who ordinarily couldn't afford to hire an architectural firm. The nonprofit design center has since become a clearing house for community-design ideas and methods and is best known for its innovative migrant housing. With research grants from the American Institute of Architects and the American Architectural Foundation, Design Corps partnered with Rural Opportunity Farmworker Advisory Councils to document the needs of farm workers in Adams County, Pennsylvania—many of them migrant. The team found that most earned less than $4,000 a year per family and lived in crowded dormitory-style "bullpens." The mixture of many cultures and languages in one large room led to fights, and the close quarters also led to a high incidence of tuberculosis and other communicable diseases, according to the Migrant Health Program.

"One cannot just design a project and shove it into a community," says Bell. In order to connect with and gain the trust of farm workers, Design Corps had to step out of the usual client-designer relationship and meet the workers on their terms.

As Sunday is the workers' only day off, Design Corps set up stalls at local farmers markets. In return for filling out a questionnaire, workers received soda and bottled water—especially welcome on hot summer days. The questionnaires revealed that there were two types of workers: single men who came for a season and then returned to their home countries, and families in search of something more permanent.

To house the single men, Bryan wanted to pull away from the bullpen approach. Instead he looked at building several smaller units that could be premanufactured, ensuring a fixed price and preapproval of housing regulations. The resulting unit is a 720-square-foot (67-sq.-m) prefabricated metal building with two bedrooms, each sleeping four men, separated by a living room, a communal bathroom, and kitchen. To date, seven units have been constructed on farms in Adams County.

Design Corps has worked to develop similar migrant-housing programs for both single men and families with farmers and workers on a nursery in Gray Court, South Carolina; on a mushroom farm in Kennett Square, Pennsylvania; and on an organic farm in Little Washington, Virginia. On the Little Washington farm the team overcame the challenge of poor septic facilities and water shortages by designing dwellings that contain greenhouse porches, where ginger lilies are grown using recycled gray water. Since the plants are pesticide free, the greenhouse provides an extra front porch for the workers among the fragrant flowers.

Prefabricated worker housing is delivered on the back of an oversize truck.
Bryan Bell

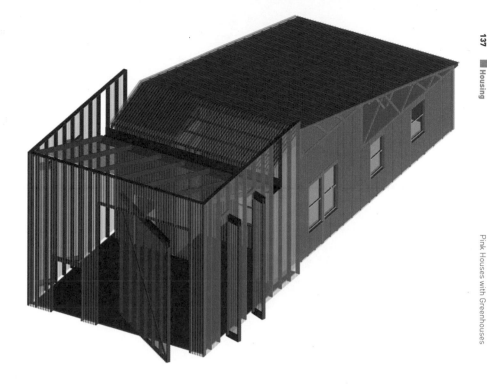

Pink Houses with Greenhouses

Location_Little Washington, Virginia, USA
Date_2002
Client_Sunnyside
End client_Migrant workers
Design center_Design Corps
Design team_Bryan Bell, Seth Peterson, Kersten Harries, Jeff Evans
Major funding_US Department of Housing and Urban Development (Rural Housing and Economic Development Program and HOME Program)
Cost per unit_$70,000, including gray-water system and greenhouse
Area_1,000 sq. ft./93 sq. m

above and right
In this housing design for a farm in Little Washington, Virginia, fragrant flowers in a greenhouse-cum-porch are watered by gray water from the unit's sinks and help mask the odors from the farm's poor septic facilities.
Both images Seth Peterson

600,000,000

urban dwellers and 1,000,000,000 people in rural areas live in overcrowded and poor-quality housing—slums and squatter settlements, old buses, shipping containers, and railway platforms

Gordan McGranahan and David Satterthawaite, "Urban Centers: An Assessment of Sustainability," Annual Review of Environment and Resources, Nov. 2003

At least

2,000,000

Europeans live in mobile, semipermanent, or other premises not fit for human habitation

"Report on Housing Exclusion and Homelessness," Council of Europe

1 in 6

people live in slums, or "contiguous settlements where inhabitants are characterized as having inadequate housing and basic services," but if no action is taken, that number could grow to 1 in 3 by the year 2020

"Report on Housing Exclusion and Homelessness," Council of Europ

Cameron Sinclair

Maasai Integrated Shelter Project

Location_Magadi Division, Kajiado District, Kenya
Date_October 1999–April 2002
Client_Arid and Semiarid Lands Program
End client_Maasai women
Design center_Intermediate Technology Development Group (ITDG), East Africa
Design team_Sharon Sian Looremetta, the Maasai community
Engineer_Edward Lein Marona
Construction manager_Sirenche ole Kanambase
Additional consultants_Dr. Nick Hall, Amon Ng'ang'a
Major funding_Danish Embassy
Cost_$721 per house
Website_www.itdg.org

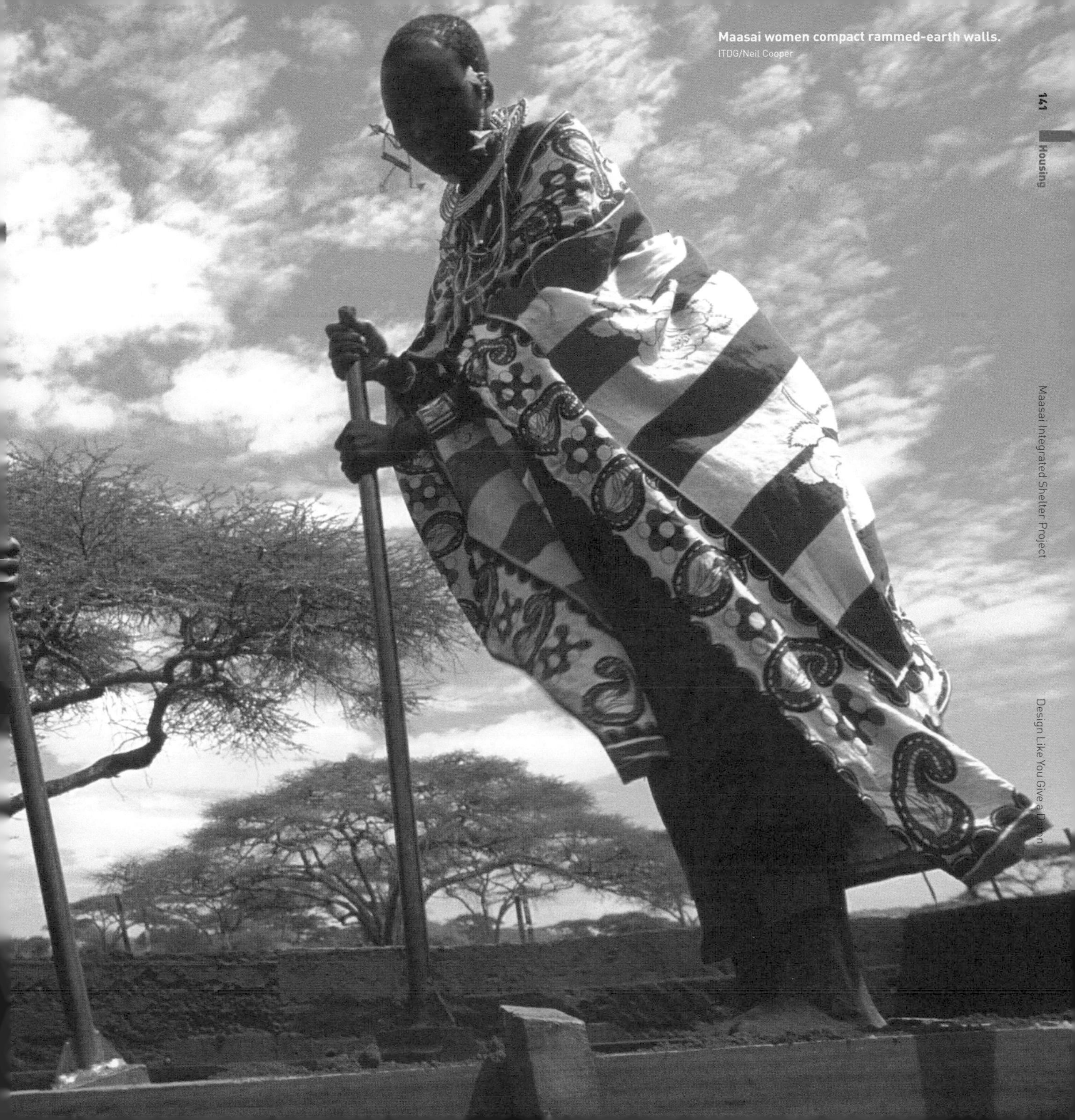

Maasai women compact rammed-earth walls.
ITDG/Neil Cooper

The Maasai of Kenya are probably one of the most well-known indigenous tribes of East Africa.

Unlike most that organized into kingdoms, the Maasai never abandoned their nomadic lifestyle, settling instead into clans and subtribes. Their housing consisted primarily of huts known as *inkajijik*, which are plastered with cow dung. Due to increased urbanization and the declaration of game reserves such as the Maasai Mara and the Serengeti in recent years, however, the tribe's ability to graze its cattle over large areas has significantly diminished, resulting in a less nomadic lifestyle—and the need for new permanent housing.

As of the late 1990s a rapidly growing population of approximately 120,000 Maasai lived in an area of 8,500 square miles (22,000 sq. km) in Kenya's Kajiado District. In 1999 ITDG in Kenya received a request for assistance by the Arid and Semiarid Lands Program to address the area's growing housing crisis.

Unlike the practice in other tribes, Maasai women maintain a prominent position within the culture and are in charge of housing construction and maintenance. ITDG's role was to work with local women's groups to give support in developing shelter strategies and new technologies.

At a workshop the women presented their ideas on housing design and construction. Their main concerns included the need for natural lighting and ventilation (most *inkajijik* have no windows and only one door opening). Smoke from cooking fires gets trapped in the houses and is a major contributor to respiratory complaints. They wanted to

opposite above
A woman plasters her roof with dung in the traditional method.
ITDG

opposite below
Mrs. Silole Malipe ene Mpariya built her own ferro-cement skin roof according to ITDG's methods. The new ferro-cement roof requires less maintenance.
ITDG/Neil Cooper

below
Women with their new ferro-cement roof, which collects rainwater and channels it into a cistern also made of ferro-cement.
ITDG/Lucky Lowe

Maasai women build a home using rammed earth.
ITDG/Neil Cooper

"I used to spend a lot of time fixing my walls and roof, and the trek to get water from long distances was very tiring. When we all have houses like mine, we shall be able to find solutions to other problems that face us."

Nolari Nkurruna, member, Naning'o Women's Group

avoid time-consuming maintenance (the traditional plaster of dung, mud, and ash needs constant attention, especially during the rainy season). And they wanted more space (*inkajijik* have such low ceilings that adults are unable to stand upright inside).

To address these concerns ITDG proposed three different housing options, each of which combined traditional building methods with new techniques and materials. The first option involved building with rammed earth; the second option was constructed from soil blocks stabilized with a small amount of cement; the third and most popular option made use of ferro-cement, cement reinforced by chicken wire.

To replace the traditional dung-based plaster, the ITDG—in a trial-and-error process with the Maasai Rural Training Center—found that it could use ferro-cement to create a more permanent and weatherproof roof, as well as walls and

water-collection jars. It was a small but significant change.

Because the new roofs were stronger and more durable, windows and living spaces could be enlarged, addressing many of the health problems associated with the traditional *inkajijik*. The new technology also enabled rain collection from the roofs, which meant women didn't have to travel long distances to get water.

Since the project began more than 2,400 houses have been built, and the region has seen a significant drop in the incidence of respiratory disease, malaria, and other illnesses. Whereas maintaining their homes and collecting water had once been taxing and time-consuming activities, the women now have time to spend on other pursuits, including starting their own small businesses—proving the strong ties between sustainable housing, economic prosperity, and independence.

above
The Lucy House at dusk
Tim Hursley

left
Carpet tiles are laid to create the exterior walls.
James Tate

opposite
The Harris family in their new living room
Tim Hursley

In 1936 photographer Walker Evans and writer James Agee spent three weeks in Hale County, Alabama, documenting the lives of Depression-era tenant sharecroppers.

Lucy House

Location_Mason's Bend, Hale County, Alabama, USA
Date_2001–2
Client_ Anderson and Lucy Harris
Design center_Rural Studio, Auburn University
Design team_Ben Cannard, Philip Crosscup, Andrew Freear, Floris Keverling Buisman, Kerry Larkin, Samuel Mockbee, Marie Richard, D. K. Ruth, Jay Sanders, J. M. Tate, Keith Zawistowski
Major funding_Netherland-America Foundation, Interface, Potrero Nuevo, individual donors
Cost_$30,000
Area_1,200 sq. ft./115 sq. m

The result was the internationally acclaimed book *Let Us Now Praise Famous Men* (1941). Many of its depictions of deep poverty still ring true over 70 years later, and many of the dilapidated homes Evans shot are still barely standing or have been replaced by ones just as unstable.

Tucked in Hale County, Mason's Bend is home to just such conditions, its 100-plus residents living in trailers or poorly constructed homes. The Rural Studio, a design/build program within the College of Architecture, Design, and Construction at Auburn University in Alabama, has made its biggest impact here, with three homes and a community space constructed under the guidance of Samuel Mockbee, D. K. Ruth, and other faculty members. In 1994 the Rural Studio completed its first building, the Hay Bale House for the Bryant family; three years later the Butterfly House was built for the Harris family; and in 2002, less than a month after Mockbee's untimely death, ground was broken for the Lucy House.

The Lucy House, for Anderson and Lucy Harris and their three children, was conceived by Mockbee and developed and built by Rural Studio students led by Ruth.

The structure draws on traditional vernacular forms such as shed roofs and barns, but with a twist—quite literally.

Anchoring the single-story home at one end is a crumpled burgundy tower housing the dining room and master bedroom. It rests on a concrete base that serves as a meditation and TV room and tornado shelter for the family. Where the tower is unique in its form, the main structure's innovation comes from use of materials. Separated from the tower by a translucent corridor, the area containing the three children's bedrooms, bathroom, kitchen, and living room is an ode to sustainable building.

Interface Carpets donated 24,000 redundant carpet tiles, which students meticulously stacked to create the structure's shell. The tiles were compressed using prestressed reinforced rods to form a solid mass, which was then capped with a wooden ring beam. A large pitch roof with heavy overhang protects the multicolored surface from the elements.

The Lucy House is just one example of the Rural Studio's maxim that the care and detail invested in building an affordable home does not need to be—and indeed should not be—directly related to the material wealth of its occupant.

If the Lucy House offers a highly personalized custom solution to affordable housing, the 20.0 House (Twenty-Thousand-Dollar House) takes the opposite tack. The project grew out of research conducted by the Rural Studio's Outreach program. In researching the housing needs of Hale County, students discovered that although many families qualified for federal housing subsidies (the rate of substandard housing in the county was five times the national average, and Hale County families were two and a half times more likely to live on annual incomes of less than $10,000) few benefited from the programs intended to help them.

The reason: Because of their low incomes and poor credit histories, most families in the area qualified for mortgages between $20,000 to $40,000 under federal programs such as the Rural Development 502 Program, but a typical home cost $75,000 or more to build. "A family's application might be accepted, but since program officials felt that no home could be built to their standards for less than $75,000, the applications just sat. People went on living in substandard housing," explains Pamela Dorr, who helped launch the project as a Rural Studio Outreach Fellow. She now directs the HERO County Housing Resource Center, which provides counseling on home ownership, home repair, and rental assistance.

What's more, substandard housing left families vulnerable to the violent storms and hurricanes that frequently pass through the region. A 2000 law enacted by FEMA provides $25,000 in funding for "replacement housing" for residents whose homes are destroyed by natural disasters. But because many low-income families could not qualify for mortgages, these funds often gave them few options but to live in trailers, leaving them vulnerable to the ravages of future storms.

The solution: The 20.0 House.

In 2004 the Rural Studio partnered with the HERO County Housing Resource Center to create one of its most pragmatic structures to date—a two-bedroom stick-frame house that can be built by a contractor—any contractor—for $20,000, including materials and labor. Careful research ensured that you can easily buy the materials at any Lowe's or Home Depot. The house is energy efficient, built on a raised foundation, and designed to comply with federal standards.

The prototype, funded and built by the Rural Studio, was donated to Elizabeth Phillips. The studio is currently building three additional homes. Prospective homeowners interested in purchasing a 20.0 House under the Rural Development 502 program, with assistance from the HERO County Housing Resource Center, can take tours of these "model homes" before they begin the application process.

20.0 House

Location_ Greensboro, Hale County, Alabama, USA
Date_2003–5
Client_ Elizabeth Phillips
Design center_ Rural Studio, Auburn University
Design team_ Andrew Freear, Philip March Jones, Min Koo Kim, Hana Loftus, Laura Noguera, Kellie Stokes
Project partner_HERO County Housing Resource Center
Major funding_ Rural Studio
Cost_$25,000
Area_616 sq. ft./57 sq. m

right
The front porch of the 20.0 House serves as an outdoor room for the family.
Both photographs Rural Studio

Hopi Nation Elder Home

Location_Hotevilla, Arizona, USA
Date_2005
Organization_Red Feather Development Group
Client_Tenakhongva family
Architect_Nathaniel Corum
Structural engineer_Beaudette Consulting Engineers
Electrical engineer_Energy A.D.
Construction_Volunteer labor
Major funding_USDA Home Mortgage, Red Feather Development Group
Cost_$79,200
Area_1,320 sq. ft./122 sq. m

It has been called a quiet crisis: According to US census figures, one in eight Native Americans lives in overcrowded or substandard housing, nearly three times the national average.

It is estimated that anywhere from 90,000 to 350,000 Native Americans, nearly half of them children, are homeless or live in substandard conditions. In severe cases 20 to 25 people live together in homes with as few as three bedrooms. And the complexity of financing construction on tribal lands means the waiting list for federal housing assistance is much longer than average.

About 10 years ago Robert Young, the owner of a sportswear company, founded Red Feather Development Group to help address substandard living conditions on reservations. Appalled to see families "stacked up like cord wood" in rundown trailers and rental units—many without running water or electricity—he organized volunteers to make home repairs and build wheelchair ramps, small fixes that helped establish trust and allowed him to get to know the community and its needs. Eventually he and volunteers built their first house, a small kit home for Lakota elder Katherine Red Feather, for whom the organization is named.

In 1996 the federal government passed the Native American Housing Assistance and Self-Determination Act, which eliminated assistance programs and replaced them with a single block grant. But as the group began to understand the issues facing tribal communities, it felt the solution depended

foundation. Then you stack hay bales like bricks to form walls. Finally, you seal the bales with stucco. In order to bear the weight of the structure, the hay must be tightly compressed, and the best bales would be free of seeds and weeds and composed of fresh, long, thick uncrushed straw to prevent rot. For this reason Red Feather buys its bales from a Navajo supplier who produces them specifically for construction purposes.

A two-bedroom home costs as little as $45,000, including plumbing and other fixtures, and can be built in four weeks, Young says. The thick walls insulate against extreme weather, saving money on heating bills—no small expense for a family living at or below the poverty line. Deep window wells, window seats, rounded corners, and contemporary, open plans lend a sense of comfort and warmth to an otherwise basic layout.

Red Feather first began experimenting with the approach five years ago, working with the university. Since then it has worked with other institutions to build six homes, including the Hopi Nation Elder Home shown here. The organization has also built a literacy center and a study hall from straw bale on reservations in North Dakota and Montana. With the addition of Rose Fellow architect Nathaniel Corum to their staff, the group has begun to explore what Corum calls "agri-tecture," using materials such as carpeting made from corn husks and particle board made from compressed sunflower seeds. Corum also has helped Red Feather standardize, simplify, and develop educational materials so families can adapt the construction technique for building their own houses.

While the waiting list for public-housing assistance remains long, some families are adopting the Red Feather model. "We lost our family home 13 months ago. Four of us built a straw structure, 10 by 30 feet (three by nine m) with posts for roof support," wrote one tribal member in an unsolicited e-mail to the organization. "Your Website gave us the inspiration to provide for ourselves when we could not get any support or help from our local Indian Housing Authority."

above
In addition to homes, the group has used straw bale to construct literacy centers and other community structures. Here, Red Feather volunteers plaster a straw-bale wall for an environmental research center on the Turtle Mountain reservation in North Dakota.
Red Feather Development Group

opposite
The Hopi Nation Elder Home under construction
Above, Red Feather Development Group; below, Jonathan Corum

less on block grants and more on finding a low-cost housing type that would allow tribal members to provide for themselves.

The group's search led it to the BASIC Initiative of the College of Architecture and Urban Planning at the University of Washington, where students and faculty suggested a surprisingly indigenous solution: straw-bale construction. "It's like Lego for adults," says Young, who was drawn to the approach by its simplicity. First you lay the

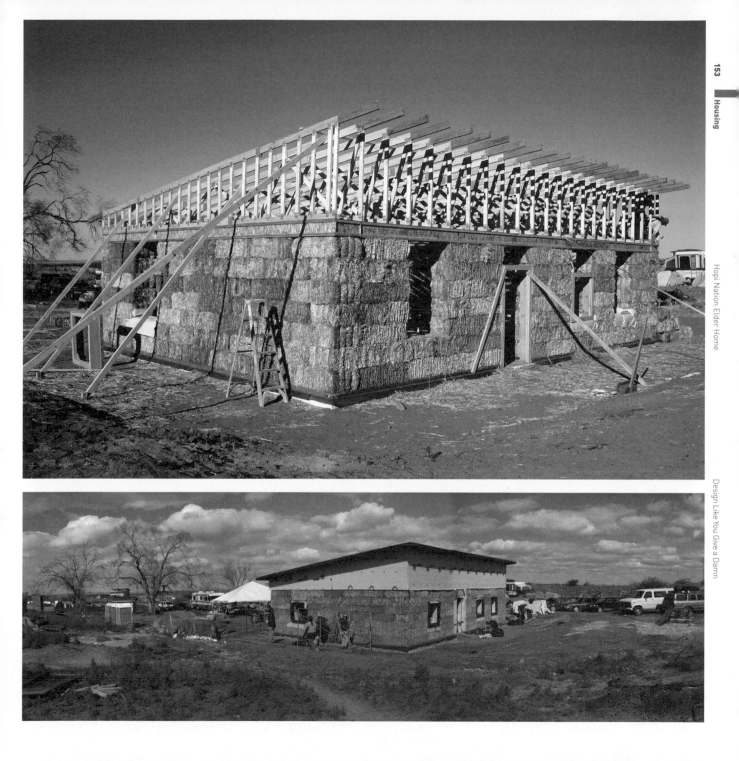

Hopi Nation Elder Home

Design Like You Give a Damn

Bayview Rural Village

Location_Bayview, Virginia, USA
Date_1997–2003
Organization_Bayview Citizens for Social Justice, Inc.
Design firm_RBGC Architecture, Research & Urbanism
Lead designer and facilitator_Maurice D. Cox
Project organizers_Alice Coles, Bola Ajayi, Frank Driscoll, Cozzie Lockwood, Vladimir Gavrilovic, William A. Drewry
Project partner_The Nature Conservancy
Design team_Giovanna Galfione, Marthe Rowen, Craig Barton
Project team_Tim Ciccone, Jeff Evans, Will Hertzog, Celia Liu, Esther Yang
Structural engineer_Nolen Frisa Associates
Civil engineer_FPS
Electrical/Mechanical engineer_ Kincaid-Bryant
Contractor_Armada Hoffler Construction
Total budget_$1.7 million
Major funding_Community Development Block Grant, US Department of Agriculture Rural Development Grant (515 Program)
Units_32 low-income rental units
Area_860 sq. ft./80 sq. m (average)
Site_160 acres/65 hectares

YEAR 1

Community leaders meet design team;
   first walk-through
$20,000 EPA planning grant to Bayview Citizens
   for Social Justice, Inc. (BCSJ)
Bayview Community kick-off meeting: short-term
   goals established
Community members organize Bayview
   Community Day
BCSJ applies for incorporation
Residents agree to pursue "new land" strategy
   and discuss housing types at 4th Community
   Workshop and Picnic
NAACP brings national attention to the
   community's substandard living conditions
First deep well drilled; pit-privies installed
Plan for New Bayview Rural Village presented at
   5th community workshop and picnic
BCSJ gains 501(c)(3) status

YEAR 2

Grant received from Dave Matthews Band to
   fund housing workshops and design services
Affordable-housing consultant joins project
Grant received to purchase land
Documentary film production begins

YEAR 3

BCSJ applies for USDA funding (515 Program)
Barn raising
BCSJ receives housing funding from UDSA

YEAR 4

Project 70 percent funded with money from
   15 different funding streams
Ongoing meetings with funders, government
   agencies, and others to obtain necessary local,
   state, and federal approvals
Delays in local approvals process cause project
   to lose partial funding

YEAR 5

Meetings and approvals process continue
BCSJ hires director to manage growing
   organization
Project fully funded

YEAR 6

Project receives final approvals
Construction begins on rental housing
CBS's 60 Minutes profiles Alice Coles
Documentary film This Black Soil released
First residents given keys to their new homes

Interview

Maurice D. Cox
Bayview Rural Village

*The story of Bayview Rural Village
is one of transformation—not just physical
but social change.*

Bayview is part of a string of historically black communities along the Eastern Shore of Virginia. Many of its residents can trace their roots back more than 350 years to the earliest days of slavery. Over time, however, this once-vibrant community steadily slipped into a state of physical and economic decay.

For years families in Bayview lived in substandard housing, most without running water or indoor plumbing. Only six of the town's 52 homes had toilets. When it rained, dilapidated outhouses overflowed, forming pools of polluted water in Bayview's streets. The community's only sources of water were shallow, contaminated wells.

Then in 1994 this forgotten rural outpost, where more than a third of the population lived below the poverty line and one in five lacked a high school education, found itself at the epicenter of a battle for social justice. Residents' success in defeating a proposal to build a prison in their backyard would galvanize the community to fight for more substantial change.

In this interview architect Maurice D. Cox, a partner in the firm RBGC Architecture, Research & Urbanism, professor of architecture at the University of Virginia, former mayor of Charlottesville, and a community leader, discusses how design became the vehicle for Bayview's transformation.

Bayview was an incredible success story that took many, many years to happen. How did you and your architectural firm get involved?
It was a case of being in a place where the community could find me. I was facilitating a community design workshop in Cape Charles, on the Eastern Shore. There must have been 100 people in the room but only a handful of African-Americans. Alice [Coles] came right over to my table and sat down. I was doing what designers do, drawing and making site plans, and she seemed absolutely mesmerized. After the workshop she pulled me aside and said, "I'm Alice Coles from Bayview, and we are trying to improve our community, too. We would be so honored to have an architect work with us." And I said, "I'll work with you."

Literally, that's how I became involved. I didn't know anything about the battles that Bayview residents had fought to defeat a maximum-security prison. All I knew was that I had met this incredibly focused, driven, and articulate black woman, and I was taken by her courage.

I often suspect had I not been in a place where the community could find me, this project would never have happened. I mean that quite seriously. If designers are not in the community, then those who might potentially need our talents the most simply might not find us.

What happened next?
One of her partners in the prison fight, Steve Parker, an outreach coordinator of the Nature Conservancy, had promised her that after their successful defeat of the prison, he would help Bayview address the issues that continued to plague her community. And he did that. On Alice's recommendation, he contacted me and said, "Here are the issues that Bayview is wrestling with. What would a team look like to address them?"

So I assembled an interdisciplinary team including an environmental engineer, an environmental planner, myself as the community designer, and a community economic development consultant. Bayview had serious issues regarding safe drinking water, and Steve found a grant for $20,000 through the EPA that was targeted for communities fighting issues of environmental justice. We applied for the grant with Alice. In just three months, we were notified that we had received the grant and would be due to begin the following month. I still had never visited Bayview, but at this point I had committed to do the project.

The Nature Conservancy arranged for all of us—Bayview community leaders with their families and our design team with our families—to spend a day on Hog Island on the Eastern Shore. Their idea was to have us meet in a neutral place, break bread, and get to know each other before we went to the larger community.

I remember so vividly walking on the beach with Alice Coles. She told me stories of the battles she'd fought, and I told her stories of the battles I'd fought for my community as an elected official in Charlottesville. That sealed the deal. She was convinced after spending that day with me that I was a fighter, and she knew, given the politics of the Eastern Shore, that I was in for the biggest political battle I had ever fought. The next day we all met again, this time in Bayview to meet the extended community.

What were your first impressions of Bayview?
It was incredible. My design partners with our families, and Bayview residents with their families all crammed onto one of the community leader's porches. They brought out platters of fried chicken and potato salad. It was to be the first of many picnics that they held around our workshops. After we finished eating, Alice Coles finally, finally led the team on a tour of Bayview.

We quickly left the paved main road and found ourselves on the side streets. The roads turned to dirt, and the houses started to look very decrepit. First she took us over to one of the community's three wells. It had this old, rusted hand pump that screeched when you pumped it. They said that this was where they drew their water—all 52 families. Families had a daily ritual of taking in buckets of water, boiling it, and using it for all of their household purposes. They took us house to house, and people invited us into their homes. I had never seen spaces

so small and deteriorated. On the one hand, I was in a state of disbelief, but on the other hand, I was trying desperately not to show them how shocked I was over their living conditions.

It got worse and worse as we got farther and farther from the main street. My children went into the homes as well. It was really quite a moving experience. When my wife and I left the Eastern Shore that evening we felt the stakes had been raised considerably. Our feelings were primarily of inadequacy; in the end we were just designers. We didn't know if we could solve a community's problems that were so incredibly dire, but we had already committed to working with them. So we went back to Charlottesville to make this work.

Had you planned and designed a project like this before?
I had never worked on a rural project of this scope before. I was raised in the city, accustomed to seeing urban blight and working with low-income residents in pretty bad urban environments. But I had never been this engaged in a rural community and never knew how different their lives could be. I certainly wasn't prepared to believe that people lived like that in the twentieth century—less than two hours from the nation's capital.

I often try to convey to people that even as these families were living in absolutely substandard conditions, there was an incredible sense of community spirit in Bayview. They were gracious hosts and did not appear to be ashamed of their situation. I'm sure they were, but it somehow didn't kill their spirit. So the character and tone of our workshops and visits to Bayview were always incredibly festive. You could close your eyes and almost blank out the physical decay for a moment. We were always laughing, sharing stories, and playing with kids. In reality, however, the physical blight was compromising every aspect of their community's health—their physical health, their mental health, their economic health. The physical decay of the place was bearing down on their ability to be a healthy community.

How did you approach the project in those first few months? How did you establish a relationship with the community?
We organized a series of nine community workshops. Once a month we would travel three hours by car out to the Eastern Shore. The first meeting was particularly memorable. We had carefully scripted how we thought the workshop would go. We went into the meeting, must have been 45 people there. We had everyone from Bayview residents to the slum landlord [who owned most of the rental housing in the community]. We had the local chapter of the NAACP [National Association for the Advancement of Colored People], the Nature Conservancy, and even county government representatives. But most of the people were from the Bayview community, and it became very apparent from the first minutes of the meeting that people had come with incredibly high expectations of what we, as community designers, could do. They talked about health care, about jobs, and about housing. We literally had to throw away our script and simply engage people in a conversation.

They talked about what it was like to live in homes without bathrooms. They talked about the pit privies, the outhouses, in their

A typical home in Bayview before Bayview Citizens for Social Justice enlisted the services of a design team to help them reenvision their community
Susannah Mills

backyards that no longer functioned. The pit privies were not even routinely emptied. So they would fill up, and when it rained, waste would spill out onto the ground and create really unhealthy conditions. And people were living right in the midst of all that. So they had these very real concerns to share with us.

Then something wonderful happened. As we talked about bringing clean water to the existing houses, a resident said, "Why would you even bother bringing water to shacks like these? This place is nothing like the Bayview we grew up in."

So we asked residents to tell us about how Bayview used to be. The exercise unleashed a whole series of incredible memories. They talked about the corner store, about the homes families owned. They talked about farming in the surrounding fields. They talked about a place that had been a rural village. This idea of Bayview as rural village became the starting point for our community design process.

Did you worry about setting unrealistic expectations?
I felt my first task as a designer was to get Bayview to dream—and to dream very big. Yes, I was concerned about our ability to deliver on their dreams, but it wasn't because their expectations for the community design process were unrealistic. I was concerned whether we, with this little EPA grant, could come up with the concrete strategies needed to implement their dreams.

What was the strategy that you eventually arrived at?
We started by helping them to imagine small, incremental changes that were within their reach. We simply asked, "What are the things we can do now to change the character of the community you live in?"

They said, "Well, we haven't hauled the garbage out of this community in years." Or, "There are burned-out buildings that are still standing and are eyesores in our community—let's demolish them." Another resident suggested, "We should plant some flowers." It was that kind of energy. By the second meeting, residents had formed a committee to clean up Bayview. They decided to hold a day to celebrate Bayview, to transform their community in small ways that their neighbors could see immediately.

We removed over 27,000 pounds (12,247 kg) of trash in one weekend, including everything from old kitchen appliances to car tires. When people saw that burnt-out buildings could be demolished in a matter of minutes, they were amazed by how rapidly they could change their community. It was a very empowering experience.

Once you'd gotten these initial projects completed and started building momentum, what was the next step?
After our initial successes in improving the existing community, we started talking to residents about taking on more challenging tasks, like refurbishing an abandoned chapel that was a beloved monument in their community, or imagining the building of a community bathhouse where residents could come to take showers, or exploring the idea of building a community kitchen. These ideas were proposed to solve short-term needs so that the community could focus on the long-term goals they really wanted to achieve. I found that every time we returned to Bayview, residents were more and more capable of tackling more difficult tasks. Our monthly meetings and the community's preparation for our arrival became an opportunity to build their capacity to make decisions and go about getting things done.

While this was going on, what was the design team doing?
We didn't start to show residents any plans for the new Bayview Rural Village until five months into the process. In the meantime the design team had lots of technical work to do, everything from environmental assessments of the pit privies and wells to documenting existing housing conditions to archival research into the history of Bayview. We felt a need to validate the stories of what Bayview once was for residents. Sure enough, in the local historical society we found photographs that showed that there was a train depot in Bayview, and other houses stood were there now were fields. There use to be neighborhood-owned restaurants and a corner store. It was wonderful to discover that residents' vision of Bayview as it once was was true.

How frequently did you meet with the community, and how did you encourage participation in the design process?
There were nine meetings over the course of the first year. Part of the way we encouraged participation was to design our workshops around things [people] already normally did. For example, we never publicized our meetings as workshops. It was always, "Come to the cookout, the architects from Charlottesville are coming." Or "Come to the fish fry and help design the community you want to live in." Their area had incredible gospel choirs, so we'd have a concert before or after the workshops. Our meetings were always held when people were not working, during the evenings or weekends, so people could gather, stay, and socialize. We simply met people where they were.

Tell us about the workshops. How did you facilitate an exchange of ideas with the community?

Most of our meetings were what I would call teach-ins. We would get started at about 10 a.m. and we wouldn't let people go until after five or six in the evening—and people stayed with us. We explained everything, even the most technical aspects of the project, so that they could make informed decisions.

For me, the most interesting part of the process was the idea of using the design process as a way to help people make decisions. Making design choices can be an extremely empowering experience for the layperson. Our design team regularly presented the community with a series of options. If we were looking at a proposal for the community catering kitchen, the bathhouse, or restoration of the chapel, we always presented the community with at least three ways of accomplishing the design task. This forced them to evaluate the pros and cons of each option and come to a group decision. We would conduct our teach-ins first, then at the end of the day, a decision would be made, and we, the designers, would live by it.

I have come to believe that if you teach people what their options are, they have this miraculous capacity to make the decision that is in their best interest. It was amazing to watch this unfold.

What were some of the hardest decisions that they faced?

The decision to tear down over 75 percent of the physical structures of their community, to tear down their blighted homes, that was pretty hard. When it came time to make that decision, we took all the black-and-white photographs that my University of Virginia students had taken to document each house, we blew them up to poster size and covered a wall with them. Because it was so visual, it had a powerful effect. For the first time people were looking objectively at these rented shacks that they had called home and were seeing them for what they were. By the end of this exercise an overwhelming majority of the residents said, "These shacks need to come down. These are places that aren't fit for living." At the same time they were talking about their own homes, so it was an emotional moment.

Another significant moment came much later, in year two of the process. The decision was whether to build single-family homes for individual ownership or rental housing for the poorest residents of their community. Here we had all these people who aspired to finally own their own home, and they collectively decided to do low-income rental housing first. It was a very altruistic thing. They said, "You know, we need to look out for the poorest of the poor in Bayview." This spirit of self-sacrifice happened time and time again during our gatherings.

So they built rentals first and then owner properties?

Yes. Today there are 32 units of subsided rental housing constructed and about 15 to 20 lease-to-purchase homes, which came afterward. From 1997 to 2003—six long years—they continued to live in the same shacks as they survived on these dreams of a new Bayview.

And that is what I thought was one of the most powerful lessons learned. These shacks were the homes that they had lived in way before I came on the scene. So when outsiders would come in and say,

"This is deplorable. How can people live like this?" they would say, "Well, we have been living this way for years. At this point waiting a few more years for new homes won't matter." They understood that their homes were substandard, but they also had a vision now of what their community could be, and they were willing to wait. And during that period of waiting is when the real work was done, the work of helping them build an organization that could deliver a $10 million community development project.

They spent five years building an organization that hired from within the community. By the time they eventually got into the development phase of the project, they had employed over 15 Bayview residents. People were doing clerical work, they were doing computer work, or home budgeting workshops with residents to get them ready for life in their new homes. And that sustained them for years.

You were asking for an incredible commitment from this community. How did you build a sense of commitment, or was that something the community brought to the table?

They took responsibility for themselves. They insisted at every step in being equal partners in this adventure. As a designer I couldn't do the community-organizing piece for them. Our design team would basically go out to the Eastern Shore once a month, but when we left, the community had assignments, they had subcommittees—they understood what they had to do. And they did it.

How did the NAACP get involved?

By 1996 Bayview had just come out of a three-year battle to defeat the maximum-security prison that was targeted for their community. The local chapter of the NAACP on the Eastern Shore was one of the partners that worked with Bayview to defeat the prison. So when we started working with Bayview, the NAACP's local leader was at the table. They were our partners from the beginning.

That was very helpful, because when things started getting rough and local bureaucrats started putting up obstacles to our getting some of community's goals accomplished, like the permitting to drill deep wells, we had a direct pipeline to the national NAACP.

I think the local chapter leader thought the national representatives could solve some of these testy local problems, but when this delegation came and saw Bayview, they were so outraged by the state of decay that people were living in that they said, "We need to blow this place wide open. We need to expose this place."

The NAACP issued a national press release, and it used some incredibly explosive language in their description: "People in Bayview are living in the Third World." It characterized Bayview's conditions as a "modern-day form of apartheid in America." Some really biting quotes, and the NAACP sent this out to the major news outlets. That's when Bayview landed on the Sunday cover of the *Washington Post*. It shined a national spotlight on one community's poverty.

Bayview was ready to capitalize on this press. Not only did they have a vision for a new rural Bayview, but they also had an organizational structure in place to manage the process. Just five months into our design process, we started talking with the community about becoming

The biggest ch
to come....Nov
beauty on the
do we come ba
the infrastruc
the human so

Alice Coles, president, Bayview

llenge is yet
there is
utside; how
k and build
ire within
?

ens for Social Justice

a 501(c)(3) nonprofit corporation—even before we presented any ideas of what a new rural village might look like. So when the *Washington Post* story broke and we started getting attention from our US senator and from the White House no less, Bayview was in a position to say, "Yes, we need your resources, and by the way, we have the organizational capacity to manage our own money."

Putting an organizational structure in place—even before we had a design concept—turned out to be the most strategic decision made during our design process.

Tell us about the design for the housing.

The community continually told us, "Whatever you do, don't stigmatize us. We want to be in affordable housing without the stigma attached." That really validated our ideas about trying to continue the vernacular heritage of the area. [They wanted] their community to blend in with the other communities that are a part of the Eastern Shore. The houses are autobiographical. They look the way they look because the people in Bayview wanted the houses to tell the story of their presence on that land. I had never designed houses that looked like that before. In fact, if it was going to be my signature, I suspect they would not have looked like that, but I was telling Bayview's story.

In a project of this nature that takes so many years to complete, there are always high points and low points. What was the low point for Bayview?

The most difficult part was when the project moved into its development phase, and a nonprofit that didn't exist two years earlier now had responsibility for millions of dollars—with no track record and lots of nervous state and federal bureaucrats all looking over their shoulders, thinking "We need to fix Bayview, get it out of our hair, and move on." And here was this community that was insisting that they become their own developers. There were many people who could not accept that. Their attitude was "We don't have time." Instead, the community said at each step, "No, we want to learn how to do this."

There were a lot of snags along the way, particularly in the approval process on the local level. It took months when it normally would have taken weeks. This was mainly due to people being concerned that they were going to be held responsible. They didn't trust the capacity of Bayview. It really was a nightmare from the agencies' perspective.

I remember that the porches on the houses became a particular point of contention. Tell us about that.

The porches took on a sort of symbolic role in the life of the community. In our design process we were always meeting on someone's porch. That was where the community received guests. A lot of their life was spent on the porch, and Alice speaks so eloquently about the role of the porch. That's where they learned to read, that's where they heard stories from their grandparents. It had real symbolic meaning for them.

So in all our designs for Bayview we had these very deep porches. The funders for this affordable housing thought we were crazy. They said. "We don't pay for those kinds of amenities." We ended up getting into a battle with the funders over the importance of a local design.

They were more in the business of delivering quantity, and it seemed Bayview was insisting on quality, which was different than what they normally encountered. We fought and we fought and we fought, and thanks to Alice and the passionate way she spoke about these porches, we won. They allowed us to build these rather spacious porches for these affordable rental properties.

How was the project funded?

The residents of Bayview didn't say, "We want quality, and you better give it to us." They said, "We want quality, and we are willing to go out to private funders to get it." So in the end there were an incredible number of financing sources, I think 17. Even this formula of mixed funding was a new form of financing for the state and federal agencies. They were accustomed to having their money in the deal—and only their money. Instead we had foundation money, state money, local money, and federal money. We found that the feds wouldn't allow one thing and the state would. Then there were things that local funds wouldn't allow but state funds would. We had to try to juggle all these conflicting requirements and try to come up with something coherent.

With all this mixed funding, there must have been a lot of reporting required for each funding source. Who was doing all that work?

[Laughs.] The community constantly struggled to build its capacity to respond. [The people of Bayview] had to hire professional accountants and an attorney. They had to write the reports. I won't sugarcoat it: It was a constant challenge to respond to their funders. And most of the funding did not come with administrative assistance. It was [restricted] to brick-and-mortar kinds of things. I didn't have to witness it on a daily basis, but I know it caused incredible strain. Alice could tell you, there were a lot of people who were lost along the way, who were disillusioned, thinking that this would never happen. She had to continue to persevere.

How were meetings with officials conducted?

Bayview taught some of its members how to operate video equipment. So there would be 20 bureaucrats sitting in a meeting, and the first thing Bayview did was set up its video equipment. This had a very powerful effect. People were literally on their best behavior because they knew they were being filmed. Afterward the community would go back and study these tapes and talk about what had happened. They were also using them as a tactic for intimidating bureaucrats and making sure they understood that everything they said was now on record.

It was mainly bureaucrats talking and Alice and [a core group of community members] or the designers reporting back on the status of the project. Very dry stuff that had to be worked through. After a while there was nothing to engage the wider community in the development process, which was going to last five years. So we proposed a number of interim things that would engage a larger group. The residents decided, for example, that they wanted to reestablish their connection to the landscape. That became a proposal for a community garden. Another project was to raise a barn.

All other photographs Scott F. Smith

This was the same strategy we used to make incremental changes in the first month. We began by cleaning up garbage, and four years later we were building a barn. Two years after that, we were delivering a new community.

When were the first houses finally built?
The project started in 1997 and wrapped up in October of 2003. The rental houses were finally complete, the roads were in place, the retention pond had been built, the sewer system had been laid—and that's when the press started coming back to celebrate the fact that the community had done this.

[Bayview Citizens for Social Justice, Inc.] is now the largest affordable housing provider on the Eastern Shore. And, quite rightfully, Alice has been honored in many venues for her leadership.

What do you think the community gained from being such an integral part the design process?
Naturally, the bricks and mortar will be there forever, but the organization that they were left with, an organization that solves affordable housing problems, is the thing that gives me the most satisfaction. To know that architecture was a part of that, that they built an organization that was about building a beautiful place.... It's one of the most fulfilling projects I have ever done. My challenge now is how do I do more of this.

How do you justify the benefits of good design, of the kind of participatory design process that you led in Bayview, to someone who doesn't appreciate the importance of aesthetics or doesn't think design is a primary concern?
I actually don't think that aesthetics should be the first concern. I didn't reach the Bayview people by talking about aesthetics, I got to them by talking about community, about creating a place where children felt safe, about creating jobs that matched the skill levels in the community.

We weren't really talking about design, but all the things we were talking about had design consequences. The task of the designer is to help people see the interface between design and the things people care about.

What about on a political level? How do you convey the benefits of a participatory design process to government agencies and other decision makers?
I am a little bit of a realist here. I'm not absolutely convinced that the innovation is going to come from those sectors. I think it will come from other places, from the bottom up. If you can get communities to be a little bit more demanding than they have historically been—to demand quality, to demand choice, and to demand their right to decide, to dream—then the rest of the structure will change. I know a lot of communities look at what Bayview did and feel inspired by it. They feel that they, too, can challenge the system to come up with new strategies, and I think that's where the power lies.

Isn't this the role of a community activist more than a designer? Is it important to have a designer involved in the process?
I absolutely think it is. [When a disaster happens] people don't think, "Oh my gosh, we need a designer." They think about all the other technical professional skills that might be needed to respond. They don't think of it as a design problem. Our challenge is to show that what we have to offer is an ability to look at things holistically and make connections. When Bayview was presented to me, it was presented as a problem of water. It wasn't about community. It wasn't about creating a rural village. It was about water. So why would you go to an architect, if your problem was water management?

We need to be in the places where problems exist. We have to be in the room when the decisions are being made to be able to voice our opinions. Then our talents will be exploited. That's how you get design to be important. Designers need to be engaged, to be civic leaders, to be in the right place at the right time.

Quinta Monroy Housing Project

Location_Iquique, Chile
Date_2002–5
Client_Regional Government of Tarapacá, Chile-Barrio Program
End client_93 illegal households
Partner organization_Serviu/Seremi Iquique
Design center_ELEMENTAL Housing Initiative, Pontificia Universidad Católica de Chile/Taller de Chile
Design team_Alejandro Aravena, Alfonso Montero, Tomás Cortese, Emilio de la Cerda
Public policy consultants_Andrés Iacobelli, Elena Puga
Engineers_Juan Carlos de la Llera, Carl Lüders, Mario Alvarez, Tomás Fisher, Alejandro Ampuero, José Gajardo
Major funding_Ministry of Housing and Urbanism, Chile-Barrio Program
Cost_$7,500 (including land)
Area_430 sq. ft./36 sq. m
Website_www.elementalchile.org

Most designers find solutions to policy limitations as a matter of course; rarely are they inspired by the limitations themselves.

In the case of this innovative housing project by the interdisciplinary design team Taller de Chile, a change in housing policy inspired them to turn to their drawing boards and prompted them to invite other architects to do the same. The result was a design-based solution to a problem that has vexed housing agencies throughout the world for decades: how to replace sprawling squatter settlements in urban centers with dignified, higher-density, low-income housing without creating vertical slums.

In 2002 the Chile-Barrio program, which works to upgrade the country's illegal settlements, changed its housing policy. Under the existing policy families were defaulting on loans. Rather than giving families loans and subsidies worth $10,000, policy makers decided to offer them mostly subsidies worth $7,500. The new program, "Dynamic Social Housing Without Debt,"

was intended to increase the number of beneficiaries without increasing the financial burden of families.

But the change posed a number of challenges for the housing developers and nonprofit groups charged with implementing it. Chief among them was the problem of building a structurally safe home for less than $7,500—including the cost of land—without pushing families into cheaper lots in the periphery of the city, where they would be far from jobs and support networks. Hoping to address this challenge, the ad-hoc team of architects, engineers, contractors, and public-policy experts of Taller de Chile, part of the ELEMENTAL Housing Initiative at Pontificia Universidad Católica de Chile, designed a pilot program. The program, which was initiated by the Chile-Barrio Program, involved resettling 93 families from Quinta Monroy, a 30-year-old illegal settlement in the center of the port city

Quinta Monroy Housing Project

Design Like You Give a Damn

opposite
**Conceptual rendering
of units after
habitation**

right
**View of new housing
units**

A DIFFICULT EQUATION TO SOLVE

Low cost (US$7,500) • **Densify (land and infrastructure savings)**
Flexibility for growth • **Structural complexity**
Protect the quality of urban space • "Orderly" growth

APPROXIMATIONS TO THE PARALELL HOUSING TYPOLOGY

- abolish the single-family per lot system
- increase the density and efficient use of land
- maintaining the possibility for growth

BASIC RULE:
The dividing walls should always coincide with habitable enclosures.

ELEMENTAL SCHEME OF THE PARALELL HOUSE

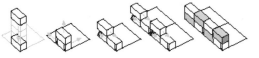

THE URBAN SCALE

above left and right
Typical residential areas in Quinta Monroy, an informal settlement in Iquique, Chile, before the ELEMENTAL Housing Initiative
Tomás Cortese

left
The design team explored a number of housing typologies before arriving at an approach that would allow families to easily build additions to their homes over time without creating overcrowding. Housing constructed using this strategy is often referred to as "incremental" or "progressive" housing.

opposite
The new housing in Quinta Monroy, with additions built by the residents, four months after construction.
All other images ELEMENTAL

of Iquique, into new housing on the same site as their original homes.

Design was constrained in several ways: The new housing had to be built on the site of the old settlement where land is more expensive, leaving less money for construction. It had to provide each family with the largest home for the subsidy provided. It had to enable occupants to easily build additions as they could afford them. And all this had to happen within a site plan that would allow the new development to grow in an orderly way. Most important, in order to ensure that the project could be replicated, the housing scheme had to be feasible within the existing policy framework—despite its limitations.

Collaborating with families in a series of workshops, the design team explored several alternatives before settling on this duplex solution. By building alternating single-story and double-story units, the scheme allows families to expand vertically rather than horizontally, thereby allowing for greater density without overcrowding. In an effort to ensure "orderly" growth, the team chose a U-shaped site plan that clearly demarcated common spaces and allowed for parking, roads, and walkways between residential clusters. Construction took a year and was completed in late 2004. During construction families were relocated to temporary housing. Within four months of their return families had

already begun adding to their units—a move the designers interpreted as a sign of the project's success.

In tandem with the pilot project in Iquique, the team also hosted an international design competition in 2003. Called Elemental, it invited designers to explore alternative solutions to Chile's new housing policy. A jury of architects, housing experts, and policy makers from the Ministry of Housing selected seven winning designs. The teams behind those designs are now working with communities and nonprofit organizations at seven other sites to help more families take full advantage of government housing subsidies using the same participatory model.

Northern Ireland Cross-Community Initiative

Location_Iris Close and Glencairn,
West Belfast; Ballysillan and Ligoniel,
North Belfast
Date_2002–present
Organization_Habitat for Humanity
Northern Ireland
Occupants_Low-income families
Design firm_David Ferguson & Associates
Project architect_Fionnuala Bradley
Structural engineer_Century Homes
Civil engineer_Whitemountain Civils
Additional consultant_Leslie Kane
(civil engineer)
Construction_1,000+ volunteers
Funding_Corporate, religious, and individual
donations
Cost per unit_$100,000
Area_742 sq. ft./69 sq. m (two bedrooms);
1,011 sq. ft./94 sq. m (three bedrooms);
1,166 sq. ft./108 sq. m (four bedrooms)

Habitat for Humanity's mandate is to build "simple, decent housing."

However, every once in a while one of the
2,100 affiliates that make up the faith-based
organization will take its mandate a step
further. These houses built by Habitat for
Humanity Northern Ireland are one example.

In the early 1990s the affiliate's executive
director, Peter Farquharson, took a leave of
absence from his job as a structural engineer
in London to volunteer along with his wife
and children with Habitat for Humanity at its
headquarters in Georgia. His three-month
stint in the Deep South turned out to be a
life-changing experience. Seeing racially
integrated housing developments in an area
of the United States once torn by segregation
inspired him to bring a similar kind of
reconciliation to his native Northern Ireland,
where 30 years of conflict had destroyed
homes and communities, leaving blighted
graffiti-strewn neighborhoods in its wake. So
when the organization offered him the chance
to start an affiliate in Belfast, he agreed.

He returned to Northern Ireland in 1993
with $20,000 in startup funds from Habitat for
Humanity International. "I started knocking
on doors and telling people that I wanted
to do an integrated housing project across
the peace lines, and people just thought
that I was mad," said Farquharson of the
difficulty he faced fundraising and generating
community support in the tense climate of
Northern Ireland at the time.

The group's first project, based on the
Habitat "sweat-equity" model, was to build
11 homes in Iris Close, a blighted and
desolate Catholic neighborhood in West
Belfast. The development—just 400 yards
(400 m) from Bombay Street, one of the
flashpoints when the Troubles first flared
up in the 1960s—brought Protestants and
Catholics together to complete the first new
construction in the area in years. For its
second project the group undertook a 16-
home development in Glencairn, a Protestant
neighborhood in West Belfast that had
been witness to some of the most horrific
atrocities of the conflict.

"We've deliberately chosen areas that
are difficult to work in as they are the
ones that are in most need," Farquharson
once explained to the *Guardian*, a British
newspaper. "These were no-go areas for
large sections of the community for years. It's

Northern Ireland Cross-Community Initiative

hard for outsiders to appreciate the courage it takes for a Catholic to go into Glencairn. This was the estate where the Shankhill butchers used to dump the bodies of Catholics. It's probably the most staunch loyalist estate in Belfast, but we have Catholics working here on homes for their neighbors."

With the ceasefire agreement in 1998, gaining support became easier. The group since has taken on tandem projects in Ballysillan and Ligoniel, neighboring communities in North Belfast fractured along sectarian lines. Doing the projects simultaneously allowed volunteers to cross the divide and participate in both. The affiliate is now partnering with local officials to build the first truly integrated housing estate in Belfast, where Farquharson hopes Protestants and Catholics will not only build together but also eventually live together.

above
**A Habitat house in Iris Close,
West Belfast, 1996**
Robert Baker/Habitat for Humanity Northern Ireland

right
**Vernon Toogood, a Protestant, and Gerry
Crossin, a Roman Catholic, share the
responsibility of overseeing the construction
of Habitat houses in Belfast, 1999.**
Robert Baker/Habitat for Humanity Northern Ireland

opposite top
**The 30-year conflict took its toll on the area's
housing stock, shown here in 1999.**
Kim MacDonald/Habitat for Humanity Northern Ireland

opposite bottom
**Graffiti marks sectarian boundaries,
segregating neighborhoods.**
Robert Baker/Habitat for Humanity Northern Ireland

Design Like You Give a Damn

Sistema Arde

Location_ Mexico City, Jilotepec, and San Miguel de Allende, Mexico
Date_1996–98
Client_ Tandacasa
Design firm_ Hierve-Diseñeria
Concept architect_ Alejandro Villareal
Design team_ Pedro Martinez, Alejandro Villarreal
Modeling_ Anima, Fernando Gutierrez
Cost_$17 per sq. ft./$178 per sq. m
Website_www.hierve.com

Cheap and widely available, concrete masonry unit (CMU) block has become one of the most commonly used materials in low-income construction. With this in mind, Alejandro Villarreal developed Sistema Arde, a patented building system that combines the ease of building with cement-block with the warmth and variety of traditional construction.

Like pieces of a jigsaw puzzle, each blocklike element is designed to solve a particular construction problem. For example, sewage lines, electrical systems, or other utilities can be run through specialized "chase" blocks. Blocks designed as key pieces simplify wall intersections and other connection points, while structural accessories such as planters and stair pieces combine to humanize the building's façade and interiors.

There are three basic groups identified within the block system: "basic technology," such as the inner walls, joists, and various other inner structural elements; "finished structural elements," which form exterior load-bearing walls and create façades with a variety of finished masonry textures; and "structural accessories," such as planters, windows, steps, closings, and decorative elements. The blocks have been used to construct a number of projects in San Miguel de Allende and other parts of Mexico.

above
A group of single-family, low-income houses outside a suburb of San Miguel de Allende, Mexico, 1999. The textured façade is created by using a variety of blocks.

opposite
Inner courtyard in a low-income housing development near San Miguel de Allende. The "block maceta," or flower-vase block, creates planters.

muros

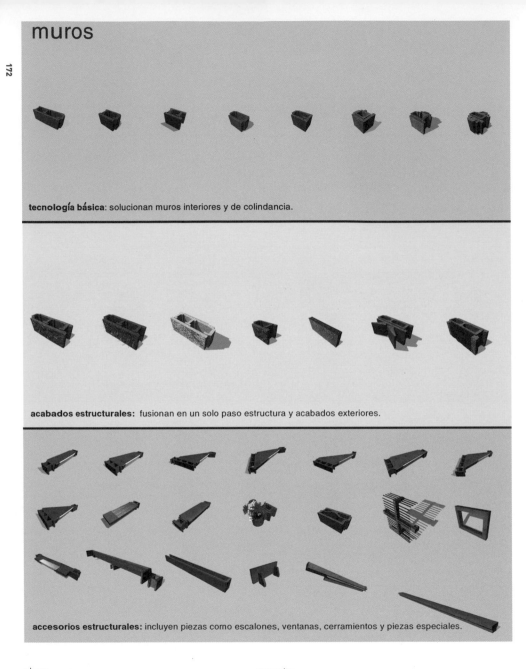

tecnología básica: solucionan muros interiores y de colindancia.

acabados estructurales: fusionan en un solo paso estructura y acabados exteriores.

accesorios estructurales: incluyen piezas como escalones, ventanas, cerramientos y piezas especiales.

above
The components of the system are divided into three types: basic technology (inner wall blocks and other structural elements); finishing blocks for façades; and structural accessories.

opposite
Structural accessories can be used to create stairs, add details such as planters, or to form chase walls for plumbing.
All photographs Hierve-Diseñeria

escalón **volado:** con un extremo conectado al sistema de muros y con un bajo relieve para recibir distintos acabados

escalón **snte:** con ambos extremos conectados al sistema de muros y con falda para frenar la vista

block **maceta:** se convierte en el receptor de una maceta plástica convencional

block **sanitario:** permite el paso libre de una tubería sanitaria de 4" de espesor

An estimated

100,000,000

children live and work on the streets in the
developing world; 40 million in Latin America

"Street Children and Homelessness," International Child and Youth Care Network,
Sept. 2004

On any given night in the
United States, at least

700,000

people are without shelter

Marielena Zuniga, "No Home
of Her Own: Homeless Women,"
Soroptimist of Americas,
Jan. 2003

At least

3,000,000

Western Europeans are homeless each winter

"Homeless in Europe," *Time*, Feb. 10, 2003

Huts and Low-Riders

Location_Atlanta, Georgia, USA
Date_1987–present
End client_The homeless
Design team_Mad Housers
Major funding_Individual donations, volunteer labor
Cost per unit_$300–500
Area_16–48 sq. ft./1.5–4.5 sq. m
Website_www.madhousers.org

In 1987 two graduate architecture students at the Georgia Institute of Technology came up with a surprisingly simple—if unorthodox—approach to providing shelter to Atlanta's homeless population.

Calling themselves the Mad Housers, they began building homes for the homeless. Over the course of the next few years—without permits or sometimmes even permission from landowners—they built more than 100 48-square-foot (4.5-sq.-m) huts. The lockable dwellings were made from wood, recycled studs, and salvaged doors, and each came with a jury-rigged stove made from shop buckets. The structures did not meet local building codes, but they did provide shelter and storage space for many people.

"It really brought to the public attention how out of balance the situation had gotten as far as homelessness, because basically the group was building shantytowns," explained Jim Devlin, an architect and Mad Houser volunteer.

Inevitably the Mad Housers' guerrilla tactics provoked controversy. When a newspaper article called attention to three of the huts, the city had them demolished. Detractors accused the group of encouraging homelessness, violating property rights, and instigating illegal squats. Still, supporters including some local politicians applauded the group's common-sense approach. The defining moment came when the Mad Housers mounted a demonstration hut during the 1988 Democratic National Convention. In the end the group forged a tacit agreement with the city that officials would look the other way unless a property owner complained or the residents were disruptive to the neighborhood. The idea spread. Huts began to appear in Illinois, California, and Wisconsin, but many were dismantled by city officials, and in the late '90s the original Mad Housers disbanded.

A few years ago a new group of stealth builders reconstituted the organization in Atlanta. Although they maintained the

original group's "build first, ask questions later" mandate, they adopted a less confrontational approach. The group is careful to build the huts in places where homeless people have been encamped for extended periods and have generally been left alone. It added insulation and made repairs to earlier huts, some of which have been in use for as long as six years. And because a number of the new Mad Housers' clients work, either recycling cans or in other informal jobs, they have taken steps to bring basic services to the camps, experimenting with water collection systems and off-the-grid energy from car engines turned into generators. Whereas residents once had to collect water off-site and could not power clocks or other essential appliances, these services now free them to pursue a more mainstream lifestyle. When possible, the group includes a cell phone, which even

without a service provider can be used to dial 911, or a bicycle, as a house-warming gift.

"Our intention is to create as much self-sufficiency and economic productivity in the homeless camps as possible, as a means of empowerment and to combat the pervasive depression and personality disintegration among homeless people," said Frank Jeffers, who engineered the generator. We want "to make the huts a base of operations people can use in their struggle to get back on their feet."

The new Mad Housers have also begun to rethink the basic structure. New development in Atlanta's urban woods, where many of the city's homeless had camped, has made it more difficult to find sites. Many individuals live under highway overpasses and other lost urban spaces, where the standard 10-foot- (3-m-) tall hut would be too visible or would not fit. Enter the "low-rider." Designed to be discreet, the 16-square-foot (1.5-sq.-m)

opposite and above
Three examples of huts built by the Mad Housers

top and above
Since the low-rider has limited space, it is built in pairs, with one unit intended for storage.

opposite
The low-rider: Sheet insulation on all four walls retains heat. The unit's "porch" was intended to prevent people from crawling in and out through the dirt. Here, homeowners adapted it to create an outdoor seating area.

Opposite top, Salma Abdulrahman/Mad Housers; all other photographs Clay Davis/Mad Housers

structure is just large enough to sleep or sit in. Because a wood-burning stove would be unsafe in this structure, the designers substituted insulation to help conserve body heat. To make up for lost space, the sleeping unit comeswith a separate lockable storage unit of a similar size.

Many of the huts also have been adapted by the residents themselves, who add portable toilets or vegetable gardens. When one resident's hut rotted and needed extensive repair, the group built a new hut on the same site. Rather than tearing down the old structure, however, the resident asked if he could maintain it as a library, lending donated books to others in the homeless community.

Huts are still razed from time to time. The Mad Housers have a policy that they will disassemble and move a hut if the current landowner decides he or she doesn't want people living there or a new owner takes over. But it rarely works out that way. "Generally if a property owner doesn't want them, they just come in with a bulldozer and level them," says Devlin. "That's happened a couple of times, and we accept that. We're not trying to build monuments or permanent structures. We are trying to build someone a shelter. When that shelter opportunity ends, the life of the shelter ends."

"I have a family. I could go home, but
I choose not to because I like to be on my
own and independent."

Barbara Quarterman, homeless client

Dome Village

Location_Los Angeles, California, USA
Date_1993–present
Organization_Justiceville, USA
End client_Homeless individuals and families
Concept_Ted Hayes, Craig Chamberlain
Design_Craig Chamberlain
Major funding_ ARCO Corporation
Cost_$250,000
Cost per unit_$10,000
Area per unit_314 sq. ft./29 sq. m
Site_1.3 acres/.53 hectares

Twenty years ago on the downtown Los Angeles site where the Dome Village now stands was a squatter camp called Justiceville—better known as "skid row."

Today this unconventional community offers homeless individuals an alternative to the traditional shelter.

Homeless activist Ted Hayes founded Justiceville in 1985 with the ambitious goal of "ending all homelessness." Along this journey Hayes decided to become homeless himself and moved to Justiceville, advocating tirelessly for the rights of its residents. In so doing he came to understand the dual nature of individuals—their need for privacy and independence versus their craving for social interaction. When the city of Los Angeles shut down the squatter camp later that same year, Hayes launched a media campaign to create an environment to house the homeless in which each of these human desires would be met. This led to a relationship between Hayes and Craig Chamberlain, a Vietnam veteran, a student of the late Buckminster Fuller, and the inventor of the Omni-Sphere dome. Together they developed a plan for a new kind of living environment that, with funding from the ARCO Corporation, became the Dome Village.

Launched in 1993 the Dome Village consists of 20 Omni-Spheres, each 20 feet (6.1 m) in diameter and 12 feet (3.6 m) tall, giving the occupants 314 square feet (29 sq. m) of living space. Each sphere is made up of 21 polyester fiberglass panels that fasten together with 150 Teflon bolts, making the structure watertight. In less than four hours, two people can assemble an Omni-Sphere dome using a stepladder, a screwdriver, and a wrench.

Partitioning each of the 12 residential domes allows the village to house up to 34 tenants at once. The remaining eight domes are for group use and include a kitchen, community room, offices, bathing facilities, and a laundry. Dome Village also offers a host of other programs and services designed to empower residents, such as a job-training program, a computer center, legal aid services, and the Compton Cricket Club, a cricket team made up of residents and former gang members from nearby Compton High School.

above
Individual Omni-Sphere domes used as dwellings

opposite
Dome building against the backdrop of the Los Angeles skyline

Several domes are linked together to form
community spaces.

above left
Resident at work in the computer center

above
The village's laundry facility
All photographs Ed Boughton

First Step Housing

Location_New York, New York, USA
Date_2001–7
Nonprofit developer_Common Ground
Community, Housing Development
Fund Corporation
End client_Homeless and transient population
Design teams_Rafi Elbaz, Nanna Wulfing,
Julia Tate (Kit of Parts); Katherine Chang,
Aaron Gabriel (The Ordering of Things)
Project architect_OCV Architects
Structural engineer_Dominick Pilla, PE, PC
Electrical engineer_Chester Schiff, PE
Mechanical engineer_Abraham Joselow, PE, PC
Additional consultants_Michael Bell, Architecture
League of New York
Major funding_City of New York Department
of Housing Preservation and Development,
New York State Homeless Housing Assistance
Corporation, New York State Homeless Housing
Assistance Program, New York City Department
of Homeless Services, Dormitory Authority of
the State of New York
Total budget_$6.4 million
Cost per unit_Under $5,000
Area per unit_60 sq. ft./ 5.6 sq. m
Website_www.commonground.org

A prototype of the First Step Housing
competition entry "The Ordering of Things,"
by Katherine Chang and Aaron Gabriel.
The design was one of two winning schemes
that will be further developed for use in
the renovated Andrews House.

In the early 1990s Common Ground proposed using historic-preservation funding to turn a derelict former luxury hotel in the heart of Times Square into housing for the homeless.

The project, which flouted the conventional wisdom that low-income tenants and the formerly homeless could not peaceably exist in the same building, became a national model for assisted-living programs. Since then the organization has rescued three other historic properties, returning them to their Gilded Age splendor while creating permanent housing for some of the city's most marginalized residents.

In its latest project the group is pioneering yet another approach. In the late '90s outreach staff from Common Ground conducted a survey of the city's chronically homeless population, typically men, to better understand why so many resisted city shelters. To their surprise they learned that many homeless preferred to stay—and in fact were willing to pay to stay—in a lodging house. In fact, most lodging-house occupants were single males who had been homeless for three years or more.

Dating back to the 1900s, cheap lodging houses, sometimes called flophouses, cubicle hotels, or single-room-occupancy (SRO) hotels, lined the Bowery of New York City. For about seven dollars a day clients could rent a bed for the night and a place to keep their belongings. For some people these were accommodations of last resort; for others they offered a no-questions-asked alternative to the streets. But as the century drew to a close the flophouse was on the verge of extinction. Considered magnets of crime, many had been shut down over the years; those that remained operated below decent standards of living and safety.

Recognizing the legitimate and important role this housing type played in providing low-cost, flexible shelter, in 2002 Common Ground purchased the Andrews House, a

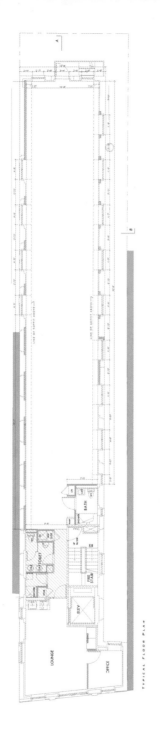

above
**An exterior view of the Andrews House,
on the Bowery**

left
**The floor plan for the Andrews House. Common
Ground hosted a design competition to rethink
the cramped interior spaces of the lodging hotel.**

opposite
**The Times Square had more than 1,700 building
code violations before Common Ground turned it
into a home for 652 residents.**
Agatha Wasilewska

partially occupied lodging house on the Bowery, with the aim of resuscitating and rethinking this dwindling shelter resource.

The requirements of the program necessitated innovation. The building was long and narrow, minimizing daylight. Stringent fire codes meant that the units had to be constructed from noncombustible materials and ensure 70 percent sprinkler coverage. What's more, in order to avoid a lengthy permit process, no unit could alter the building's structure, systems, or permanent walls and spaces. Each unit had to be, in a sense, a piece of furniture.

In 2003 Common Ground hosted an international design competition to enlist the help of architects in overcoming these structural and programming challenges. Designers were charged with developing a prefabricated "individual dwelling unit" no larger than 60 square feet (5.6 sq. m). More than 180 teams entered the competition, from which the jury selected five finalists. Today Common Ground is working with two of the finalists ("Kit of Parts," by designers Rafi Elbaz, Nanna Wulfing, and Julia Tate from the New York firm LifeForm; and "The Ordering of Things," by New York designers Katherine Chang and Aaron Gabriel) to bring their projects to life. Prototypes were built in summer 2005, and the renovation is expected to be complete by spring 2007.

top and above
A prototype of "Kit of Parts," designed by Rafi Elbaz, Nanna Wulfing, and Julia Tate of the New York firm LifeForm. The unit, along with Chang and Gabriel's "The Ordering of Things," will be used in the Andrews House.

opposite
Details of Chang and Gabriel's prototype, "The Order of Things."
All other photographs Beth Bates

paraSITE

Location_New York, New York; Baltimore,
Maryland; Boston and Cambridge,
Massachusetts, USA; and other locations
Date_1998–present
Client_The homeless
Designer_Michael Rakowitz
Additional consultants_Various
homeless clients
Funding_Self-funded
Cost per unit_$5 or less
Website_www.michaelrakowitz.com

In New York City alone there are over 36,000 homeless people seeking refuge in shelters each night.

Another estimated 4,400 live unsheltered on the streets—true urban nomads who feed off the city. They glean from dumpsters for food and sleep on subway cars or steam vents for warmth. In response to this condition, artist Michael Rakowitz has been constructing what he calls paraSITEs, temporary shelters for people living on the streets.

A paraSITE is inflatable and tentlike, fabricated from two layers of plastic bags and tape (materials easily attainable for the homeless). A series of interconnected hollow tubes make up the framework, with a tube tailing at one end. To inflate the structure you connect this extending "intake" tube to the exhaust duct of the heating or ventilation system of a building or other "host." The warm exhaust fills the tubes and inflates the double membrane structure, instantly providing shelter and radiant heat for the user. You can then deflate the structure, pack it away, and easily transport it to a new site and host.

Rakowitz built the first prototype in 1997 in Cambridge, Massachusetts, for a homeless man named Bill Stone. Since then he has built and distributed over 30 prototypes of the paraSITE shelter—each one customized for its intended occupant. Units have popped up in New York, Boston, and Baltimore—and, according to Rakowitz, there are still about 10 paraSITEs in use on the streets of New York, despite the tight security measures put in place after the attack of 9/11.

To the user a paraSITE shelter represents a refusal to surrender to the life one faces in the welfare and shelter systems; it provides a sense of autonomy and a more self-sufficient lifestyle. For the average pedestrian, however, a paraSITE functions as an agitational device, instigating a relationship between those who have homes and those who do not and calling attention to the epidemic of homelessness.

"I proposed my concept and first prototype to a homeless man named Bill Stone, who regarded the project as a tactical response. At the time, the city of Cambridge had made a series of vents in Harvard Square 'homeless-proof' by tilting the metal grates, making them virtually impossible to sleep on."

Michael Rakowitz, artist

paraSITE

Design Like You Give a Damn

opposite
Urban nomad with paraSITE in hand

right
Neighborhood residents, including a police officer, react to the paraSITE as it is attached to a host building.
All photographs Michael Rakowitz and Lombard-Fried Projects

Comm

Gathering Spaces

Women

Health

Education

community

Mason's Bend, located deep in Alabama's former cotton belt, is home to four extended families. Most live in trailers or poorly constructed homes.

This rural cluster of homes never had a community gathering space until residents approached the Rural Studio to build a place where they could hold meetings, provide childcare, and worship. In addition to creating a central node within the hamlet, residents hoped the structure would serve as a transportation point for a mobile library and a traveling health center, bringing education and medical services to the community.

Because the site bordered the properties of three of the area's four families, Rural Studio students at Auburn University's College of Architecture, Design, and Construction held intense community discussions during the development of the project. Due to the fluid nature of the studio's design/build process, the team abandoned architectural drawings in favor of "in the field" development. As a result, adaptive reuse of found materials played a major role in the design.

Students used rammed earth for the center's walls. With a donation of cypress trees from a studio supporter, they created simple laminated-timber trusses and handmade furniture. The bold glass structure that wraps the chapel, however, is the project's most delightful form. The sculptural glass skin gives the building an unanticipated appeal, made all the more surprising when the visitor realizes that the individual scales are actually Chevy Caprice windshields (bought from a junkyard for $120 by student Jon Schumann)—a rare find that became the signature of the chapel.

Mockbee once described the building as "as cutting edge as any piece of architecture you can find in the United States," a statement that's hard to refute. As the light filters through the blue-tinged glass wall onto the open-air seating, the beauty of the chapel's form marries with its ingenious use of materials, creating a sense of spirituality and place.

Mason's Bend Chapel

Location_Mason's Bend, Hale County, Alabama, USA
Date_1999–2000
Client_Residents of Mason's Bend
Sponsoring organization_Rural Studio, Auburn University
Design team_Bryan Bell, Adam Gerndt, Forrest Fulton, Samuel Mockbee, Dale Rush, D.K. Ruth, Jon Schumann
Major funding_Potrero Nuevo Fund, Bob Wilson
Cost_$15,000
Area_1,000 sq. ft./93 sq. m

At night the chapel acts like a beacon, signaling
Mason's Bend to passersby.

The sculptural glass skin gives the building an
unanticipated appeal, made all the more surprising
when the visitor realizes that the individual scales
are actually Chevy Caprice windshields (bought from
a junkyard for $120 by student Jon Schumann)—
a rare find that became the signature of the chapel.

The chapel is always open, to provide a space for
contemplation and respite from the heat.
All photographs Timothy Hursley

Appirampattu Village Center

Location_Appirampattu, Tamil Nadu, India
Date_2003
Client_Appirampattu Panchayat
Designer_Logan Allen
Consultant_Auroville Earth Institute, Auroville,
Tamil Nadu
Structural engineer_Piero Cicionesi
Major funding_Fatima and Faris al Mazrouei,
Richard and Jo-ann Amick, Carl Sterner, and
others
Cost_$2,500
Materials_Rammed earth, compressed-earth
blocks, bamboo, concrete
Area_460 sq. ft./43 sq. m
Website_www.earth-auroville.com

The Appirampattu Village Center pairs two structures with a stair rising between them, meant to symbolize the interdependence of individual study and learning in a group.

Built from blocks made from compressed local soil, shaded by large trees, and with window openings designed to allow maximum ventilation, it is also a case study in low-tech environmental design. But perhaps the most remarkable aspect of the building is that it was inspired by a 20-year-old architecture student from the University of Cincinnati and was designed and built in just under four months.

Appirampattu is a small community of about 300 Dalit (formerly "untouchables") in the southeast Indian state of Tamil Nadu. During monsoon season, little public activity happened in the community; the rains put a stop to the tutoring sessions that took place on a concrete plinth outside the temple. The new center allows gathering year-round. It provides two indoor spaces, a meeting room, and a room that serves as both computer lab and library. Weather permitting, two spaces on the roof are used for tutoring groups of children after school, and a bamboo plinth around the entry doubles as a stage during festivals.

The center got its start when Logan Allen, who came to Tamil Nadu to study earth architecture at the nearby Auroville Earth Institute, began looking for an opportunity to pass on what he was learning there. Working with the Auroville Village Action Group, he heard about Appirampattu and the Dalits' need for a community center. Though the label "untouchable" has been officially obsolete since the mid-1950s, the caste system still operates on a de facto basis, says Allen. "I am under the impression that government-funding organizations often still ignore these groups," he said, which is part of the reason he was attracted to the project.

Logan devised the building program in collaboration with the community, relying on architectural models and the translation skills of a friend, at least initially, to aid discussion. The center was constructed primarily from blocks made mostly of sand and soil. The earth blocks were compressed with a binder such as cement or lime, which hardens the blocks and prevents them from washing away during heavy rains. The blocks look like bricks but are unfired, and therefore require less energy and fewer resources to produce. The meeting room was whitewashed to give it a more formal air, while the library was left as exposed compressed block. A staircase to the roof hangs on a thin slice between the two volumes and leads to the rooftop meeting spaces.

With only two and half months left on Logan's visa, construction began with a crew consisting of Logan, two masons, and four assistants. Not until three days before his visa expired did they pour the roof slab (engineered by Piero Cicionesi, an engineer based in Auroville). Though the center is sure to become a fixture of the community, especially during monsoon season, the architect himself only had a few hours to admire his first completed building.

Barefoot College

Location_Tilonia, Rajasthan, India
Date_1986–89
Client_Residents of Tilonia, India
Sponsoring organization_Social Work and Research Center
Project organizer_Bunker Roy
Design team_Main campus by Bhanwar Jat, Neehar Raina, and Barefoot Architects; geodesic domes by Rafeek Mohammed and Barefoot Architects
Construction_Bhanwar Jat with rural masons and day laborers
Major funding_Social Work and Research Center; Government of India; United Nations Development Program; German Argo Action; HIVOS-Humanist Institute for Development Cooperation; Plan International
Cost_$21,430
Area_Building: 30,140 sq. ft./2,800 sq. m; site: 377,000 sq. ft./35,000 sq. m

Inspired by Gandhi and moved to respond to India's famine of 1967, Bunker Roy moved from his family's affluent suburb to Tilonia, a rural community in the state of Rajasthan.

His aim was to help rural villagers improve their lives. The organization he founded in 1972, the Social Work and Research Center, would eventually come to be known as the Barefoot College.

Work on the Barefoot College began in 1986. Remarkably, the college was designed and built by the very same rural villagers, many of them semiliterate, that it was intended to train. As the group later explained, "We believe, like Gandhi, that there is a difference between literacy and education." This philosophy guided every aspect of the campus's construction and, eventually, all the activities that would take place there. After a

preliminary scheme was drafted by Neehar Raina, a young architect, a farmer named Bhanwar Jat and 12 other so-called Barefoot Architects developed and constructed the buildings.

The process became very fluid; the group refined and redrew the plans on the spot to accommodate traditional building techniques and specific site issues. "The project was a joint effort. Everyone who was going to live there was consulted. Everyone's views had to be respected," Jat explained. Several women from the village assisted the team, taking active roles in the decision-making process and joining in construction.

The buildings are arranged around traditional, highly decorative courtyards. Local materials were used throughout the construction process. Load-bearing walls were constructed from stone with lime mortar; the flat roof was constructed from stone slabs. Collected rainwater gathers in a tank beneath a courtyard, a space that doubles as a stage and gathering place for residents. Scattered throughout the campus are solar panels—built by the Barefoot Solar Engineers—that generate power for the college. These engineers maintain the panels at a fraction of the cost of Western units.

The Barefoot Architects also gave Buckminster Fuller's geodesic dome a sustainable makeover. Deforestation is a major threat in the area, as traditional housing has made wood a scarce resource. Rafeek Mohammed and seven other Barefoot

Architects fabricated domes from discarded agricultural implements, including bullock carts and pump sections. They covered them with thatch, giving a traditional look to a new idea. Geodesic dome structures are currently used for a pathology lab, a dispensary, a post office, and an Internet café.

Communities from all over India have sent representatives to the college to study to become "barefoot" paraprofessionals, as Bunker calls them. Through night classes and other programs, the center demystifies education for the rural poor through technology training. Over the past 30 years the school has trained more than 750 health workers, teachers, and engineers. Many return to their villages to use their knowledge of water engineering, solar power, income generation, medicine, and other topics to improve their own communities.

above
The college sits like an oasis in the arid Rajasthan plains.

opposite
Local women use traditional technologies to waterpoof the roof of a college building.

above left
Discarded agricultural implements are repurposed to create the structural members of a geodesic dome.

above right
A completed dome serves as a pathology lab.

right
Solar panels, built by the Barefoot Solar Engineers, generate enough power to run the college.

above
A stage in the central courtyard serves as the college's main gathering space. Rainwater is collected through the grates and stored in a holding tank beneath the stage.

left
The designers drew on traditional construction techniques in building the college.
All photographs The Barefoot Photographers/Aga Khan Foundation

Homeboy Industries

Location_Los Angeles, Calif., USA
Date_2000–2001
Client_Jobs for a Future
End client_Former gang members
Design center_Detroit Collaborative Design Center
Design team_Dan Pitera, Kelly Powell, David Garnet
Site architect_Whitney Sander, Sander Architects, Los Angeles
Contractor_Ruiz Construction, Inc.
Cost_$300,000
Area_4,628 sq. ft./430 sq. m

In 1992 a Jesuit priest started Homeboy Industries for gang members from Los Angeles who wished to start afresh.

With slogans like "Jobs, Not Jails" and "Nothing Stops a Bullet Like a Job," Father Gregory Boyle (or G-dog, as ex-gang members call him) designed the center to provide job training for gang members, many from rival groups, and help them find work.

By the late 1990s the center needed a bigger space, and Boyle contacted Father Terrence Curry, a fellow Jesuit who was then the director of the Detroit Collaborative

Design Center, a community design studio based at the University of Detroit Mercy. The call came as Curry was moving on to a new position in New York, but the center's new director, Dan Pitera, embraced the project.

Working with the LA-based architect Whitney Sander, the team held a series of workshops with stakeholders, including former gang members, on the planning and design of the space, which would contain a bakery, a silk-screening workshop, and other small businesses and job-training services. This engagement continued long into the project, as Ruiz Construction employed ex-gang members to work on the new center from demolition to construction. As soon as they saw the site, the architects knew that the way the center engaged the street would be a critical component of its design—and ultimately its success.

Most buildings in the neighborhood were boarded up or covered in security bars. Drive-by shootings were not uncommon. In an act of defiance, the designers chose to draw attention to these basic safety and security issues. "There is always a fear when taking boys away from gangs and women away from pimps [that] there would be retaliation," Pitera explained. "The space was filled with bars and rolling security gates. It read of fear.... We wanted to create an unflinching, fearless approach to openness."

Rather than creating barriers between the building and the street, Homeboy Industries removed all the security elements and replaced them with large bulletproof-glass windows. In an act of solidarity and a show of resilience, Homeboy and Homegirl meetings take place right in front of the windows for all the neighborhood to see.

Architecturally, one of the major challenges was connecting the offices and the printing facility, which were built on different levels. A number of the Homeboys and -girls are disabled due to gang-related violence. So instead of hiding wheelchair access off to the side, the team decided to celebrate it, creating a ramped spine that wraps around a central, columned, canopied space where Homeboys and Homegirls work. This central space is the only area where you find any hint of a religious connection.

It was important to Father Boyle to bring a sense of spirituality to the space without sending any overtly religious messages. "We created a canopy made from four pieces of theater scrim. When the lights shine on them, a cross appears in the negative space," Pitera said. "I doubt many of the kids even know it's there."

What started as a small nonprofit determined to create a safe place for recovering gang members is now a $3 million organization. It runs five businesses of its own, including a silk-screening operation, a landscaping service, and a café, and even offers free tattoo removal for former gang members. Homeboy Industries' core mission, however, remains finding jobs for former gang members and convicts in businesses willing to take a chance on young people at risk.

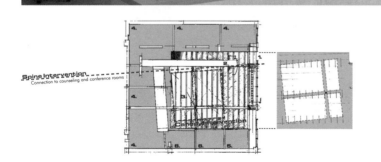

Spine Intervention
Connection to counseling and conference rooms

opposite
Former gang members outside the center. The expanse of bulletproof glass opens the space to the street, advertising the work taking place inside.
Sharon Risedorph

top
Main workspace with ceiling scrims.
Dan Pitera/Detroit Collaborative Design Center

above
Floor plans for the center: At left, the shaded areas represent raised offices (4 & 6); the spine through the space represents the center's wheelchair ramp (2). At right, the ceiling plan for the main workspace. The subtle use of scrim forms a cross, the center's only religious iconography.

Center for Disabled Workers

Location_Orange Farm, South Africa
Date_2004–5
Client_Modimo O Moholo Association for the Disabled People in Orange Farm
End client_40 disabled residents
Project organizer_Thandi Mjiyakho
Design center_Department of Housing and Design, Technical University, Vienna, Austria
Design team_Peter Fattinger, Sabine Gretner, Thandi Mjiyakho, Franziska Orso, Cornelius Pfeiffer, Michele Riedmatten, students
Contractor/Manufacturer_Designers, local builders, disabled residents of Orange Farm Township, students
Major funding_Brainbows, Federal Office for Environment Protection, Gold Reef, Investkredit, Kallco, Kunst, Lederer Communications, Sedus Stoll, s²arch, Zehetbauer/Salzer
Cost_Approx. $40,000

above
Cornelius Pfeiffer works with one of the residents to lay bricks.
Michele Riedmatten

top and opposite
The shed roof straddles the bedroom pods.
Leon Krige

Orange Farm township is situated 25 miles (40 km) south of Johannesburg and is home to more than 300,000 inhabitants, most of them Zulu.

Modimo O Moholo Association for the Disabled People in Orange Farm was founded in 1994 by Thandi Mjiyakho to help disabled persons in the township meet one another and develop skills. In the beginning Mjiyakho, who is physically disabled, opened her house to physically or mentally disabled persons to run programs such as instruction in silk-screening, sewing, basket-weaving, carpentry, and building simple furniture or coffins. Within a few years the program was so successful that Mjiyakho decided to expand, to provide the area's disabled community with better living and working conditions. That meant building a facility that would include a daycare center, workshops, and, eventually, housing for 16 disabled people.

She got help from Christoph Chorherr, an Austrian politician who had supported her work in the past. Inspired by an exhibit on the work of the Rural Studio, he proposed turning the initiative into a socially active design project for students at the Technical University in Vienna. He connected Mjiyakho with Peter Fattinger, assistant professor at the university, and planning for the project began. Phase one, the daycare center and workshops, was built in five weeks in early 2004 by local workers and a group of 16 students (who paid for for their own flights

and accommodations) on land donated
by the city of Johannesburg. This success
of this initial project prompted Chorherr
to found the nonprofit s²arch (social and
sustainable architecture).

The second phase was planned by
Michele Riedmatten, a participant in
phase one, and Cornelius Pfeiffer in spring
2005. Concerned by the dire housing
conditions in which some of the center's
members lived, they undertook a 16-unit
residential extension. In all, the second

phase included living accommodations,
a veranda, a common room, kitchen and
sanitation facilities, and an extension of the
workshops. Together these new structures
created an ample courtyard with open views.

The most distinctive aspect of the
design for the housing unit, the pods
tucked underneath the oversize roof, was
a result of sheer practicality as much as
anything else. As the team worked during
the rainy season, the shed-roof structure
was erected first, and rooms were then built

beneath them. This system created natural
ventilation by allowing air to circulate
between the roof and the building. The
walls were constructed using an interlock
system of adobe bricks (mixed with 5
percent cement to help bind them and to
overcome the social stigma attached to
traditional adobe bricks). Each brick fit on
top of others without mortar. Using this
"dry stacking" system meant that unskilled
workers, including the disabled community
members, could contribute to the project.

Siyathemba Soccer "Clinic"

Location_Somkhele, KwaZulu-Natal, South Africa
Date_2004–present (unbuilt)
Client_Somkhele youth ages nine–25
Sponsoring organizations_Architecture for Humanity, Siyathemba Consultants, Africa Centre for Health and Population Studies
Concept architect_Swee Hong Ng
Site architect_East Coast Architects
Projected budget_$350,000
Major funding_American Society of Interior Designers, INDEX, Marty and Dorothy Silverman Foundation, Red Rubber Ball Foundation, design competition fees

above
Rendering of Swee Hong Ng's winning competition entry for the proposed Soccer "Clinic"
Swee Hong Ng/Architecture for Humanity

right
An existing soccer pitch, one of many makeshift pitches that dot the area surrounding the site
Cameron Sinclair/Architecture for Humanity

Siyathemba Soccer "Clinic"

Design Like You Give a Damn

Somkhele, KwaZulu-Natal, South Africa, in the heart of Zululand, is one of the many rural communities hardest hit by the HIV/AIDS epidemic.

According to a report released by the South African Medical Research Council, the pandemic accounts for 42 percent of all deaths in KwaZulu-Natal. At the center of this quiet crisis are the region's youth, in particular, girls ages nine to 14, who are three times more likely to become HIV positive than youth in other parts of the world.

Siyathemba (Zulu for "we hope") began as a small community-driven project. Part of a collaboration between the Africa Centre for Health and Population Studies (a rural health research center based in Somkhele; see "Africa Centre") and Architecture for

Humanity, the goal of the initiative was to use sports as a vehicle for bringing health services and HIV/AIDS awareness to this hard-to-reach demographic.

In 2004 Architecture for Humanity hosted an international competition for the design of a soccer field and small changing room that could serve as a natural gathering spot for the area's youth and eventually as a base for mobile health care. An international jury reviewed more than 320 entries from 40 countries and picked nine finalists. The selected designs were posted in schools and health clinics throughout the area so that young people could make the final

choice. The winner: an elegant and simple scheme by Singapore-born designer Swee Hong Ng. With its V-shaped earthen terraces and textile canopy, Ng's design seemed a natural fit for the rolling hills of Zulu Somkhele.

In 2005 Ng, an emerging architect currently working in Pittsburgh, traveled to South Africa to collaborate with site architect Steve Kinsler of East Coast Architects, volunteers from the Africa Centre for Health and Population Studies, community members, recreation officials, and the players themselves to adapt and refine Ng's design.

During meetings and workshops the project began to take on a new dimension. Although there are more than 10 soccer fields in the immediate vicinity of the Africa Centre, none is graded. Wooden goalposts tilt in the breeze as goats and cattle graze midfield. In the past officials spent upward of $8,000 to bus players from the district to better-equipped, more secure facilities in Durban—a four-hour round-trip journey from Somkhele. From the perspective of Somkhele's talented players, "Siyathemba" offered the hope of a level playing field where they could not only host games but also compete at a provincial and national level.

Construction of the field and outreach center—which will now meet FIFA (Fédération Internationale de Football Association) regulations and include two practice fields as well as facilities for other sporting activities such as netball, basketball, cricket, and rugby—is planned for fall 2005. A healthcare worker will serve as the facility coordinator, providing basic medical services and organizing both sporting events and HIV/AIDS prevention programs. A computer lab is also planned for the site.

More significant, the field and clubhouse will be home to Somkhele's first girls' soccer league as well as the regional women's team. Organizers hope that by emphasizing a team approach, Siyathemba will not only act as a catalyst for youth empowerment but also create lasting ties of friendship and trust between the area's healthcare workers and its future mothers.

Siyathemba Soccer "Clinic"

Design Like You Give a Damn

above right
Members of the regional women's team discuss their design ideas for the field with competition winner Swee Hong Ng.
Doug Halsey/Architecture for Humanity

right
Competition winner Swee Hong Ng (left) and a player present the outcome of a breakout brainstorming session to the rest of the group.
Steve Kinsler/Architecture for Humanity

opposite
Detailed renderings of Ng's winning design
Swee Hong Ng

Favela-Bairro Projects

Location_Rio de Janeiro, Brazil
Date_1994–present
Client_168 favela communities
Design firm_Jorge Mario Jáuregui Architects
Design teams_Various
Major funding_Inter-American
Development Bank
Total budget_$1 billion

The favelas of Rio de Janeiro are unplanned, illegal shantytowns housing one-third of the city's population.

Though favelas are typically seen on the fringes of a city, Rio's unique topography of mountains and sea forced squatters to build within city limits. For over 100 years, simple makeshift houses climbed on top of one another up Rio's steep surrounding hillsides.

Though the government long ignored the favelas, efforts were finally made in the mid-twentieth century to eradicate them and move occupants to public housing. These efforts met with strong opposition from residents, and the favelas survived, growing at a faster rate than the city itself. By the early 1990s the favelas had become dangerous clusters of substandard housing, lacking basic sanitation and reliable electricity, terrorized by drug lords, and disenfranchised from the greater community.

In the mid-'90s the city changed tack, launching the Favela-Bairro program, which engaged the community in a participatory design process with architects and other

IGREJA EVANGELICA
ASSEMBLEIA DE DEUS
AGUA VIVA
CULTOS: SEG. QUART.
SEX. DOM.
TEL. 594 5212

New roadway and daycare center,
Fuba-Campinho
Jason Schmidt

When a new, planne
the slum—be it a pu
co-operative—it im
a monument. It was
architect, it indicate
People understand
right to what was on
so-called "formal ci
Jorge Mario Jáuregui, architect

building rises in
ic toilet or a sewing
ediately becomes
onceived by an
things are changing:
ey now have the
available in the
."

technical experts. Its goal was to upgrade existing favelas and integrate them with the larger city. The result was a wide range of proposals including the award-winning projects shown here by Jorge Mario Jáuregui Architects.

Since the program's inception this firm has built projects in more than 10 favelas, including Fernao Cardim, Fuba-Campinho, Salgueiro, and Vidigal. Grafted into the heart of the favelas, the new structures, with their Carnival coloring and functional modernist design, signal the arrival of basic services and the favelas' assimilation into the formal city.

Where tangles of wiring once snaked their way up the hillsides to informal shantytowns, new power lines have been buried and brightly colored stair rails mark the boundaries of newly formalized neighborhoods. In Fuba-Campinho, a gateway made from brick and steel I-beams brings order to the once-chaotic jumble of pathways and demarcates a new public square. In Vidigal, a semiabandoned sports center once overrun by drug dealers has been transformed into the official venue for Rio's soccer championships. In other neighborhoods, daycare centers, communal laundries, and salsa halls stand shoulder to shoulder with makeshift housing and storefronts, as if to invite and encourage the community to embark on its own journey of self-improvement.

In many areas streets are being built for the first time, allowing police and sanitation departments critical access to once-inaccessible parts of the city. Where streets cannot be built, connecting pathways are being improved to overcome the constant erosion of the hilly topography. In some cases housing must be removed to accommodate the new infrastructure. Affected residents are offered compensation to relocate or a spot in new housing units. Most choose the latter.

Since 1994 the Favela-Bairro Project has reached about 500,000 people in 168 of Rio's marginal settlements, and the government plans to continue and extend the program. Each project is designed independently of the others, maintaining the unique characteristics of neighborhoods ranging in size from 850 to 12,000 families. To encourage dialogue the project requires architects and planners, including many students, to be present in the communities on a daily basis—an experience most say they find liberating.

above
Soccer field and clubhouse, Fuba-Campinho
Toshiko Mori

right
Public square entrance, Fuba-Campinho

far right
Community buildings, Fuba-Campinho

opposite left
Daycare center, Rio das Pedras

opposite right
Communal laundry, Vidigal
All other photographs Jason Schmidt

women

WORK
2/3 of the world's working hours,

PRODUCE
1/2 of the world's food, and yet

EARN
10% of the world's income and

OWN LESS THAN
1% of the world's property

Walter Kalin et al., eds., *The Face of Human Rights*, Baden: Lars Müller, 2004

2/3 of the **110 million** children not in school are girls

Walter Kalin et al., eds., *The Face of Human Rights*, Baden: Lars Müller, 2004

Women constitute **70%** of the estimated **1,300,000,000** people living in absolute poverty

Walter Kalin et al., eds., *The Face of Human Rights*, Baden: Lars Müller, 2004

BETWEEN
40-60% of sexual assaults are committed against girls younger than 16.

"Prevention and response to sexual and gender-based violence in refugee situations", UNHCR

Rufisque
Women's Centre

Location_ Rufisque, Senegal
Date_ 1996–2001
Client_ Comité de Gestion du Foyer de la
Femme de Gouye Aldiana à Rufisque
(Board of Management of the Hearth of the
Woman of Gouye Aldiana in Rufisque)
Design firm_ Hollmén Reuter Sandman
Architects
Design team_ Saija Hollmén, Jenni Reuter,
Helena Sandman
Consultants_ MBacke Niang, Anne Rosenlew
Structural engineer_ Galaye Niang
Contractor_ Abdourahmane MBaye
Major funding_ Finnish Ministry of Foreign
Affairs, Fenno-Senegalese Association
(Centre-ARC), SOCOCIM, SOSETRA
Cost_ $100,600
Area_ 7,535 sq. ft./700 sq. m

Juha Ilonen

In 1906 Finland blazed the trail for women's suffrage across Europe when it granted women the right to hold public office.

Finland is also home to a rich history of social democracy. This socially conscious agenda, translated to the soils of Senegal, informs the design of the Rufisque Women's Centre.

Designed by three Finish architects, Saija Hollmén, Jenni Reuter, and Helena Sandman, the project stemmed from the work of Centre-ARC, whose focus is Senegalese-Nordic cultural exchange. The center's director, Anne Rosenlew, a Finnish sociologist, spent nearly twenty years observing the political and social infrastructure of Senegal. By tracing the population explosion there, she noticed a rise in both urban sprawl and locally active women's groups. Senegal's high unemployment rate meant that women, who traded fish, vegetables, incense, fabrics, brooms, and other basic goods in the country's crowded markets, were often the sole breadwinners in their families. These women's groups, which emerged spontaneously by the hundreds within traditional social structures in all parts of the country, enabled women to form microlending societies. Segregated within their culture from the male sphere of commerce, the women created an emotional and fiscal support network, which provided opportunities for economic growth and stability and, in some cases, a means of survival for them and their children.

But while some of the women's groups were sanctioned by the government through a program called Groupement de Promotion Féminine, they lacked adequate facilities, funding, and centralized coordination. Meetings would often be held in the courtyards outside private homes. "Always after having a meeting, we had to repair the fence because we just didn't have space enough in the courtyard," commented one member. The Rufisque Women's Centre arose from this need for a central gathering space big enough to accommodate group meetings and other activities.

The center, built on land donated by the city of Rufisque, is composed of three buildings situated around a central courtyard in the underdeveloped district of Gouye Aldiana. Architects used scale models to facilitate an exchange of ideas with the women, who were involved in the design process from the beginning. With its space ordered around a courtyard, the center echoes the traditional Senegalese gathering space and serves as a metaphor for democracy.

Reuse and recycling, along with an emphasis on locally available materials, guided the design team's choices. For example, the biggest cement factory in West Africa is just up the road from the center, so the buildings were constructed of cement. The team used recycled metal for the doors, windows, and reinforcing bars; old car-wheel rims became vents; and recycled bottles—"glass bricks"—were used as fenestration. Every effort was made to avoid utilizing wood, one of the region's scarcest natural resources. The walls facing the courtyard contain open colonnades, which also function to ventilate the buildings. Rich red walls separate it visually and functionally from neighboring businesses.

Today as many as 30 women's groups use the center, including the 110-member Bokk Jomm association, which participated in its design. The center also serves as a hub for women from groups throughout Senegal who come here to learn trades and exchange ideas. For the women of Rufisque the center's courtyard has become a symbol of unity, a modern-day version of the communal hearth, where they can share their concerns and aspirations.

above
Courtyards are important in Rufisque domestic architecture, so the design team organized the center around a series of courtyards.
Juha Ilonen

right
Plan of the center

> "What I find to be the best thing about the group [is the ability] to meet every day and talk, [to discover] that which concerns another person also concerns me."

Bokk Jomm member

above
The interior and exterior spaces are designed to flow together.

right
A view from one of the center's workshops into a courtyard. The ceiling is insulated with straw, a technique borrowed from Finland that keeps the space cool.

Opposite top, Juha Ilonen; all other images Helena Sandman

How can a project be both discreet and distinctive? That was the challenge posed to architect Christopher Livingston and his students at Montana State University in designing Shelter 2.

In 2002 a women's group approached the university about making some repairs and renovations to one of its battered women's crisis centers, an average-looking home that had been damaged by a water leak. That simple collaboration led to another request: Could the university help expand the shelter itself?

What the students designed and built over the course of a number of semesters was the antithesis of the "everything vanilla" approach that typifies most crisis centers, where efforts to create a safe haven to protect women from their violent spouses often result in purposefully bland structures in undisclosed locations. Rather than trying to have it blend in, Livingston and his students found a way to build a two-bedroom detached dwelling behind the center's existing residence that was both protective and bold, a place where the architecture reflected the catharsis and healing occurring inside.

"A building can stand out if you don't know what's in it. What happens inside is very important, but it's just a building after all," explains Livingston of the group's choice to put, in a sense, a brave face on pain. "If you didn't know what it was, you'd think it was just a funky apartment. We'd get subcontractors to come over and I would just say, 'Oh it's just an apartment for the house,' and that seemed to work for everyone. And the client was fine with that. From their perspective, having *some* people in the neighborhood know where it is is actually good for security."

Other parameters also guided the group's design choices. The size of the lot dictated a certain footprint. The need for off-street parking to protect residents' identities meant that the ground-floor garage had to contain as many spaces as possible. Finally, because many women leave violent relationships with their children, the living quarters needed to be flexible enough to accommodate whole families. The most critical concern, however, was privacy. (To protect the shelter's existing and future occupants, all the students were asked to sign nondisclosure agreements before beginning work. For the same reason, we have chosen to show only the interiors.)

As a result, the finished addition plays an interesting game of peek-a-boo. On the one hand, although the apartment sits back from the street, the distinctive protrusions and roofline of its façade stand out. On the other hand, covered stairs to the second-floor entrance, small windows high enough to obstruct the view of passersby, and a secluded ground-floor entrance safeguard the identities of occupants.

But if the exterior is eccentric, the unit's interior radiates familiarity. Like a little red barn, the kitchen and common areas are finished with varnished wooden siding. Small nooks, including a computer room, allow residents to escape into semiprivate spaces, while separate hallways lead to two comfortable bedrooms. An organically shaped reading loft that protrudes into the living space is the only reminder of the dwelling's unconventional exterior.

Although the overall feeling is one of safety and comfort, the apartments are intended only as temporary living quarters—a reality Livingston and his students were mindful of, especially when designing the finishing details of the space. For example, sliding doors on the bedrooms force residents to choose between an exposed closet and a private moment. Like an open suitcase, they serve as a tangible and spiritual reminder of the transitional nature of the space: This not a place to hide, they counsel, but a place to begin again.

Shelter 2

Location_Undisclosed
Date_2002–4
Client_Women suffering from domestic abuse
Sponsoring organization_Women's Crisis Center
Lead designer_Christopher Livingston
Design team_Students of Montana State University School of Architecture
Construction_Students of Montana State University School of Architecture
Cost_$75,000
Area_2,000 sq. ft./186 sq. m

opposite above
The kitchen is designed to provide an open, communal space for cooking and dining.

opposite left
The windows in the hallway are placed high so that people can't see inside from the street.

opposite right
The formal living room adjacent to the dining area provides an adult counterpoint to the play loft above.

All photographs 2005 Shelly Saunders

There were

20,000,000

AIDS-related deaths in the world between 1981 and the end of 2003, and

12,000,000

children orphaned by AIDS living in sub-Saharan Africa at the end of 2003

"Action Against HIV/AIDS in Africa," UNAIDS, 1999

At least 2/3
of the world's HIV/AIDS population of

22,500,000

lives in sub-Saharan Africa

"Action Against HIV/AIDS in Africa," UNAIDS, 1999

By the end of 2002 there were up to
4,600,000 people with HIV/AIDS in India

Of these, fewer than **30,000** are currently receiving antiretroviral therapy

"Epidemiological Fact Sheet on HIV/AIDS and Sexually Transmitted Infections: INDIA," UNAIDS, 2004

At the end of 2003 an estimated
1,039,000 to **1,185,000**
persons in the United States were living with HIV/AIDS, with **24** to **27%** undiagnosed and unaware of their HIV infection

"Estimated HIV Prevalence in the United States at the End of 2003," National HIV Prevention Conference, Atlanta, Georgia, June 2005

Mobile
Health Clinic

Location_Paris, France (prototype)
Date_2002–5
Sponsoring organization_Architecture for Humanity
Design firm_atelier [gilliland tolila]
Design team_Nicholas Gilliland and Gaston Tolila
Structural engineer_ARUP (formerly Ove Arup & Partners) (Botswana and South Africa)
Cost per unit_$16,500

Mobile Health Clinic

Design Like You Give a Damn

above
During the day the clinic doubles as a
marketplace. Local artisans set up stalls to sell
their wares while people wait to see doctors.

below
At night the facility becomes a traveling
community center for events, including film
screenings.

The statistics are staggering. An estimated three-quarters of the world's AIDS population lives in sub-Saharan Africa;

most have no access to lifesaving drugs, testing facilities, or even basic preventive health care. One of the major obstacles medical professionals in Africa face in treating this disease is their inability to reach vast areas of the continent.

To meet this need, Architecture for Humanity challenged the world's architects and health-care professionals to submit design ideas for a mobile HIV/AIDS health clinic. Designers were given six months to develop schemes for a fully equipped, mobile medical unit and HIV/AIDS treatment center that could be used not only for testing, prevention, and treatment of the disease but also for disseminating information regarding the virus and providing basic health-care services.

In submitting designs, entrants were asked to consider a number of criteria—chief among them, ease of deployment and maintenance by a small team of medical professionals, community acceptance, and cost. Over 530 teams from 51 countries entered the competition, and in November 2002 a panel of doctors and architects from Ghana, Kenya, and the United States selected four finalists. The Paris-based team of Nicholas Gilliland and Gaston Tolila received the Founders Award.

Selected for its approach to community involvement, the design consists of two parts: a permanent component, made up of one or two "granaries" (a building form common to sub-Saharan Africa constructed from earthen materials) built by the community several weeks before the arrival of the clinic, and a mobile component, which arrives by truck with the medical team. "Although some advance work is required to build the infrastructure, the two buildings left behind create a permanent space for a local contact person and a pharmacy," said jury member Dr. Shaffiq Essajee, director of the AIDS Research and Family Care Clinic in Mombasa. In addition, explained designers Gilliland and Tolila, "a veil of local African textiles gives protection from the sun and presents a familiar face to the village."

During the day the permanent clinic buildings double as a marketplace. With the construction of each new clinic, a natural trade route expands for artisans to sell their wares. In the evenings the clinic turns into a community gathering space, where events can be held or films projected against the wall of one of the earthen structures. By combining a number of services the facility is seen not as an "AIDS clinic" but as a traveling community center.

After a development workshop in South Africa the team continued to work on refining its design. In summer 2005 a prototype was built and displayed at the Pompidou Center in Paris.

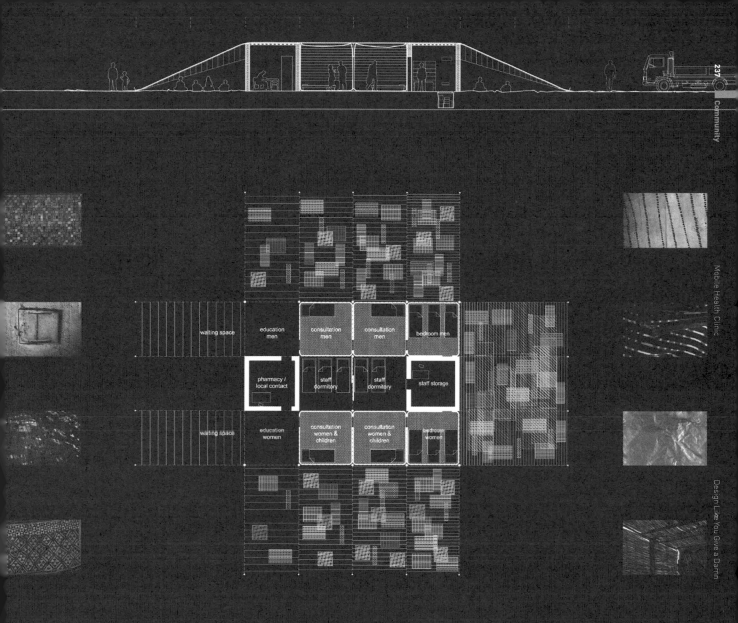

237

Community

Mobile Health Clinic

Design Like You Give a Damn

waiting space

education men

consultation men

consultation men

bedroom men

pharmacy / local contact

staff dormitory

staff dormitory

staff storage

waiting space

education women

consultation women & children

consultation women & children

bedroom women

Two permanent earthen buildings are constructed to support the temporary clinic. The mobile clinic's tentlike structure is transported from site to site and is hung from supports between the buildings when the clinic is in use.

All photographs atelier [gilliland tolila]

Africa Centre
for Health
and Population
Studies

Location_Somkhele, KwaZulu-Natal, South Africa
Date_2003
Client_Africa Centre for Health and Population Studies
Design team_East Coast Architects
Structural engineer_James Rivett-Carnac/Astcon
Electrical/Mechanical engineer_C. A. du Toit
Contractor/Manufacturer_Condor Construction
Environmental consultant_Geoff Nichols
Major funding_Wellcome Trust
Cost_$1 million
Area_29,000 sq. ft./2,694 sq. m
Website_www.africacentre.org.za

Angela Buckland

left and opposite
**The Africa Centre's tower serves as
a landmark in the community.**
left, Doug Halsey/Architecture for Humanity;
opposite, Angela Buckland

In the rolling hills of the Hlabisa district of KwaZulu-Natal sits one of the largest medical research facilities in rural South Africa.

Its central tower pierces the sky, declaring its presence with traditional forms, materials, and colors. It lies in the rural village of Somkhele, home to high unemployment and situated at the epicenter of South Africa's HIV/AIDS epidemic.

In 1996 the UK-based Wellcome Trust decided to build a modern research facility focusing on reproductive and population issues. The intention was to bring together African and international scientists in a rural setting to better understand how the virus was affecting rural populations and identify ways to overcome rural South Africa's health challenges.

As the people of Somkhele and the surrounding villages would form the research pool, the Africa Centre sought to develop long-lasting ties with the community, and the design process became an opportunity to establish and foster good relations. In a gesture of goodwill, iNkosi M. Mkhwanazi, the local tribal chief, donated 32 acres (13 hectares) in the heart of the village. The Durban-based firm East Coast Architects then took on the challenge of creating a community-engaged design by encouraging numerous opportunities for local involvement and input. They also worked with researchers to survey local skills, identifying artisans and craftspeople in the immediate vicinity of the planned center. This guided many of the design decisions and resulted in a building both indigenous to the area and iconic.

Materials for the center included timber from nearby saligna and gum trees, local thatchwork, and Zulu-made mosaics, plasterwork, murals, and sculptures. "It's very low-tech," project manager Steve Kinsler says of the design philosophy behind the center. "You should be able to go down to the hardware store and pick up everything you need there."

In addition to considering cultural issues, the architects were equally sensitive to environmental concerns. Rainwater is collected and conserved in large tanks held in a 49-foot- (15-m-) tall central tower that serves as a landmark for the region, while waste from the center is filtered and treated naturally in a series of tanks and wetlands filled with indigenous plant life. Known as a Living Machine, these tanks serve as a natural on-site waste treatment system. (For a full explanation of Living Machines, see "Living Machine").

While sustainability is at the heart of the building, the real joy is in the spirit and openness of its space. As you cross a bridge over the wetlands, you enter a reception area flooded with light. A central courtyard situated under the landmark tower defines the interior, while its wood-slatted top captures prevailing winds to help ventilate the building. Four two-story office wings, or "pods," house the research and administrative offices. Open space between the pods serves for socializing, with patios that echo the traditional bomas used in Zulu gatherings. The entire building is filled with color, bringing a sense of life and vitality.

top and above
The building's open central tower provides ventilation and holds two water collection tanks.
Cameron Sinclair/Architecture for Humanity

top right
Much of the building was constructed using local labor, including the window shades, which were woven by craftswomen.
Doug Halsey/Architecture for Humanity

right
The center's back porch is used for events and social gatherings.
Angela Buckland

clockwise from top left
Wooden truss details and connections
Nicholas Gilliland/Architecture for Humanity

The building is divided into four office "pods." Each pod has its own meeting rooms and open spaces.
Nicholas Gilliland/Architecture for Humanity

Visitors cross a bridge over a reed bed to enter the center. The reed bed is part of the center's on-site wastewater treatment system.
Michelle Myers/Architecture for Humanity

The village of Wadi-Naam in Israel's northern Negev Desert holds its annual festival during the week of Passover.

Here, during the spring celebration of 2003, several hundred volunteers descended upon the village to build a clinic that would serve as a powerful testament to the marriage of design and what its designers call "the public performance of civil disobedience."

Home to some 4,000 Bedouins, Wadi-Naam is a no man's land, one of many in the Negev. Sometimes called Israel's "last frontier," the Negev is a triangular stretch of desert bordered by Egypt on one side

Medwed Clinic

Location_Wadi-Naam, Israel
Date_2003
Client_Bedouin community
Sponsoring organization_Bustan
Design team_Michal Vital and Yuval Amir
Structural engineer_Ofer Cohen
Mechanical engineer_Dror Zchori
Consultant_Kibutz Lotan Ecological Center
Construction_Volunteers
Major funding_Private donations from the United States
Cost_$25,000
Area_753 sq. ft./70 sq. m

above
The semi-translucent façade made from two layers of polycarbonate sheeting filled with twigs allows light into the interior while maintaining a sense of privacy.
Both photographs Tal Adler, Yosefa Dresher

and Jordan on the other. Here squatter settlements of once-nomadic Bedouins and wealthy suburbanites compete over land rights and scarce resources. Israel is not the only country experiencing land conflicts between formal communities and unplanned settlements, but its politically charged history makes these conflicts all the more complex.

The group behind the clinic's sudden appearance was Bustan, a partnership of Jewish and Arab eco-builders, architects, academics, and farmers. Since 1999 Bustan—"grove" in both Hebrew and Arabic—has been working to promote social change and environmental justice in Israel and Palestine, with a particular focus on the Bedouin villages of the Negev. According to the group's founder and director, Devorah Bruos: "The Bedouin have become an underclass, unrecognized and therefore not connected to water, electricity, sanitation, or any other state infrastructure. [They are] denied permits for sewers, access roads, and municipal garbage-collection services."

In the case of Wadi-Naam, she says, heavy pollution worsens its plight. The village is located less than 1.25 miles (2 km) from Israel's largest toxic-waste incinerator, Ramat Hovav. During the 1980s an electric company built a power plant in the center of the village, but the village's "unrecognized" status meant residents could not benefit from its output. Many live in overcrowded shanties, and without adequate access to potable water, sanitation, or power, these conditions are detrimental to people's health. "Incidents of asthma, bronchitis, skin cancer, miscarriages, and eye infection are substantially higher among Bedouin children than all other segments of the Israeli population," says Bruos.

In early 2003 her group began circulating plans to build an environmentally sustainable medical facility in Wadi-Naam, where earlier efforts to install a clinic had faltered due to the village's unrecognized status, despite a court order mandating its construction. Notified by word-of-mouth, several hundred Israeli and foreign volunteers traveled to the

village during Passover to build a medical clinic alongside residents in less than six days. "The Medwed project was undertaken with the understanding that it is an unauthorized structure in an unrecognized place that may be bulldozed without any advance notice," Bruos explains.

The unusual circumstances of construction led to a number of design challenges. The entire clinic had to be as low-tech as possible while providing proper medical care. It had to function outside the official system and be built using inexpensive natural resources and unskilled volunteer labor. And it had to be erected quickly. Given these constraints, architects Michal Vital and Yuval Amir turned to straw-and-adobe construction, which has a long history in Bedouin culture. (For more about hay-bale construction, see "Hopi Nation Elder Home.")

The clinic's butterfly roof recalls the traditional Bedouin tent, and three of its exterior walls are made from mud-covered straw bales. The fourth wall is made from two layers of polycarbonate sheeting with

©Alon Hertz

vegetation grown in between. The clinic is divided into two parts, dry and wet areas, separated by an adobe brick wall. Inside the clinic a solar-powered refrigerator holds medical supplies. The team sited the building according to area wind patterns to allow for natural ventilation.

The clinic is situated within a shaded garden and enclosed by a perimeter fence made from adobe-covered tires. A rainwater collection system irrigates fruit trees and a medical herb garden. Outside there is also a traditional mud-brick oven, or *taboun*, designed and built by the village women. On busy days the garden doubles as a waiting area for mothers and children.

The result is a self-sustaining shaded structure that finds dignity in simplicity. For its originators, however, the complexity and politics of the project make it all the more meaningful. "This clinic is not just about medical rights for the citizens of Wadi-Naam," says Brous. "It is about health security for all the Bedouin citizens in our shared homeland."

Volunteers set tires in concrete to form a wall around the clinic. The tires are filled with sand to ensure stability.
Both photographs Alon Hertz

"Pass the incinerator on Rt. 40 and 2 km down the road make a right at the sign reading Electric Company. That is the village entrance. Follow the two smoke stacks and the high-voltage pylons up the road and swerve left over the hill. There you will find us."

Message posted to guide volunteers to the Medwed Clinic building site

275,000,000
children never attend or complete
primary school education

870,000,000
of the world's adults are illiterate

Thomas Kostigen, "Rich-Poor Gulf Widens; 'Inequality Matters' Conference
Puts Nations on Alert," CBS News MarketWatch, June 14, 2005

There are
103,000,000
out-of-school children; **57%** are girls

**Three-quarters are concentrated in
sub-Saharan Africa and South and West Asia**

"Towards EFA: The Quality Imperative," EFA Global Monitoring
Report 2005

In Africa a child will spend on average
7.8 years in school
Tertiary studies represent only
3% of the total years of schooling

In Europe a child can expect
to receive three years of
schooling at the tertiary level
out of a total of
15.4 years
of schooling at all levels

"The Haves and Have-nots in Tertiary Education," UNESCO Institute for Statistics, Jan. 2005

Cameron Sinclair

Gando Primary School

Location_Gando Village, Burkina Faso
Date_1998–2001
Client_Office of Education, Gando Village, Burkina Faso
Sponsoring organization_Schulbausteine für Gando
Designer_Diébédo Francis Kéré
Site coordinator_Wénéyda Kéré
Structural engineering_Technical University, Berlin
Craftsmen_Sanfo Saidou, Oussmane Moné (master mason), Minoungou Saidou (welder)
Consultant_Issa Moné, LOCOMAT
Assistants_Anna von Schulenburg, Christiane Putschke, Katja Neuheiser, Rüdiger Tomm
Cost_$29,830
Area_5,662 sq. ft./526 sq. m
Website_www.fuergando.de

The Gando Primary School was the result of one architect's mission to give the children of his village better educational opportunities than he had as a young boy.

Not only did Diébédo Francis Kéré design the school, but he also secured government support for the project and raised all the funds to build it.

In a country where only half of all primary-school-age children are enrolled in school, Kéré was the first person from his village to study abroad. "When I was seven years old I had to leave my family to attend school in the town. Even today I can still remember that time well. We were up to 160 children in a single room they called the 'classroom.' So many children were all crowded into a space of around 60 square meters [645 sq. ft.]," recalls Kéré, who says the school's corrugated roof trapped heat, raising temperatures to a stifling 104 °F (40 °C). "It was like a room to make bread, but not to teach somebody."

The village of Gando, population 3,000, lies on the southern plains of Burkina Faso, 124 miles (200 km) from the capital, Ouagadougou. Gando's only school was built in 1990 but was on the verge of collapse after just a decade of use. In 1998, while still a student himself at the Technical University, Berlin, Kéré decided to help. Enlisting the support of his classmates, whom he persuaded to dip into their coffee and cigarettes funds, he founded the nonprofit Schulbausteine für Gando (Bricks for the Gando School).

Although Kéré was trained in advanced techniques, climate and budget considerations combined with a desire to include the village in construction of the school prompted him to design the school using traditional mud-brick methods. The only concession to his Western training was the school's innovative soaring roof, which Kéré designed to be built without any need for imported materials or heavy-lifting equipment. Local craftsmen cut ordinary rebar with a handsaw and welded the pieces together to form lightweight roof trusses—and, according to the designer, an unintended playground for children who like to climb the roof's metal supports.

The building is a model of passive solar design, from the cooling and ventilation provided by its double roof structure—each classroom has its own mud-brick ceiling that insulates it from hot air circulating above—to its innovative use of widely available local

"People started talking about this pretty schoolhouse in Africa whose walls are so beautiful and pleasantly cool and whose roof floats as if it were able to fly."

Diébédo Francis Kéré, architect

top left
**Rebar truss systems are assembled
and then carried up to the roof.**

top right
**A worker takes a break by sitting
on the roof frame.**

above
**Women perform a traditional ceremony
at the school's opening in 2001.**

opposite
**A double-roof superstructure overhangs the
building, creating shaded areas and preventing
the classrooms underneath from gaining heat.**
All photographs Diébédo Francis Kéré/Aga Khan Foundation

materials. Still, the village's initial response
to Kéré's design was disappointment.

"According to people in my region,
Europeans use more solid materials,
like concrete or steel, when they build
houses for themselves. This is [seen as]
progress," comments Kéré. "But Europeans
suggest a different solution for Africans:
Africans should keep living in their small,
dark clay huts. The villagers found that
unacceptable because they equate clay
with backwardness." It wasn't until a heavy
rain proved the durability of clay-brick
construction that Kéré was able to convince
the village of the merits of his design.

The villagers were involved in every
aspect of the school's construction, says
Kéré, who enlisted the help of LOCOMAT
(a Burkina Faso government agency) to
provide training in brick-making. "[The
people] used their bare hands to dig out
and sieve the clay, which was transported
in donkey carts to the building site. Very
early in the morning, sometimes before
seven o'clock, [children] were at the school
carrying stones to the construction site,
some of which weighed more than they did.
And the women of the village would bring
water needed for construction, carrying it on
their heads sometimes from over a distance
of seven kilometers (4.4 mi.)," Kéré explains.

Today the school, which received the
2004 Aga Khan Award for Architecture, is
overflowing with students and has become
a model not only of sustainable building but
also of the power of architecture to uplift
and inspire. Designed for 120 children, the
school now has 350 students and another
150 on the wait list. Nomadic families who
shunned formal education in the past have
enrolled their children. Girls, too, now
attend classes. Two neighboring villages
have built their own schools following
Gando's cooperative approach, and local
authorities have employed many of the
young people trained during the school's
construction to build other public projects
using the same techniques.

"Without education, development is a dream."

Diébédo Francis Kéré, architect

Bamboo
Primary School

Location_Luong Son Village, Nha Trang, Vietnam
Date_2000–2002
Client_L'École Sauvage; Ministry of Education,
Vietnam
Design firm_theskyisbeautiful architecture
Design team_Nguyen Chi Tam, Charlotte Julliard
Site architect_Nguyen Vu Hop
Concrete engineer_Bui Van Minh
Major funding_Marcel Bleustein-Blanchet
Foundation, La Caisse des Dépôts et
Consignation, RENAULT, Liliane Bettencourt,
and other individual donations
Cost_$30,250 (including furniture)
Area_4,000 sq. ft./372 sq. m
Website_www.theskyisbeautiful.com

A few miles north of Nha Trang lies the small seaside
community of Cuu Ham in Luong Son Village, whose main
income derives from fishing and agriculture.

The area didn't have a primary school until L'École Sauvage, a French humanitarian organization that brings education to underprivileged children of the area, teamed up to build one with Paris-based architects Nguyen Chi Tam, who was born in Vietnam, and Charlotte Julliard.

Starting in 2000 the designers began to conceptualize and actively raise funds to build the school. In 2002 they approached the Vietnamese Ministry of Education with their proposal, and the state agreed to donate a vacant piece of land between a railway line and small river less than 3,000 feet (800 m) from the sea.

The site created a unique opportunity to build an alternative to the "all concrete, all glass" architecture seen across much of modern Vietnam. By using a locally abundant, sustainable natural resource, bamboo, the project employed the traditional skills and craftsmanship of the community. "We wanted to show that we can make beautiful architecture with a simple material," architect Tam explains.

The heat of central Vietnam determined many of the team's creative decisions. The school is composed largely of exterior spaces and relies heavily on natural ventilation. It includes three large classrooms, a small

opposite and right
**The architects planned the space
under the school's covered
overhang to be used as play
space, but it quickly became an
ad-hoc bicycle storage area.**

classroom, a teachers' room, a library, and a washroom. Each of these enclosed areas is separated by small open gardens. The exterior walkway that provides access to the school was intended to double as a playground, "but in the end it became a place for bicycles, because it is protected from the rain," Tam says.

Bamboo has its flaws and must be pretreated to prevent decay and termite infestation. The project used over 5,000 13-foot- (4-m-) long stems, which were submerged in mud for a month to dry them. Next the sugar, which attracts insects, was removed. Finally, the stems were gently scorched over an open flame, cleaned, and polished.

Working closely with a local architect, Nguyen Vu Hop, the designers aimed to simplify the construction process. The roof structures were prefabricated off-site and then assembled. The bamboo stems were tied with rattan cords and bolted at regular intervals, a standard method, to create roof trusses. Reinforced-concrete column beams support the roof, and the floor was made from rough concrete that will become smooth over time. Brick walls were coated in lime. Instead of using expensive glass, the architects opted for windows of corrugated plastic, which bathe the school in a bluish light, bringing a small piece of sky into each classroom.

"With the local architect, we had to draw details so that they could be built by the local workers. Think globally but act locally."

Nguyen Chi Tam, architect

right
Light blue corrugated sheeting used as an inexpensive alternative to glass lends the classrooms a soft blue light.

opposite
Roof trusses are constructed from bamboo.
All photographs Nguyen Vu Hop

Druk White Lotus School

Location_Shey, Ladakh, India
Date_1992–2011
Client_Drukpa Trust and its founder,
His Holiness the Twelfth Gyalwang Drukpa
Design firm_Arup Associates
Design team_Jonathan Rose (lead architect),
Caroline Sohie, Roland Reinardy, Sean
Mackintosh, Ian Hazard
Engineering firm_ARUP
(formerly Ove Arup & Partners)
Engineering team_Jim Fleming (lead
engineer), Martin Self, Francesca Galeazzi,
Omar Diallo, Masato Minami, Dorothee Richter,
Davina Rooney
Construction manager_Sonam Wangdus
Cost_$2 million
Patrons_Rt. Hon. the Dowager Countess
Cawdor; the Viscount and Viscountess Cowdray;
Richard Gere; Joanne Lumley, OBE; Raya
Thinles Namgyal, King of Ladakh; the Rt. Hon.
Lord Weatherhill, PC DL

above
**The nursery and infant school as completed
in 2001**
Caroline Sohie/Arup Associates

right
Nursery and infant school courtyard
Arup Associates

Set deep in the Indian Himalayas on the western edge of the Tibetan plateau, Ladakh, or "Little Tibet," is considered one of the last strongholds of indigenous Buddhist Tibetan culture.

In the early 1990s His Holiness the Twelfth Gyalwang Drukpa recognized a need to prepare the children of this remote mountain kingdom to face a changing world. The area's existing schools were either based in monasteries or ill-equipped for modern learning. His Holiness envisioned a school that would teach the children of Ladakh skills relevant to life in the twenty-first century without sacrificing their Buddhist traditions. The Druk White Lotus School was born out of this vision.

In 1992 the Drukpa Trust, a British charity, approached Arup Associates to develop a master plan for the school. From concept to ground-breaking, the project took more than five years and as of this printing is still under construction. However, the result is a design that fuses modern technology with traditional building techniques and stands as a model for appropriate and sustainable modernization in regions with limited resources.

The Tibetan plateau is remote and prone to seismic activity, but its harsh climate posed the most significant challenge to Arup's design team. The area is isolated by snow six months of the year, and winter

temperatures can drop as low as –22 °F (–30 °C). Limited rainfall and a lack of sewage services or electricity, combined with the cost of importing materials, further constrained the design.

The school's master plan is informed by the sacred geometry of Buddhism, forming a nine-square mandala and an eight-spoke dharma wheel. South-facing buildings take advantage of the area's abundant sunlight. Ventilated Trombe walls made from granite and mud brick trap the sun's heat during the day and release it slowly throughout the night, insulating the school's dormitories from extreme temperatures. The design team used timber framing to bolster traditional mud roofs against seismic activity. Finally, solar-powered wells pump groundwater into a gravity-fed distribution and irrigation system, and excess energy will be stored in batteries and used to power school computers.

But perhaps the most innovative aspect of the school's design is its latrines. Ladakh, like many remote regions, does not have a waterborne sewage system. Forced to find an affordable and self-sustaining solution, Arup developed a waterless "ventilation

improved pit" latrine, which uses passive solar engineering to encourage airflow and eliminate odors (see "VIP Latrine").

Arup has provided much of its design services for the school on a pro bono basis, and each year a member of the firm volunteers on-site for three to four months. Scheduled to be completed in 2011, the school will include classroom space for 800 students ages three to 18, a library, an open-air temple, computer and science labs, sports facilities, a kitchen and dining hall, and housing for pupils and staff.

above
Solar panels power the school's water pump.
Arup Associates

opposite
Because of the difficulty of transporting materials to the site during the region's long, harsh winter months, construction of the school took place over the course of several years.
Arup Associates

top and above
Loadbearing timber roof members offer seismic resistance in the school's classrooms.
Caroline Sohie/Arup Associates

School Solar Kitchen

Location_Jiutepec, Morelos, Mexico
Date_2004
Client_Municipality of Jiutepec
Design center_BASIC Initiative, College of Architecture and Urban Planning, University of Washington
Design team_Sergio Palleroni with students and faculty of the Global Community Studio
Electrical/Mechanical engineer_
Javier Castellanos
Solar consultant_Antonio Cuellar, SOLAIRD AG
Major funding_COSTCO Mexico and US; Municipality of Jiutepec, Morelos, Mexico; Communidad AC; BASIC Initiative
Cost_$67,200
Area_3,283 sq. ft./305 sq. m

When architect Sergio Palleroni and his students arrived at the site of their first design/build project in Mexico, they were greeted only by a simple sign stating, "A school will be built here."

"We sort of sat around and wondered what to do," Palleroni remembers. Then a woman came around with oil and a taco drum and began making tortillas for the group. "The students began talking with her and forming ideas. After this first exchange of ideas we decided that we should have the design process happen in a public place. So every time we were ready to exchange with the community we brought all our drawings up to the tortilla shop and posted them there." This small incident says much about Palleroni's approach and the work of the Global Community Studio at the University of Washington.

In 1995 Palleroni, who now teaches at University of Texas at Austin, founded what would become the BASIC Initiative with fellow University of Washington professor Steve Badanes. Since then the Global Community Studio, one of three program areas of the BASIC Initiative, has completed dozens of projects, from schools to libraries to housing to projects that address a broader need for infrastructure, such as roads and environmental projects. Much of the studio's work has been centered in Mexico's free-trade industrial zones, where the effects of globalization can be seen and felt.

The José Maria Morelos Elementary School Solar Kitchen is just one example of how the studio has managed to do just that. As part of a nutritional program students were asked to build a kitchen and dining hall on a narrow, steep slice of land behind a the existing school. "We were trying to help the mothers who set up their stands [outside the school] everyday to feed their kids," Palleroni explains. "The University of Seattle brought in strategies of nutrition, and we worked with the mothers to help them improve their diets and offer them a different way of cooking, without using fossil fuels, that they could later use in their own kitchens."

Working with the community, students imbedded the kitchen into the hillside. As with all the studio's projects, students were required to include strategies for on-site water harvesting and waste treatment. A small basin at the dining hall entrance encourages children to wash their hands before eating, and gray water from the basin helps nourish a small garden that grows food for the school. By far the most ingenious aspect of the project is a solar dish made from vanity mirrors and recycled bicycle parts that heats the ovens. The dish radiates the sun's rays onto the kitchen's hearth, generating 2,000 °F (1093 °C) of heat. "So it cooks," Palleroni says.

The solar kitchen is just one of many projects in which the Global Community Studio has created opportunities for students to engage in a dialogue and rethink the role of the architect in an increasingly interconnected world. Each project invites students to discover for themselves not just what makes a building sustainable, but what makes a community sustainable.

top
A sign reading "a school will be built here" marks the site of one of the Global Community Studio's first projects in Mexico.

above
The narrow, rocky site of the José Maria Morelos Elementary School dining hall before construction

right
View of the kitchen and dining hall during construction. The basin is decorated with a mosaic of tiles made by local craftsmen. Water from the basin irrigates the school's garden.

Skylights fill the interior of the school kitchen with light.

opposite
A solar panel made of recycled vanity mirrors and bicycle parts directs rays toward the school's ovens.
All photographs Sergio Palleroni/UW BASIC

"We often live and work in the United States unconscious that the way we live, the economic policies we are establishing, have a tremendous impact on the rest of the world. It's transforming the rest of the world in ways that are irreparable. I realized I needed to take students out of the United States into these areas so they could see how they could be rethinking their profession as designers—to become citizens of the world, to be aware of the social, cultural, environmental impact of architecture. "

Sergio Palleroni, architect

Hole-in-the-Wall Schools

Location_New Delhi, India, and 30 other
locations in rural India and Cambodia
Date_1999–present
Sponsoring organizations_NIIT Centre for
Research in Cognitive Systems, Hole-in-the-
Wall Education, Government of Delhi
Concept_Dr. Sugata Mitra
Design team_Ravi Bisht, Ashoo Dubey,
Sanjay Gupta, Vikram Kumar, Dinesh Mehta,
Dr. Sugata Mitra, Nitin Sharma
Major funding_NIIT, Government of Delhi,
ICICI Bank, World Bank
Cost per unit_$10,000
(three-computer VSAT kiosk)
Area_324 sq. ft./30 sq. m (per kiosk)

Dr. Sugata Mitra's Hole-in-the-Wall school program has become a portal to the future and a connection to the outside world for many Indian children.

Mitra, a professor and chief scientist at NIIT's Centre for Research in Cognitive Systems, has been working to provide high-speed Internet access to children in rural areas of India since 1999 with rewarding, and often surprising, results.

The first computer terminal Mitra installed was in an abandoned, garbage-strewn lot near NIIT headquarters in New Delhi. He mounted the computer in a concrete wall and monitored the activity via video camera from his own computer. He discovered that most of the people using the computer were children between the ages of six and 12 who spoke little English. What they were learning astonished him. He then launched a campaign to install computer kiosks on school playgrounds, where children were encouraged to learn free from adults, exams, and all the other trappings of formal education.

Mitra says his original concept was based on the assumption that children could learn basic computer skills without instruction—an assumption that proved true. He reports that children learned to surf the Internet, download music, use a mouse, copy, drag, and save—all without direction. They also created their own computer terminology. When asked by a journalist, "How do you know so much about computers?" one child responded, "What's a computer?"

Even more telling, Mitra and his team of researchers found that children were able to transgress communication barriers,

Children crowd around a kiosk in Vivekanand Basti, New Delhi, India.
All photographs Hole-in-the-Wall Education

abandoning their native language Web browser for the English version of Microsoft Explorer. In one case children created a drawing using a Microsoft Word template that Mitra himself didn't know existed. By providing computers he found that children will work in groups to teach themselves basic skills and knowledge. However, Mitra is careful to point out that the kiosks are not intended to replace education but to give it a boost, freeing up scarce dollars for instructors to teach subjects children cannot learn on their own.

Since the introduction of the kiosks, parents have reported other interesting developments. They say their children have learned to share and work together, assigning time slots for terminal use without the aid of adult supervision. Often parents become the project's most ardent advocates, in some cases paying the electric bill for the kiosks from their own earnings in order to keep the computers up and running. (To avoid these costs, some kiosks, such as the one in Stok, a village in the Ladakh district of northern India, are being run on solar power.)

The Hole-in-the-Wall schools do have potential drawbacks. Mitra fears children may become targets of Internet crime. There's the task of monitoring who uses the computer and for what purposes. And there's the problem of maintenance. Design plays a role in mitigating many of these issues. For example, to deter adults from monopolizing the computers, the kiosks are designed to be more physically comfortable for children. To cut down on maintenance, the computers have very few moving parts and only the most basic function keys. Sensors on the terminals detect the presence or absence of finger movement and help conserve power. Finally, to discourage misuse, a sign above the kiosks warns that the terminals are being monitored in New Delhi.

Original funding for the project came from sources including NIIT, the World Bank, and the Indian and Delhi governments. Mitra estimates that an additional $2 million would help educate as many as 500 million children; he says he is committed to making the kiosk design and plans available without charge to anyone willing to build one.

"The Hole-in-the-Wall experiments have given us a new, inexpensive, and reliable method for bringing computer literacy and primary education to areas where conventional schools are not functional. Such facilities are not meant to replace schools and teachers; they are meant to supplement, complement, and stand-in for them—to help in areas of the earth where good schools and good teachers are, for whatever reason, absent."

Dr. Sugata Mitra, chief scientist, NIIT

A Bridge Too Far

Location_Po River, Maosi, Gansu Province, China

Date_2004–5

Client_Villagers of Maosi

Design centers_Chinese University of Hong Kong, Hong Kong University of Science and Technology, Hong Kong Polytechnic University, Xi'an Jiaotong University

Design team_Chan Pui Ming, Mu Jun, Karen Kiang, Polly Tsang, Ryan Cheung, volunteers from Maosi, students

Environmental consultant_K. S. Wong, Professional Green Building Council

Engineering team_Andrew Luong, Steven H. Chow with Paul Tsang, Ove Arup

Major funding_Sir David Akers-Jones, Peter Man Kong Wong, H. M. Chan, Chi Yan Yip, Chung Man Ng, Ying Lun Ho

Cost_$141,900 (including in-kind labor and materials)

Length_328 ft./100 m

Website_www.bridge2far.info

The Po River, a tributary of China's great Yellow River, divides the village of Maosi. In the rainy season it is common for the river water to rise 16.5 feet (5 m).

Every year Maosi's 2,000 villagers would see their simple bridge of planks, stones, and mud washed away by this swell. In addition to slowing commerce, the high water prevented children from going to school. After observing this phenomenon in 2000, a small team of architects from the Chinese University of Hong Kong decided there must be a way to engineer a bridge that could withstand the floods. Their project became known as A Bridge Too Far, and architecture students from as near as Xian and as far as Hong Kong focused their energies toward developing a structure that would be affordable and straightforward to build, easy to repair, and made only of locally available, sustainable materials.

The first design breakthrough came when the team realized that the bridge didn't need to breach the high-water mark. The main advantage the villagers had seen in their old bridges was that they never risked damming the river and flooding their valley. If a bridge were built to sit about 5 feet (1.5 m) above the riverbed, people could cross the river 95 percent of the year, in all but the worst of storms. The bridge could be a porous submersible structure and still meet the village's needs for most of the year. This epiphany led to the design of porous piers. The students and advisors of A Bridge Too Far chose gabions—steel-mesh containers loaded with rubble—because water could flow through them. The gabions had the

added advantage of being cheap and easy to repair, since their weight and substance comes from rocks from the riverbed itself. All of the 20 piers that dot the riverbed have tapered edges oriented in the direction of the water flow, making them more streamlined and less subject to wear and tear from river currents.

The decking of the bridge also considers the inevitability of its yearly submersion. Just as the gabions reduce the force of the water's drag on the piers, the low arches of bamboo that form "leg guards" along the bridge's surface are designed as thin pieces so that in flood season they won't be deformed by the force of the water. If the current is especially strong, the bamboo arches pop out and float away, and the villagers easily replace them. The steel path sections are meant to be forgiving to the force of the river as well. Each pier is connected by a steel-edged deck that spans 16.5 feet (5 m). Split bamboo struts bolted with thin steel rods make up the walking surface, and if one of these sections should become dislodged, a team of six villagers can lift it back up on the pier.

The staggered planks of decking mimic the old patterns of the boards on mud that the villagers once used to cross the river. The very simple configuration provides stability for the whole system, because each deck section has twice the surface area over the pier that it would if the pieces were joined end to end, like an industrial bridge. In August 2005 villagers of all ages and students who worked on the project gathered at the river's banks for what would be the village's last annual bridge-building. The new, more permanent bridge has allowed for uninterrupted commerce and enabled children to attend school year round.

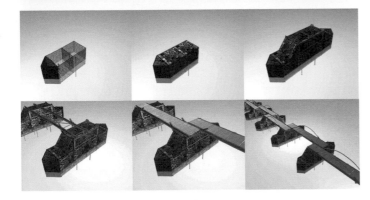

above left
The original bridge

above
The new permanent bridge

opposite above
Leg guards shaped from bent bamboo

opposite
**Wired gambion mesh is tied and filled
with rubble to create a pier. The piers, about
20 in all, are connected by a steel frame
covered by bamboo planks.**
All photographs The Chinese University of Hong Kong

Water,
and Sal

Energy,
ilitation

1,700,000,000
people in the world lack access to clean water, and

3,300,000,000
are without proper sanitation facilities

"Water Issues: The Need for Action at Different Levels," Aquatic Sciences, Mar. 2003

More than
2,200,000
people die from preventable water- and sanitation-related diseases each year

"Report on the Global Water and Sanitation Crisis," United Nations Human Settlements Program, Mar. 2003

In urban Asia
700 million
people, or half the population, do not have adequate water, and

800 million
people, or 60 percent of the urban population, are without adequate sanitation

"Report on the Global Water and Sanitation Crisis," United Nations Human Settlements Program, Mar. 2003

Child mortality rates in cities without proper sanitation are

10 to 20 times
higher than those in cities with adequate sanitation

"Report on the Global Water and Sanitation Crisis," United Nations Human Settlements Program, Mar. 2003

Helena Sandman

The Hippo Water Roller literally lifts the weight off the shoulders of millions of people—mostly women and children who have been collecting water at distant sources and carrying it home in five-gallon (20-L) buckets on their heads. The component parts are a 23-gallon (90-L) polyethylene barrel and a clip-on metal handle. The roller allows one person to collect four times the amount of water she could with a bucket. And because the roller is designed to be pushed across the ground, it feels like you are managing 22 pounds (10 kg) instead of the actual 200 pounds (90 kg) the barrel contains. The design saves time and energy and eliminates unhealthy skeletal stress.

Hippo Water Roller

Location_Throughout Southern Africa
Date_1993–present
Project leader_Grant Gibbs
Design team_Pettie Petzer and Johan Jonker
Manufacturer_Imvubu Projects
Additional consultants_Robin Drake, Piet Hickley
Major funding_Africa Foundation
Cost per unit_ Approx. $75
Website_www.hipporoller.org

above
Traditional method of water transport

opposite
Children bring water home with a Hippo Water Roller.
Both photographs Grant Gibbs

Trevor Field
Roundabout Outdoor

*The idea behind the PlayPump is simple:
Use the energy of children at play
to pump water.*

*When first designed by Ronnie Stuiver, the pump had enormous potential
to bring clean water to South Africa's rural communities. Children, who
are often responsible for water collection, spin on the roundabout, forcing
318 gallons (1,400 L) of water per hour from 130 feet (40 m) below ground
into a 568-gallon (2,500-L) storage tank, tapping enough water to meet the
daily household needs of a small community. There was only one problem:
How to make the pump, which cost three times as much as a typical pump,
economically viable in places where it was needed most. Enter advertising
executive Trevor Field.*

How did the idea for the PlayPump come about?

The equipment that goes underground is windmill equipment—it's not
rocket science. We've not reinvented the wheel; we've just taken the
best parts of the design and modified it so that we have a consistent
energy source, which is the children.

I found the pump in 1992 [and] bought the patent from Ronnie
Stuiver, who invented the system in South Africa. He got a [standard
playground] roundabout pumping water, and I saw it and said, "Sell it
to me." He was going to sell it because it was five times the cost of a
hand pump, and he couldn't make it profitable on its own.

What changes did you make to sell it as a community water pump?

We had to make it affordable. So I came up with the advertising idea to
subsidize the cost of the pump.

We also designed a force head, a one-way valve that holds the water
at the surface and allows it to be pumped to an overhead storage tank.
[Roundabout Outdoor] partner Paul Ristic designed the system. When
the pump is operating it holds the water at the top of the tank, so that
water is available immediately.

My wife installed the first ones in 1994 while I was working in
advertising and couldn't get away from my desk. They are still
operating. We've updated them, but they are very reliable. We try to
install them near schools, so kids will go. If you want to get a girl to go
to school, put water in the school. Girls miss out on 25 percent of their
education because of lack of water and sanitation at schools, which
leads many girls to stay home when they are menstruating.

How much does it cost and how do communities pay for it?

Users don't pay for the pump at all, advertisers do. It's a bit of a Robin
Hood exercise. The cost for the pump is just under $9,000, but that
includes the cost of full installation anywhere in rural South Africa
and 15 years of maintenance. If you don't consider maintenance, the
stuff begins to fall apart instantly. Especially because ground water is
free, and because people don't pay for water, [the pump generates]
no maintenance budget. So we pay for maintenance with the revenue
we get from advertising. Each pump has a toll-free number on it, and
anyone can call and notify us that a pump is out of order.

The advertising is critical to paying for the pump. A lot of Doubting
Thomases say that you can't get effective advertising into remote
places in South Africa. We've proved the opposite. This is one of the
only opportunities in rural areas.

Who are some of these advertisers?

All sorts of people: Coke, Unilever, Colgate Palmolive, big super-
markets like Spar. The [South African government] Electricity Board.
It's a very good platform for introducing new products like electricity,
for instance, for warning people about the dangers of electricity. All
manner of things are advertised because there isn't another medium.
There is no TV, rarely even any radio.

Not only have we got a water pump, we've got a medium for
important messages. In Africa we have the equivalent of the Indian
Ocean tsunami every three or four months. [For example] the Kaiser
Foundation advertises HIV awareness.

[The world] loses 6,000 people every day due to inadequate water
or poor sanitation. It is the equivalent of 20 747 jets crashing every day
with no survivors. And this disaster is preventable.

[Africa loses another 6,000 people each day to HIV/AIDS.] Women
and young girls are the most vulnerable population on the planet for
HIV and AIDS, and they don't understand this. Most of the education
efforts are in cities. Eighty percent of the problem in Africa is in rural
areas, and we are trying to reach them. We've got to try to keep them
HIV negative, and if you can put a message in a place where you make
somebody's life easier, you had better believe they will remember it.

PlayPump

Location_South Africa
Date_1996
Design team_Trevor Field, Ronnie Stuiver
Engineer_Paul Ristic
Manufacturer_Roundabout Outdoor
Major funding_International Finance Corporation (World Bank), UNICEF, Kaiser Foundation, South African Department of Water Affairs and Forestry, various advertisers
Cost_$8,500 (including maintenance)

When the children ride the merry-go-round, water is pumped into the nearby water tower. Public health and HIV/AIDS awareness posters always occupy two of the water tower's four billboards.

All photographs Roundabout Outdoor

Ceramic Water Filter

Location_Bisbee, Arizona, USA;
Managua, Nicaragua
Date_1981
Organization_Potters for Peace
Design center_Central American Institute of
Industrial Technology
Designer_Dr. Fernando Mazariegos
Additional consultant_Ron Rivera
Cost_$10–15
Website_www.potpaz.org

The Ceramic Water Filter provides households with safe drinking water and promotes community-based cottage industry. As water passes through the filter, most bacteria are too large to follow through its tiny clay pores. Any bacteria and fungi that do make it through the clay are eliminated by the ionic colloid state of the filter's silver coating. Each filter can purify nearly one to 1.8 quarts (1.75 L) of safe drinking water an hour, easily filling up a five-gallon (20-L) dispenser, enough to meet a household's daily drinking-water needs.

In October 1998 Hurricane Mitch tore through Central America. One of the most destructive hurricanes ever recorded, it left millions of people without access to safe water. In response Potters for Peace launched an effort to mass produce and distribute the filter in areas affected by the hurricane.

Since then Potters for Peace has continued to team with local partners and groups throughout Central America as well as in twelve other countries throughout the world to establish production facilities and provide training in the filter's manufacture. Using local clay, sawdust, and 10 cents worth of colloidal silver per filter, one press mold can produce 50 filters per day.

Peter Chartrand/Potters for Peace

Watercone

Location_Yemen
Date_1999
Designer_Stephan Augustin
Manufacturer_Wisser Verpackungen
Major funding_Hans Sauer Stiftung
Cost_$60–100
Website_www.watercone.com

At last, some good news about the greenhouse effect: It's the secret to Stephan Augustin's Watercone, an elegant low-tech water-purifying condenser. The design is a simple clear polycarbonate cone, 23 to 31 inches (60 to 80 cm) in diameter, that rests on a black polycarbonate pan. The shapes are stackable for efficient shipping all over the world. It works by filling the pan with seawater and leaving it in the sun; the air's natural heat-trapping gases cause the water to evaporate. The water beads up on the inside of the cone, and runs into the channel around its bottom edge. By flipping the cone upside down and unscrewing the cap, a person can collect up to one to 1.8 quarts (1.7 L) of safe, desalinated water a day. That's enough to meet a child's daily needs; two Watercones will take care of one adult.

counter-clockwise
from bottom left
Saltwater is poured into the Watercone's dish; the heat of the sun causes the water to condense; the desalinated water collects in the lip of the cone and is ready for drinking.
All photographs Stephan Augustin

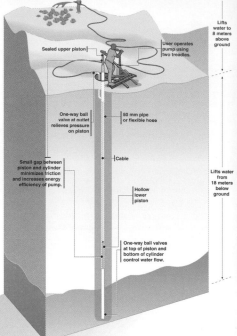

MoneyMaker Pumps

Location_Nairobi, Kenya
Date_1996
Design team_Mark Butcher, Dr. Martin Fisher, Abdi Mohammed, Alan Spybey, Mohammad Swaleh, Ben Tarbell, IDEO volunteers
Design consultant_IDEO
Manufacturer_KickStart
Major funding_UK Department for International Development (DFID), USAID, Skoll Foundation, John Deere Foundation
Cost_$38–150, depending on model
Website_www.kickstart.org

The MoneyMaker pump allows small farmers unprecedented access to water—a resource in rural Africa as valuable as any currency. The product of careful research and development by KickStart, a Nairobi-based NGO formerly known as ApproTEC, the MoneyMaker pump is a portable, manually operated, self-installed deep-lift pump that can both pull water from a deep well and pressurize it through a hosepipe. Based on feedback from farmers, the nonprofit now manufactures two models of the basic pump, the Super MoneyMaker Pump and the MoneyMaker Plus Pump, which allows one person to irrigate 1.5 acres (0.6 hectares) a day, pumping water from as far underground as 23 feet (7 m) and uphill as high as 69 feet (21 m).

KickStart makes each model from widely available steel parts so farmers can easily afford and maintain them. The pedal-driven pumps are light enough to be carried on public transport and safe enough to be operated barefoot. Posture was also a design consideration: The pumps' pedals operate at a low angle so that women wearing skirts or dresses can be comfortable using them. Today 50 percent of the pumps' buyers are women. Its makers estimate that in Kenya alone the pump has resulted in the farming of over 15,000 acres (6,070 hectares) and $37 million per year in profits and wages for the small-business entrepreneurs who sell the pump throughout Africa.

above left
The MoneyMaker pump was designed to be used by people of all ages.
KickStart

above
Diagram showing how the deep-lift pump operates
IDEO

Long-Lasting Antimalaria Bed Nets

Location_Arusha, Tanzania
Date_2002–present
Design firm_Sumitomo Chemical Corp.
Manufacturer_A to Z Textile Mills
Project partner_Acumen Fund
Major funding_Acumen Fund, A to Z Textile Mills, Exxon Mobil, Sumitomo Chemical Corp., UNICEF, World Health Organization
Cost per unit_$7–8

above right
Installing antimalaria netting at roof vents

below right
Netting enveloped around a bed

All photographs Susan Meiselas

Standing water is a breeding ground for mosquitoes and is the main contributor to the spread of malaria. There are 300 million new infections of acute malaria worldwide every year; 90 percent occur in Africa—primarily among children under five.

Treated nets kill mosquitoes on contact, but the cost of re-treating conventional bed nets can be a heavy burden on many families. In 1978 the Sumitomo Chemical Corp. of Japan developed a highly effective insecticide-treated antimalaria bed net that lasted three to five years instead of the usual six months.

In 2001 the World Health Organization initiated a project to manufacture beds using the chemical. But making this lifesaving yet expensive new technology available to as many people as possible posed a challenge. This is where the Acumen Fund, a philanthropic foundation based on a venture-capital model, stepped in.

First the Acumen Fund facilitated the transfer of the technology license and manufacturing contract to Africa's largest bed-net producer, Tanzania's A to Z Textile Mills. With investment from Acumen, A to Z purchased equipment to produce about 380,000 bed nets per year. Then, through a public-private partnership between A to Z, the World Health Organization, UNICEF, Exxon Mobil, and Sumitomo, the fund helped create a distribution channel for selling the bed nets at gas stations, clinics, and charitable organizations. The result: an improved product made accessible and affordable to those who need it most.

Aquacube

Location_Banda Aceh, Indonesia; Gulf Coast region, USA; various locations in Africa
Date_2005
Client_Sampoerna Foundation
Manufacturer_Water and Process Technology Division, Süd-Chemie
Funding_Süd-Chemie
Cost_Approx. $9,500
Website_www.sud-chemie.com

First developed by the German company Süd-Chemie for use in undeveloped areas of Africa, the Aquacube is a miniature water-purifying plant that packs for transport into a steel frame slightly larger than 35 cubic feet (one cubic m). With its own integral generator it can purify approximately 400 gallons (1,500 L) of water per hour.

After the Indian Ocean tsunami of December 2004, a Süd-Chemie team drove through Indonesia with an Aquacube mounted in the back of a truck. In the months following the disaster, several Aquacubes remained in Indonesia as interim replacements for municipal water systems. The company also donated a system for use in the Gulf Coast in the wake of Hurricane Katrina to provide safe drinking water to temporary health-care facilities and emergency shelters.

above left
The white storage tank slides into the steel frame to protect the main mechanism during shipping. Here it is positioned to purify water.

above right
In Indonesia, Aquacubes purify water drawn directly from local rivers.
Both photographs Süd-Chemie

Clean Hub System

Location_Minneapolis, Minnesota, USA
Date_2005
Organization_Architecture for Humanity–Minnesota
Design firm_Shelter Architecture
Concept_John Gavin Dwyer
Estimated cost_$15,000
Area_180 sq. ft./17 sq. m
Website_www.afh-mn.org, www.shelterarchitecture.com

Clean Hub is a compact, manufactured structure that provides sustainable electricity, clean water, toilets, and bathing facilities. Based on a concept by John Dwyer, principal of Shelter Architecture and co founder of Architecture for Humanity Minnesota, the structure is self-contained, self-reliant, and intended to serve up to several hundred people for 30 years or more.

The structure's components include a roof of light-gauge metal for rain collection and 16 photovoltaic panels producing up to 2,640 watts for solar collection. The shell is constructed of polycarbonate panels, and the foundation is set on piers to accommodate uneven ground.

A reverse-osmosis water system is located in the mechanical space and pumps water from a reservoir stored beneath the shell and below grade to regulate the water's temperature to the showers and sinks. The reservoir can be tapped into an existing water source or fed water and is designed to handle contaminated water or seawater. The current design can produce about 3,500 gallons (13,000 L) of clean water a day with a continuous water source. The showers and sinks return gray water to the reservoir for reuse, and the toilets are waterless and self-composting.

Architecture for Humanity–Minnesota is currently working to develop a prototype of the design. Although it was intended as an all-purpose structure to fit a wide range of situations, Dwyer says that "given its ability to weave into dense urban fabric, we believe its most effective application is for urban slum upgrading and disaster recovery and rebuilding."

above left
Exploded axon of rendered Clean Hub unit showing the rain-collecting roof, body made from polycarbonate panels, adjustable feet for uneven terrain, and water reservoir beneath

above center
Rendering of the Clean Hub in a disaster settlement

above right
Rendering showing the unit deployed over uneven ground, with the water reservoir tapped into a river

All images Shelter Architecture

Power Shade

Date_2004
Client_US Army Soldier Systems Center
(NATICK)
Design firm_FTL Design Engineering Studio
Design team_Nicholas Goldsmith,
Robert Lerner
Structural engineer_Sui Ming Louie
Solar technology_Iowa Thin Film
Tent manufacturer_Eureka/Johnson Outdoors
Major funding_US Department of Defense
Cost per unit_$15,000 (prototype)
Area_500 sq. ft./46 sq. m
Power generated_1 kilowatt
(65 amps at 15.4 volts)
Websites_ www.ftlstudio.com,
www.iowathinfilm.com, www.eurekatents.com

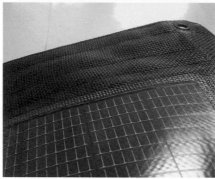

Developed with two grants from the US
Department of Defense, the Power Shade
is designed to provide shade for vehicles,
humanitarian aid workers, or troops while it
generates one kilowatt of energy. Thin-film
solar technology integrated into the tent
fabric offers an easily portable, totally quiet
power source for anyone on the move. The
energy is stored in a bank of batteries that
can then be used to power field equipment.
The 20-x-22-foot (6.7-x-6-m) structure folds
flat to 28 x 72 inches (71 x 183 cm).

above
Detail of the solar film and reinforced tent edge
Both photographs FTL Studio

Seba Dalkai School Solar Classroom

Location_Seba Dalkai, Arizona, USA
Date_2000
Organization_Native American Photovoltaics (NAPV)
Client_Seba Dalkai School
Design firm_Kiss + Cathcart Architects
Designer_Gregory Kiss
Project engineer_TerraSolar
Major funding_Federal Energy Management Program, US Department of Energy, NAPV
Manufacturer_NAPV
Cost_$50,000
Area_1,200 sq. ft./111 sq. m

When architect Gregory Kiss cofounded the nonprofit organization Native American Photovoltaics (NAPV) with Gregory Smith, Peterson Zah, and Roman Bitsuie, he knew he could put the experience he had gained in solar technology from his New York–based architectural practice, Kiss + Cathcart Architects, to good use. Since 1998 NAPV has been manufacturing and installing stand-alone solar-powered energy systems for Native American households and other facilities on Arizona's Navajo reservations. Says Kiss, "Since the Navajo reservation has perhaps the greatest need for photovoltaic technology in the United States, it seemed like an obvious challenge."

Unlike New York, where solar panels are occasionally used to augment reliable power from the municipal power grid, much of the Navajo nation had no power at all. This meant that up to 25,000 households lacked the basic benefits of refrigeration and electric light. These infrastructural problems translated into poor diets and fewer working hours for a population that has one of the world's highest incidences of diabetes and a rate of unemployment hovering around 75 percent.

Education is one avenue for helping overcome these obstacles, so it is fitting that one of the NAPV's first tribal projects was for a school. The Seba Dalkai school is a Bureau of Indian Affairs institution for children in kindergarten through twelfth grade. The solar-powered pavilion Kiss + Cathcart designed for the school creates a shady space for use as a classroom or a performance stage, while the five-kilowatt photovoltaic system on the roof creates auxiliary power for computers.

The group hopes that in addition to augmenting the school's environmental sciences curriculum, the pavilion will also be used to train people from the Navajo nation and beyond to build, install, and service photovoltaic systems—eventually fostering an industry in alternative power sources.

Solar panels shade a classroom. The simple building form is derived from the traditonal southwestern ramada.
Both photographs Kiss + Cathcart Architects

Himalayan Rescue Association Pheriche Clinic

Location_Pheriche, Nepal
Date_2001
Client_Himalayan Rescue Association
Pheriche Clinic
Designer_Lotus Energy
Manufacturers_Synergy Power Corporation
(turbine), Shell Solar (PV panels)
Cost_Approx. $30,000

Lotus Energy, a renewable-energy company
based in Nepal, designed a hybrid wind and
solar system to power the world's highest
hospital, the Himalayan Rescue Association
Pheriche Clinic. With a rotor diameter of just
over three feet (1 m) and a weight of only 11
pounds (5 kg), the small but efficient turbine
is appropriate for the remote location. The
altitude was the determining factor for the
design of this power system, because the
air is literally too thin to support a wind-only
configuration. The output power of the wind
turbine is 500 watts; that of the 16 75-watt solar
PV modules is 1.2 kilowatts. The hybrid system
supplies the necessary power for lighting the
hospital and powering medical equipment
such as X-ray and oxygen machines, EKGs,
and other life-supporting devices.

top right
**The solar panels are positioned to
optimize sunlight.**

above right
**A technician checks the battery bank on
the solar and wind system at Pheriche.**

above left
**The wind turbine at Pheriche Clinic,
one day's walk from the Mt. Everest
base camp**
All photographs Lotus Energy

The waterless VIP (Ventilated Pit) latrine, designed for a school on the remote Tibetan plateau (see "Druk White Lotus School"), offers an improvement over the standard pit latrine. Designed by Arup, the system uses a solar-heated flue to force fresh air through the toilet cubicles and waste pits and out a vent, taking with it unpleasant odors and flies. Solid waste dries in twin composting pits for use as fertilizer.

"Everyone thinks that modernization means flushing toilets. It means water infrastructure, waste infrastructure, all those things. Here we are saying you can do something simply in a very remote area and still deal with these problems in a very modern, civilized way," explains lead architect Jonathan Rose. The firm is working with local groups to replicate the design throughout the region.

VIP (Ventilated Improved Pit) Latrine

Location_Shey, Ladakh, India
Date_2001
Client_Druk White Lotus School
Design team_Arup Associates
Engineering team_ARUP
(formerly Ove Arup & Partners)
Construction manager_Sonam Wangdus
Cost_$18,600

above
Completed solar-assisted VIP latrine blocks for the Druk White Lotus School. The granite finish, required because of the buildings' exposure to Ladakh's harsh climate, makes them relatively expensive. The dark south façade, with the solar flue, draws air through the cubicle and pit, which eliminates flies and odors.
Caroline Sohie/Arup Associates

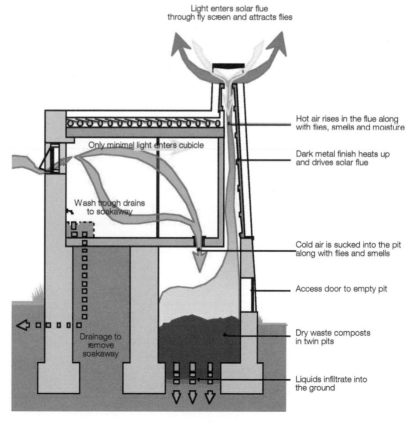

Light enters solar flue through fly screen and attracts flies

Hot air rises in the flue along with flies, smells and moisture

Only minimal light enters cubicle

Dark metal finish heats up and drives solar flue

Wash trough drains to soakaway

Cold air is sucked into the pit along with flies and smells

Access door to empty pit

Drainage to remove soakaway

Dry waste composts in twin pits

Liquids infiltrate into the ground

Living Machine

Location_US Pavilion, Auroville,
Tamil Nadu, India
Date_2002
Client_Auroville International, USA;
City of Auroville
Design center_BASIC Initiative,
College of Architecture and Urban Planning,
University of Washington
Design team_Sergio Palleroni with students
and faculty of the Global Community Studio
Environmental consultant_Charles Henry
Major funding_BASIC Initiative; Auroville
International, USA; University of Washington;
private donations
Cost_$8,600 (composting toilets and waste
treatment only)

Finding environmentally safe ways to handle human waste can be one of the most challenging aspects of building in areas with little or no infrastructure.

Most of the world's communities, especially its informal settlements, are not linked to waterborne sewage systems.

Septic tanks are often improperly maintained, leaking hazardous wastes into groundwater. However, in recent years environmental designers have developed a number of self-sustaining natural systems to safely treat waste on-site.

University of Washington students worked to incorporate such a system into the building pictured here, a dormitory for visitors from the United States to the experimental community of Auroville in Tamil Nadu, India. Working with Charles Henry, a professor of forest resources, the students devised a dual system, where black water (highly toxic solid waste) is treated in dry-composting pit latrines while gray water (urine and wastewater from sinks and showers) is treated in what's known as a Living Machine.

The system, part of a holistic approach to the building's design, including rainwater catchment and solar energy, requires that liquid and solid wastes be separated into two different streams. While the design team built showers in each dorm room and sinks throughout the building, toilets are centralized in a large bathroom at one end of the building. Certain toilets are designated for solid waste, others for liquid waste. The solid-waste toilets pass material to a cabinet beneath the bathrooms, where the waste sits in modified water bins for six months. The resulting compost can then be used to fertilize the building's gardens.

The toilets for liquid wastes siphon urine into the buildings' gray-water system, or Living Machine. In this system, first invented by eco-pioneer John Todd in the late 1980s, gray water passes into a tank where any leftover solids settle out. The liquids are then diverted to a closed reed bed where plants take up the toxins or bacteria break them down and turn them into nutrients. Finally, the nearly clean water passes through open trenches where snails, algae, frogs, small fish, and a variety of plants, including banana trees, take up any remaining toxins in the water. Living Machines such as this one have been used to treat waste for individual buildings (see "Africa Centre for Health and Population Studies"), industrial plants, and entire municipalities.

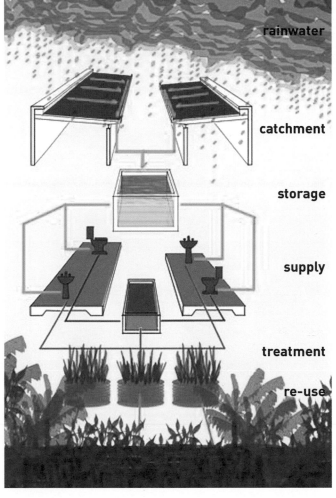

rainwater

catchment

storage

supply

treatment

re-use

top left
Pipes ventilate the American Dormitory's six composting toilets.
Pino Marchese/UW BASIC

above left
When planted, three reed beds, part of the building's Living Machine, will naturally filter pollutants out of the water.
UW BASIC

above
Diagram of a rainwater collection system combined with a Living Machine
UW BASIC

Ecological Dry Toilet

Location_Cuernavaca, Mexico
Date_1980
Organization_Centro de Innovación en Tecnología Alternativa
Designer_César Añorve
Additional consultants_Gustavo Esteva, Iván Illich, Jean Robert
Manufacturer_Tecnologías y Sistemas Ecológicos (TESEC)
Cost_$27–54 (stand-alone toilet), $150–550 (complete system)

Nearly half the water used in a typical Mexican home goes straight down the toilet. The Ecological Dry Toilet both conserves increasingly scarce water and creates fertilizer. The design mounts a conventional toilet seat over two chambers—one active, where waste is collected, the other passive, where waste composts while the other chamber is in use. The toilet diverts urine to a tank where it settles before being used as fertilizer. Solid waste passes to the active chamber, which is "flushed" with ash or lime rather than water to speed composting and neutralize odors. When the active chamber is full, it is sealed off and the waste is left to compost for 18 months or more. Meanwhile, composted waste is emptied from the second chamber, which then becomes active again. Because the waste streams must be separated, the group also created a dry urinal for men and recommends that homeowners install both.

While the toilet can be utilized with traditional plumbing, it is especially useful in areas that lack full sanitation services. TESEC, a small local business development firm, helps communities build new industry by setting up low-tech facilities to cast the toilet bowls from fiberglass or cement.

above left
Section diagram showing how gray water is diverted

above
The toilet with its diverting panel in place, and with the panel lifted
All images CITA AC

UnBathroom

Location_Pasadena, California, USA
Date_2003
Design center_Art Center College of Design
Designer_William Hsu
Cost per unit_$2 (prototype)

In a disaster situation, a critical part of preventing an outbreak of disease is the hygienic disposal of human waste. The UnBathroom biodegradable cardboard toilet offers a recyclable, sanitary solution. Allowing one liner bag and cardboard seat per use, it packs flat for shipping, assembles easily, and can support up to 200 pounds (91 kg). The waxed cardboard structure is intended to be burned after all the liners are used.

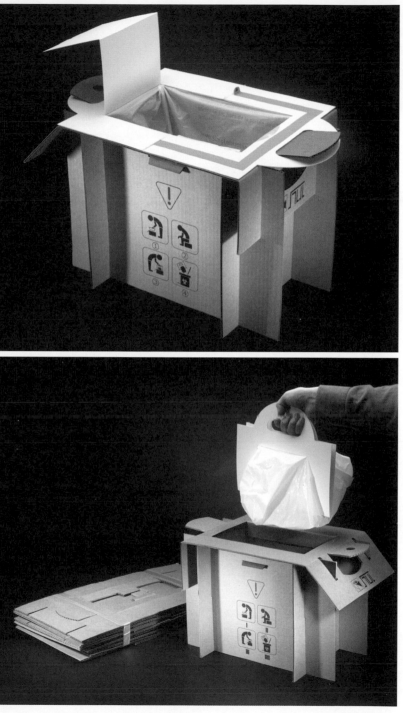

above
The UnBathroom ready for use

below
Removing the liner bag from the UnBathroom
Both photographs Steven Heller

Politics
and Pla

Policy
nning

Effects of Zimbabwe's "Operation Murambatsvina" slum-clearance program in 2005:

92,460 housing structures demolished

133,534 households affected

32,538 enterprises demolished

700,000 people displaced

2,400,000 people, or **18%** of the population, directly or indirectly affected

"Report of the Fact-Finding Mission to Zimbabwe to Assess the Scope and Impact of Operation Murambatsvina," UN Habitat, July 2005

In the first forty years after the 1949 Revolution, China resettled an average of

800,000

people per year

Forced Migration Review, Jan.–Apr. 1998

The Three Gorges Dam project in China will resettle more than

1,200,000 people

Forced Migration Review, Jan.–Apr. 1998

The official notice of enforcement for "Operation Murambatsvina," published May 26, 2005

REGI

These o
developr

To the d
Enforce
Harare,
is being
Harare i

Unautho
outbuild
purpose

And wh

CITY OF HARARE

L, TOWN AND COUNTRY PLANNING ACT
PTER 29:12 REVISED EDITION 1996
FORCEMENT ORDER SECTION 32

relate to all residential properties in Greater Harare for illegal

s, occupiers and users of such stands/properties.

Order Section 32: Whereas it appears to the City Council of
the Local Planning Authority that development or use of land
s been carried out on the said stands/properties in Greater
ravention of the Act.

erection and use of illegal structures - namely illegal
wooden and metal shanties mostly used for human habitation
other illegal businesses.

it appears expedient to the Local Planning Authority and

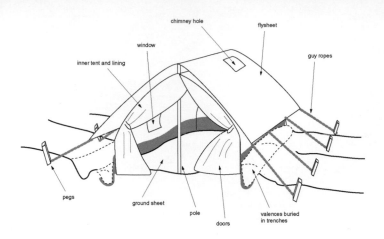

chimney hole
window
flysheet
inner tent and lining
guy ropes
pegs
ground sheet
pole
doors
valences buried
in trenches

shelterproject

Date_1997–present
End client_Displaced populations
Design center_Martin Centre for Architectural
and Urban Studies, University of Cambridge
Design team_Joseph Ashmore, Dr. Tom
Corsellis, Peter Manfield, Antonella Vitale
Project partner_Oxfam, Great Britain
Consultants_Peer reviews by technical
consultants from a range of humanitarian aid
organizations
Website_www.shelterproject.org

shelterproject is an informal research project based at the Martin Centre for Architectural and Urban Studies at the University of Cambridge.

In 1997 architect Dr. Tom Corsellis, whose background included field work with aid organizations such as CARE and UNHCR, teamed with a group of researchers to rethink the way emergency shelter was designed and implemented.

For years the design of relief tents revolved around two main considerations: cost and ease of assembly. Most tents were made from canvas. But canvas tents were heavy and costly to ship, and because canvas rots, the tents deteriorated quickly and could not be stockpiled for long periods. Wear and tear on the weakened material in the field significantly shortened the useful lifespan of the shelter.

To further complicate matters, there were no standards for the way tents were manufactured and dispatched. In an emergency everything got used. Refugees in snow-prone regions might receive plastic sheeting, while winterized tents might get shipped to warm, desert climates. The logistics of procurement and shipping meant that tents sometimes arrived after the greatest need for them had passed. What's more, once they were distributed tents were often assembled without consideration for drainage, firebreaks, and other critical siting issues. As a result they were used with

varying degrees of success; sometimes they were effective, other times not.

Starting in 1995 shelterproject collaborated with Oxfam GB to develop a guide to tents. The project was significant because of its scope and the collaborative nature of the group's approach. The team sought input from numerous aid organizations including UNHCR, Oxfam, Care, and CHF. Called simply "Tents," the booklet underwent a series of peer reviews and was published in 2004 by the UN Office for the Coordination of Humanitarian Affairs (UNOCHA).

More recently shelterproject has worked with the humanitarian community to address the broader issue of creating transitional settlements and to better bridge the gap between relief work and future development. In 2005 it consolidated information from a number of sources to publish a set of best practices guidelines ("Transitional Settlement: Displaced Populations"). The guidelines offer a broad overview of emergency shelter and planning as well as technical recommendations on a wide range of issues, from protecting shelters from rodents to building with bamboo to preventing the sexual exploitation of women.

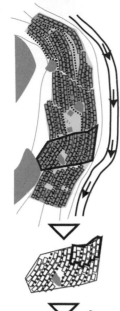

camp: approximately 20,000 inhabitants

4 sectors

- fire breaks: 30m per built-up 300m
- roads follow contours and lead out from centre
- run-off water also follows contours
- features used to break repeating pattern
- administrative centre located at the centre of the camp.

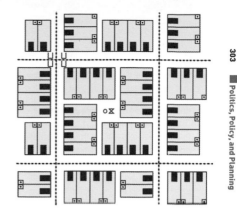

sector: approximately 5,000 inhabitants

4 blocks

- fire breaks: 15m between blocks
- should contain central recreational/commercial spaces

block: approximately 1,250 inhabitants

16 communities

- fire breaks: 6m (pathways)

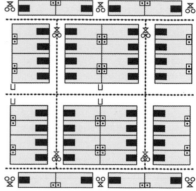

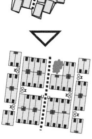

community: approximately 80 inhabitants

16 plots with 16 shelters

- fire breaks: 2m between dwellings
- drainage should be well planned and maintained
- drain water must not pollute existing surface water or groundwater, or cause erosion.

opposite
Parts of a tent

above
A camp subdivided into sectors, blocks, and communities

right
Three community plans for transitional settlements: the Hollow Square plan, the Staggered plan, and the Community Road plan
All diagrams www.shelterproject.org

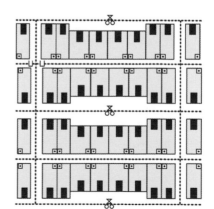

Sphere Project

Date_2000
Sponsoring organization_Steering Committee for Humanitarian Response; InterAction
Website_www.sphereproject.org

In 1997 a group of humanitarian aid agencies collaborated to create a set of standards for disaster response, aiming to improve quality and enhance accountability.

The project came of age during a moment of self-reckoning in the humanitarian community. The world was facing ever-more complex emergencies. Just a few years earlier, the Rwandan genocide had resulted in the deaths of between 500,000 to 800,000 people. To add to the already extraordinary human tragedy, as many as 80,000 more people died in the refugee camps, mainly from cholera and dysentery—both preventable.

In 1996 a group of researchers and field workers released a report on the humanitarian community's response to the Rwandan crisis. "Study III" of the Joint Evaluation of Emergency Assistance to Rwanda criticized the lack of coordination and preparedness among the agencies that responded to the disaster and called for greater accountability within the aid community. At the same time there was a growing sense of unease among field workers and others about varied and sometimes poor response by some aid groups. As one policy researcher put it, "The days of accepting the 'good work' of humanitarian agencies were over."

The Sphere Project, initially spearheaded by the Steering Committee for Humanitarian Response and InterAction, offered a starting point for the discussion of a shared code of conduct. Field workers, policy analysts, and experts from a wide range of UN agencies,

NGOs, and other groups participated in formulating the policy guidelines. In 2000 the group published the first edition of its *Humanitarian Charter and Minimum Standards in Disaster Response*. The standards covered five key areas: water and sanitation, nutrition, food aid, shelter, and health services. They outlined for the first time what people affected by disasters had a right to expect from humanitarian assistance.

Although the standards were intended to set a baseline for safeguarding the health and dignity of displaced persons, the organizers acknowledge that they may not be appropriate in all situations. For example, aid workers may find themselves in a situation where the normal standard of living in a country is so poor that the Sphere minimums actually offer a better standard of living, notes Jean McCluskey, a project coordinator. "So you have situations where you might want to alter the indicators to match the context.... Obviously, it's best not to lower the standard, but if it creates problems in the local population, then something has to change."

Since their inception the Sphere standards have been widely adopted. It is not uncommon for funders or project managers to ask whether a particular shelter design or settlement plan "meets Sphere standards," and understanding those standards has become an essential tool for shelter experts responding to disasters.

Humanitarian Charter and Minimum Standards

5. Natural hazards: risks posed by the localised impact of natural hazards such as earthquakes, volcanic activity, landslides, flooding or high winds in any given location should also be assessed. Locations close to buildings or structures vulnerable to earthquake aftershocks, land formations vulnerable to landslides, low-lying sites prone to further lava flows or the build-up of exhaust gases, riverbanks and depressions at risk from further flooding and sites exposed to high winds should be avoided, until the assessed risks of returning to such locations have satisfactorily diminished.

6. Hazardous materials and goods: potentially hazardous materials and goods can be deposited or exposed following natural disasters such as earthquakes, floods and typhoons; mines and unexploded ordnance can be present due to previous or current conflicts. The presence of such items and the potential risks involved in their removal should be identified by appropriately experienced personnel. The time and expertise required for their safe removal may preclude the use of part or all of any locations affected.

7. Structural assessments: the stability of building structures in inhabited areas should be appraised by appropriately qualified personnel. Assessments should include the effects of further structural weakening from earthquake aftershocks, further flooding and high winds, etc. For mass shelters, the ability of existing building structures to accommodate any additional loading and the increased risk of the failure of building components such as floors, internal dividing walls, roofs, etc. should be assessed.

8. Land and building ownership and usage: such issues are often controversial, especially where records may not have been kept or where conflict may have affected possession. Ownership of the site or building(s) should be established and the holders of formal or customary use rights identified to the extent possible. The land or property rights of vulnerable groups should be identified and supported. This includes formal or understood rights of inheritance, particularly following a disaster in which the holder of the rights or title may have died or been displaced.

9. Availability of services and facilities: existing or repaired services or facilities should be identified and used, where there is sufficient capacity, before the construction of new facilities is considered (see Water Supply, Sanitation and Hygiene Promotion chapter on page 51).

Minimum Standards in Shelter, Settlement and Non-Food Items

10. Access to settlement locations: access to the settlement, the condition of local road infrastructure and proximity to airstrips, railheads or ports for the supply of relief assistance should be assessed, taking into account seasonal constraints, hazards and security risks. For mass shelters and temporary planned or self-settled camps, the site itself and any primary storage and food distribution points should be accessible by heavy trucks from an all-weather road. Other facilities should be accessible by light vehicles.

11. Livelihood support: an understanding of the pre-disaster economic activities of the affected population, and the opportunities within the post-disaster context, should guide the settling of affected populations. This should include land availability and access for cultivation and grazing; the location of and access to market areas; and the availability of and access to local services that may be essential to particular economic activities. The differing social and economic needs and constraints of particular vulnerable groups within the displaced or any host communities should also be assessed and accommodated accordingly (see Food security standards on page 119).

Shelter and settlement standard 2: physical planning

Local physical planning practices are used where possible, enabling safe and secure access to and use of shelters and essential services and facilities, as well as ensuring appropriate privacy and separation between individual household shelters.

Key indicators (to be read in conjunction with the guidance notes)

- Area or cluster planning by family, neighbourhood or village groups as appropriate supports existing social networks, contributes to security and enables self-management by the affected population (see guidance note 1).

- All members of the affected population have safe access to water, sanitary facilities, health care, solid waste disposal, graveyards and

Shelter

Roots of Peace

Location_Croatia, Afghanistan, Angola, Cambodia, Iraq
Date_1997–present
End clients_Farmers and schools
Project team_Heidi Kühn, Gary Kühn, Kyleigh Kühn, Brooks Kühn, Tucker Kühn, Christian Kühn
Project partners_HALO Trust, M.A.G., Chemonics, AgLand
Cost_$1,000 per land mine
Major funding_USAID, US State Department, individual donations
Website_www.rootsofpeace.org

Land mines are like anonymous terrorists, killing or maiming one person, usually an innocent civilian or de-miner, every 22 minutes.

They are inexpensive to produce (the cost of a hamburger), expensive to remove, and can be set off with less than eight pounds (3.6 kg) of pressure. More than 70 million are planted in over 70 countries, waiting for victims.

The effects don't end there. Landmines stifle transportation routes and make agricultural fields inaccessible, crippling economies. Founded in 1997 by Heidi and Gary Kühn, the nonprofit Roots of Peace turns minefields back into working agricultural land through a program called Mines to Vines. Beginning in 1998 the group de-mined six Croatian villages, making way for vineyards to be planted. Currently in Afghanistan the group grows grapes, pomegranates, and almonds, and in Angola it plans to plant bananas and other subtropical fruits in former mine fields.

In 2003 Kyleigh Kühn followed in her parents' footsteps by raising funds from children to create safe places for children to play in Afghanistan. Through the program, called "Making Change Work," children across the United States raised 7,000,000 pennies to pay the cost of clearing minefields and turning them into soccer fields. So far by partnering with de-miners from the HALO Trust, a UK-based de-mining group, Roots of Peace has created two playing fields, one at a boys' school in Bagram, the other at a girls' school in Parwan province. The group has also de-mined a field next to the Bajgah village school in Baghlan province.

All three sites are located in Northern Afghanistan, which over the last two decades has seen some of the country's fiercest fighting and where roads and fields are littered with mines. Despite lingering fear in the community, the "Making Change Work" soccer fields are in constant use: At the boys' school in Bagram students play in the morning; by midday former child soldiers are kicking a ball around; and in the afternoon aid workers and local men wind down with informal games.

above
The grounds of the Bagram Boys School near Kabul, Afghanistan, were unsafe for play until a de-mining team cleared them of mines and unexploded ordnance.

above right
The Bagram boys' soccer team with Gary Kühn (center) in the newly de-mined school grounds

center right
After de-mining the fields the group trellises the vines. Lifting the vines from the ground prevents mold, increasing the crop yield.

bottom right
Heidi Kühn with a farmer whose field was de-mined, in his vineyard in the Shomali Plains north of Kabul

opposite
A farmer shows off grapes grown in a field de-mined by Roots of Peace.
All photographs Roots of Peace

European Greenbelt

Location_ Europe (path of the former Iron Curtain)
Date_ 2004–10
Developer_ World Conservation Union
Major funding_ Global Environment Fund, Phare CBC, NATO (science program), World Heritage Fund, European Rural Development Fund, European Regional Development Fund, Neighborhood Program, Sixth Framework Research Funding, other private, corporate, and government-sponsored funding sources

PARKS ON THE BORDER

Oulanka National Park

Paanajärvi National Park

FINLAND

Baltic Sea

RUSSIA

Podyjí National Park

GERMANY

Sumava National Park

Bavarian Forest

CZECH REP.

AUSTRIA

SLOVAKIA

Neusiedler See National Park

HUNGARY

Ferto-Hansag National Park

ALBANIA

Black Sea

The proposed chain of parks stretches from the Arctic shores of Finland and Russia to the arid frontier between Bulgaria and Greece.

The Iron Curtain was a political, economic, ideological, physical, and cultural divide that separated Eastern and Western Europe throughout the cold war.

The 4,000-mile-long (6,400-km-long) zone formerly filled with barbed-wire fences, walls, minefields, guard towers, and bunkers is today a no man's land that stretches 30 to 4,000 yards (27 to 3657 m) wide in some places. If successful, the European Greenbelt, a project started by the World Conservation Union, based in Gland, Switzerland, would convert this vast zone into a network of parks spanning the length of the former Iron Curtain and crossing through 22 countries.

Much of the work has already been done by individual nations. Since 1989 governments have been creating their own series of border parks and other protected areas, removing fences and other obstacles that blocked wildlife migration and limited recreational use along the frontier. Germany has been leading the movement, protecting more than half of

the border area that once divided West from communist East. Finland and Russia have created Europe's largest protected area with a pair of national parks spanning their shared Arctic frontier. Other parks link Austria with the Czech Republic and Hungary.

What distinguishes the Greenbelt initiative from other conservation programs is not only its emphasis on "green diplomacy" but also its goal of pairing conservation with rural development. By encouraging sustainable development, the project's coordinators hope areas that have suffered from shrinking populations and eroding economies since the fall of the Iron Curtain will benefit from new income sources provided by the parks. "The idea is to interlink the needs of people and nature," explains Andrew Terry, project officer for the World Conservation Union.

Politics and religion have combined to create a sensitive patchwork of divided territories in Israel's West Bank.

The conflict has also played out, among other places, on the drawing boards of architects and planners. In 2002 Eyal Weizman and Rafi Segal undertook a study of the physical transformations of the West Bank, documenting the growth patterns of Jewish settlements and Palestinian villages in the disputed territory.

The architects found that ownership policies dating back centuries had resulted in a kind of "vertical planning." During the time of the Ottoman empire, residents paid tax only on lands they cultivated. Later land that could be proven to be under continuous cultivation reverted to private Palestinian ownership. Lands not privately owned reverted to the state. As a result Palestinian villages were concentrated in the fertile valleys, while Jewish settlements took root on hilltops. After the Six Day War the extension of the occupied territories coincided with the growth of suburbs, creating in the architects' words an architecture of "civilian occupation."

Originally the Israel Association of United Architects (IAUA) commissioned the study for the International Union of Architects' congress in Berlin in 2002. But after the catalogue was completed, the IAUA withdrew its support for the project. The exhibition was canceled and the catalogue banned. Subsequently published by Verso Books and exhibited in New York and Berlin, the work instigated a wide discussion of the conflicted role of architecture within the disputed territories. By mapping the physical transformation of the occupied territories, the architects raised ethical and humanitarian questions about the way roads, water systems, and telephone lines—the everyday elements of urban planning and architecture—had become "tactical tools," shaping not only the landscape but also the spatial dimensions of the Israeli-Palestinian conflict. Those questions have only increased in significance with the construction by Israel of a proposed 416-mile- (670-km-) barrier between itself and the West Bank.

A Civilian Occupation: The Politics of Israeli Architecture

Location_West Bank, Israel
Date_2002–3
Design team_Rafi Segal, Eyal Weizman

above left
An example of high-rise apartments in an Israeli settlement overlooking Palestinian lands

above right
Traditional Palestinian vernacular architecture

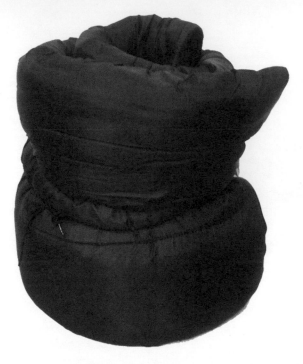

Sleeping Bag Project

Location_Baltimore, Maryland, USA
Date_2003–4
End client_Homeless population in Baltimore
Design center_Project Locus
Project organizers_Patrick Rhodes, Melissa Coleman
Major funding_Wal-Mart Foundation, individual donors
Cost_$25,000
Website_www.projectlocus.org

Sometimes an architect can make a difference in a community without building.

For Patrick Rhodes, who founded Project Locus, a nonprofit dedicated to bringing design to underserved neighborhoods, a simple act of kindness would become the catalyst for providing temporary shelter for hundreds of homeless throughout Baltimore.

In 2003 Rhodes, a recent graduate from Southern California Institute of Architecture, was leaving a movie theater with his girlfriend, Melissa Coleman, a couple of days before Christmas when they stopped to hand some spare change to a homeless man. It happened to be the winter's first cold spell, and Rhodes realized he had a sleeping bag in his car. The man was more than just pleasantly surprised when Rhodes returned a couple of minutes later and handed him the bag. His gratitude inspired Rhodes to organize a sleeping-bag drive throughout Baltimore.

Rhodes began by researching Baltimore city health department statistics and found that more than 70 people had died of hypothermia in the past decade. Feeling that something needed to be done, he and Coleman canvassed businesses for donations but raised only $15.

Undeterred, Rhodes produced a flyer and handed it out at his weekly soccer game. As chance would have it, one of the players worked in the art department of the *Baltimore Sun*. He passed the story idea on to a features editor, and the following week an article about the project appeared in the newspaper. The response was overwhelming: In less than six weeks, the pair raised $25,000. The Wal-Mart Foundation donated 400 sleeping bags, and several organizations offered volunteer support. All told, more than 800 sleeping bags were distributed. That winter the city recorded only one death from hypothermia—and it occurred two weeks before the sleeping-bag campaign began. Interest in the project and the publicity it generated threw a spotlight on Baltimore's shortage of accommodations for the homeless, eventually prompting the city to add more permanent beds to its emergency shelters.

above left
Volunteers distribute sleeping bags during the winter of 2004 in Baltimore.

left
Baltimore shelters were forced to turn away 15,000 people in 2003. In response Project Locus initiated the Sleeping Bag project, which helped keep people warm and called attention to the inadequacy of the city's shelter system.
All photographs Colby Ware

The Housing for Health project began when an interdisciplinary team realized that health services alone were not improving the welfare of some 3,000 aboriginal peoples living in remote communities in central Australia.

Housing for Health

Location_Australia
Date_1999–present
Client_Indigenous households
Organization_Healthabitat
Project coordinators_Paul Pholeros, Stephan Rainow, Dr. Paul Torzillo
Major funding_Federal, local, and state housing and health agencies
Number of homes repaired to date_4,000
Average maintenance costs per house_ $2,658–$3,797

Despite efforts by various health organizations, more than 60 percent of the illnesses being treated at community clinics were basic infectious diseases stemming from poor living conditions.

In 1985 Yami Lester, the director of Nganampa Health Council in South Australia, put together a task force including thoracic physician Paul Torzillo, environmental health expert Stephan Rainow, and architect Paul Pholeros to better understand the causes behind the health issues these communities faced. While previous programs had focused on "education," attributing the poor health and sanitation conditions in many aboriginal households to poverty or cultural differences, Pholeros and his team members learned that in most cases faulty home construction and poor maintenance were to blame.

"In the first house I entered to commence the survey fix work, there were two families consisting of 12 people trying to use the two-bedroom house, four of them children under five years of age," Pholeros recalls. "To make matters worse, there was raw effluent flowing from the direction of the bathroom toilet. After much digging and searching, we found that the toilet bowl had not been connected to a wastewater drainage pipe and was just sitting on the concrete slab! So at the first flush the toilet had overflowed. Government officials and politicians would drive by and remark on the pointlessness of building houses for indigenous people, because they preferred to sit outside the house. [The officials] clearly had never attempted a visit inside."

Rather than spending more tax dollars on awareness and education, the panel recommended that funds be put to better use toward basic repairs and maintenance on individual houses. Working with health officials and the community, the group identified nine "healthy living practices" in addition to basic safety issues, such as the ability to bathe and wash clothes and bedding, the safe removal of wastewater, and improved nutrition.

The team then evaluated the functionality of each house in terms of how well it allowed families to perform these basic practices. And from the start, the Housing for Health program established a simple rule: No survey without service. Small fixes (everything from repairing showerheads and blocked drains to installing insect screens to updating wastewater systems to accommodate larger households) were done on the spot, larger repairs as soon as possible.

These jobs also provided vital feedback on ways the houses could be designed and built better in the first place, information that Housing for Health has published in a guide to indigenous housing and passes on to architects and contractors working in the community. For example, data collected about bathing facilities such as showers can inform contractors as to which parts of the plumbing work well and which ones do not.

The group also created a training program to teach repair and maintenance trades to community members. The program not only creates jobs but also ensures that local expertise will be available to carry out these tasks in the community. According to Pholeros, Housing for Health, which is now a national program, has employed more than 1,500 indigenous people, "giving the first paid work to many and giving training opportunities to others."

opposite
The nine "healthy living practices" identified by the Housing for Health team
Healthhabitat

WASHING PEOPLE

WASHING CLOTHES

REMOVING WASTE SAFELY

IMPROVING NUTRITION

REDUCING CROWDING

SEPARATING PEOPLE FROM ANIMALS,
VERMIN OR INSECTS

REDUCING DUST

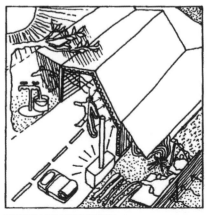

CONTROLLING TEMPERATURE

REDUCING TRAUMA

Viewing Platforms | Stair to Park

Location_Los Angeles, California, USA
Date_Viewing Platforms, 2005;
Stair to Park, 1997
Organization_Heavy Trash
Design team_Anonymous
Website_www.heavytrash.blogspot.com

On the morning of April 24, 2005, residents of three Los Angeles subdivisions awoke to discover bright orange structures peeking over the gates of their communities.

Some assumed public-works officials had placed them there for tree maintenance, but others soon discovered their true purpose. Stenciled on the structures in a militaristic style was the Web address of an organization calling itself Heavy Trash.

Since 1997 this anonymous grassroots organization of architects, designers, and urban planners has been forcing Angelenos to confront the planning and policies that shape their everyday lives. Heavy Trash installed its first project—a 2,000-pound (907-kg) stair in a park after the city had fenced it in to prevent homeless people from using it. For three weeks the stair allowed community members to access the park, calling attention to the way tax dollars had helped remove the park from public use.

The group struck again in 2000, this time with a series of official-looking "Future Subway Station Site" signs outlining the route of the "Aqua Line," a fictional transit corridor between Los Angeles and Santa Monica. Part tongue-in-cheek art installation, part architectural agitprop, the project drew attention to inadequate public transportation.

Most recently Heavy Trash took on the gated community, America's fastest-growing form of housing. Gated neighborhoods are marketed as friendly, safe places to raise families. But according to the group these gated subdivisions rarely cultivate the sort of front-porch dialogue with neighbors that has come to represent the "good life" and instead may actually erode the texture of urban life.

Heavy Trash argues that by walling themselves in to "flee a disintegrating society," residents actually accelerate the decline around them by replacing a city tax system that feeds a wider community with private homeowner association fees whose benefit ends at the subdivision's gates. The group also claims that gated communities sever links between neighboring developments, segregating not only their residents but all those surrounding them. Armed with plywood and two-by-fours, Heavy Trash sought to subvert the notion of the walled city. While the viewing platforms provoked amusement, anger, and intrigue, they also inspired conversation between residents on both sides of the gate.

above
A viewing platform outside the gates of Laughlin Park, Los Angeles, April 2005

left
Another Heavy Trash viewing platform outside the Park La Brea apartments in Los Angeles, April 2005

opposite
Stair allows public access to the "closed" Triangle Park at Santa Monica and Bundy, June 1997

All photographs Heavy Trash

Finding
Public Space
in the Margins

Location_Hollywood, California, USA
Date_2002–5
Client_Yucca Corridor Coalition
Design center_Center for Community
Research and Design, Woodbury University
Design team_Jeanine Centuori, Russell
Rock, Sonny Ward, Jesie Kelly, and Woodbury
University students
Consultant_Kim Shkapich
Major funding_National Endowment for
the Arts; Graham Foundation for Advanced
Studies in the Fine Arts; American Institute of
Architects, California Council and California
Architectural Foundation, William Turnbull, Jr.,
FAIA Environmental Education Grant;
Woodbury University

Many community design centers are eager to engage in design/build projects in their cities, but often land is either too costly or too far from the population the center is mandated to reach.

Such was the case in Los Angeles, home to some of the most expensive real estate in the world. However, a studio hosted by the Center for Community Research and Design at Woodbury University in Los Angeles found a novel solution. Rather than competing with developers for prime lots, they focused on finding what they called "public spaces in the margins."

The studio was taught by Jeanine Centuori, the center's director, and Russell Rock, her partner at the firm UrbanRock Design, who challenged their students to design public amenities in the disregarded recesses of the city. In this new view of the urban landscape, grass-trimmed edges of parking lots became incubators for business, blank walls become hosts for public showers and water fountains, and chain-link fences intended to mark property lines became spontaneous sites for "congregation and conversation." Although the project began as a theoretical exploration, the group is working with the Yucca Corridor Coalition to implement one of its ideas: to turn parking meters into markers of historic sites and other points of interest.

opposite
"Give and Take" fills in chain-link fences at property lines, transforming the structure intended to divide properties into a gathering place. Rubber tubes slipped into the fence openings can be pushed or pulled to create topographic furniture.

top
A street marker highlighting the Capitol Records Building. "Site Portals" turn ordinary parking meters, street lights, and tree guards into ocular guides to historic sites and other neighborhood landmarks.

above
"Water Bar" provides a consolidated set of public amenities: showers, restrooms, drinking fountains, and a car wash cantilevered off blank walls along sidewalks. Plumbing is contained within a bar attached to the wall.
All renderings UrbanRock Design

City Without a Ghetto

Location_New York, New York, USA
Date_2003
Design center_Center for Urban Pedagogy (CUP)
Project organizers_Damon Rich, Rosten Woo
Project team_Danny Aranda, AJ Blandford, Stella Bugbee, Zoë Coombes, Meghann Curtis, Leigh Davis, Beth Lieberman, Andrea Meller, Sam Stark, Celina Su, Oscar Tuazon
Partner organizations_Interboro Institute, Storefront for Art and Architecture
Volunteers_James Case, Cynthia Golembeski, Alyssa Gerber, Anette Gallo, Rob Giampietro, Edwin Huh, Jackson McDade, Gaetane Michaux, Jennifer Minnen, Elizabeth Solomon, Lila Yomtoob
Major funding_Brooklyn Arts Council, Center for Arts Education, Storefront for Art and Architecture, City-as-School High School, Parsons School of Design Integrated Design Curriculum, Lily Auchincloss Foundation, Rooftop Filmmakers Fund
Cost_$19,353

Designed and researched by the Center for Urban Pedagogy, a New York-based nonprofit, City Without a Ghetto examined the urban-renewal programs of the '50s and '60s and their effects on the American city.

The project began in 2003 as a curriculum for students at New York's City-As-School High School and the Parsons School of Design. Under the direction of Damon Rich and Rosten Woo, it eventually grew to become an exhibit that traveled to the Storefront for Art and Architecture, New York, and Mess Hall, Chicago, among other venues.

An immensely successful educational tool, City Without a Ghetto used the Housing Act of 1949 (which gave rise to Urban Renewal, a policy aimed at revitalizing blighted urban areas), as a springboard for discussions of design, urban planning, and low-income housing policies. The act's use of eminent domain had far-reaching and controversial effects in cities throughout the country. Designers, public policy students, political figures, and community activists collaborated to create the teaching materials, which asked students questions such as: "According to certain narratives of design history, the destruction of Pruitt-Igoe, begun in 1972, forced design into a retreat, abandoning its heroic pose. If we as designers want to effectively relate to politics, what should we take from this example?"

Likewise, the traveling exhibit featured six modules that encouraged viewers to "appreciate how legislation, architecture, finance, popular culture, and social attitudes shape human environments." It put public-housing programs under a colorful microscope, dissecting the policy and planning arguments that shaped urban renewal. Detailed graphics showed "before" and "after" examples of iconic housing projects and explained how their designs were influenced by legal battles such as *Gautreaux v. Chicago Housing Authority*, the 1966 court case in which a group of plaintiffs argued that the very location of their housing project violated their civil rights. Five tables displayed photographs, timelines, and interactive elements, each table highlighting the history of a different blighted area in New York.

Above all, City Without a Ghetto discussed policy issues in a way that was at once tangible and provocative. Even the project's name was intended to give students and gallery visitors alike pause for thought.

above and opposite
To explain the complex intertwining of design, politics, and finance in federal efforts to remake cities, CUP designed a series of Urban Renewal activity tables and exhibition boards. Each table was made in the shape of the relevant Urban Renewal area and held a series of games and informational devices.

right
From 1949 through 1974 Urban Renewal programs drastically reshaped built landscapes across the United States.

far right
Futuristic visions provided by architects popularized massive redevelopment, often in the interest of real estate developers.
All photographs CUP

Shrinking Cities

Location_Berlin, Germany
Date_2002–5
Sponsoring organization_Federal Cultural
Foundation of Germany
Project office_Büro Philipp Oswalt
Partner organizations_Leipzig Gallery
of Contemporary Art, Bauhaus Dessau
Foundation, archplus
Budget_Approx. $4.3 million
Website_www.shrinkingcities.com

For decades population experts and urban planners have warned of overcrowding in the world's major cities.

But paradoxically, even as the world's population increases by one million a week, for every city that expands another loses population. Whether slow or sudden, drastic population shifts can lead to a cycle of job loss, poverty, crime, and even greater exoduses. Around the world cities such as Johannesburg, Detroit, and Liverpool are rotting from the inside out. The resulting blight and abandonment can be a cruel reward for those who stay behind, often the elderly or people subsisting on the economic fringes of society.

In planning circles the prevailing wisdom has been that the solution to urban blight is new growth. Throughout the 1970s and 1980s urban revitalization projects—from public housing to subsidized office blocks to stadiums—were built in cities like Manchester and Detroit, only to be torn down 20 years later and replaced with another dose of optimism and capital. How then does one rebuild in a city that doesn't need buildings?

Based in Germany, the interdisciplinary Shrinking Cities project began as a response to the mass exodus from East to West following the fall of the Berlin Wall in 1989. Reunification emptied once-thriving industrial areas such as Halle-Leipzig seemingly overnight. In an attempt to spur investment, Germany poured money into rebuilding the area's infrastructure. The approach failed, leaving the region dotted with "illuminated meadows" where municipalities had laid foundations, power lines, sewage mains, and even streetlights on plots of land that went undeveloped by the private sector.

By the late 1990s the problem had become so acute that Shrinking Cities hosted an international competition to address it. Funded by the Federal Cultural Foundation of Germany, the project focused on four metropolitan areas that had experienced drastic population declines: Halle-Leipzig; Manchester-Liverpool; Ivanovo, Russia; and Detroit.

"The idea of the project is to compare the cultural and urban changes in Germany with other international cases," says Philipp Oswalt, the project director. "Even though the development in Germany is quite shocking, it is not the first or only place where this kind of crisis is taking place."

According to the group's research more than 450 cities with populations above 100,000—59 in the United States alone—have lost 10 percent or more of their populations since 1950. By enlisting teams of architects, artists, journalists, and others to study the problem, the Berlin-based group hoped to learn from the successes and failures of other shrinking cities. "The classic urban-planning tools don't work," Oswalt says. "And there's a lack of ideas or methodology as to how to solve the problem."

Ten projects from each area—ranging from photographic studies of housing to cultural studies of reappropriated commercial buildings—were selected for a traveling exhibition. The show, held in Berlin in 2004, offered a survey of the physical and cultural landscapes of shrinking cities, revealing the often-surprising ways that countercultures can take root in the decaying, abandoned spaces of cities. A second competition, also held in 2004, will result in specific interventions to be built and tested in the former East Germany.

opposite
Smart growth in reverse: A satirical look at the challenges posed by shrinking cities from the bad-architects.network, one of the many architectural, artist, and planning groups to participate in the Shrinking Cities project.
Anders Melsom, Kathrine Nyhus, and Ursula Faix/bad-architects

Shrinking Cities

Penang, Malaysia
Population in 2003: 25,000
Population loss: 35,000 | 58%
Period: 1990–2003
Katja Kruckow

Leninsk-Kuznetski, Russia
Population in 2002: 110,200
Population loss: 24,000 | 18%
Period: 1989–2002
Isolde Brade

Design Like You Give a Damn

Tiflis, Georgia
Population in 2002: 1,081,600
Population loss: 165,400 | 13.3%
Period: 1989–2002
Stefan Thimmel

Beirut, Lebanon
Population in 2000: 1,200,000
Population loss: 300,000 | 25%
Period: 1996–2000
Ali Saad

Cherski, Russia
Population in 2003: 6,000
Population loss: 11,500 | 65%
Period: 1990–2003
Daniel Göler

Karaganda, Kazakhstan
Population in 2002: 412,000
Population loss: 196,600 | 32%
Period 1991–2002
Bernhard Köppen

above right
An abandoned building in Halle-Weißenfels, 2001. Since 1989 Weißenfels has lost one-seventh of its population.
Shrinking Cities Office, Berlin

right
Often spaces in shrinking cities are repurposed in surprising ways. Detroit's Beaux-Arts Michigan Theater is now an office parking lot.
Stan Douglas, courtesy of David Zwirner, New York

Urban
Acupuncture

Location_Curitiba, Brazil
Date_1971–92
Planners_Mayor Jaime Lerner and the
City of Curitiba

*Jaime Lerner, an architect turned politician who has served
three terms as mayor of Curitiba, Brazil, since 1971, is fond
of using the phrase "urban acupuncture" to describe his
approach to urban planning. In this article, excerpted from
"Curitiba: Story of a City," writer Bill McKibben reflects on how
Lerner's small but targeted changes have made the city an
international model of people-friendly planning and design.*

opposite
**The municipal flock of sheep tends the grass in Curitiba's
parkland. Since the 1970s more than 1.5 million trees
have been planted by volunteers and parkland has grown
from five square feet (.46 sq. m) per person to 500 square
feet (46.4 sq. m), despite a tripling of the population.**
David Springbett /Asterisk Productions Ltd.

Excerpt

Curitiba:
Story of a City

Bill McKibben

The first time I went there, I had never
heard of Curitiba. I had no idea that its
bus system was the best on Earth or that
a municipal shepherd and his flock of 30
sheep trimmed the grass in its vast parks.

It was just a midsize Brazilian city where an airline schedule forced
me to spend the night midway through a long South American
reporting trip. Though I flew out the next day as scheduled, I never
forgot the city.

From time to time over the next few years, I would see Curitiba
mentioned in planning magazines or come across a short newspaper
account of it winning various awards from the United Nations.
Its success seemed demographically unlikely. For one thing, it's
relatively poor: the average per capita income is about $2,500. Worse,
a flood of displaced peasants has tripled its population to a million
and a half in the last 25 years. It should resemble a small-scale
version of urban nightmares like São Paulo or Mexico City. But I knew
from my evening's stroll it wasn't like that, and I wondered why.

Maybe an effort to convince myself that a decay in public life was
not inevitable was why I went back to Curitiba to spend some real
time, to see if its charms extended beyond the lovely downtown.
For a month, my wife and baby and I lived in a small apartment
near the city center. Morning after morning I interviewed cops,
merchants, urban foresters, civil engineers, novelists, planners; in
the afternoons, we pushed the stroller across the town, learning the
city's rhythms and habits.

And we decided, with great delight, that Curitiba is among the
world's great cities.

Not for its physical location; there are no beaches, no broad
bridge-spanned rivers. Not in terms of culture or glamour; it's a fairly
provincial place. It has slums: some of the same shantytown favelas
that dominate most Third World cities have sprouted on the edge
of town as the population has rocketed. But even they are different,
hopeful in palpable ways. They are clean. For instance under a city
program, a slumdweller who collects a sack of garbage gets a sack
of food from the city in return. And Curitiba is the classic example of
decent lives helping produce a decent environment.

The main purpos
should be quality
the large majorit
If you don't have
of cities, then you
a generous view

Jaime Lerner, mayor of Curitiba,

e of development
of life for
y of people.

generous view
don't have

f people.

azil

Planning a city's future

Curitiba started out as a backwater town, a good stopover on the way to São Paulo. By 1940, there were 125,000 residents. By 1950, the number had jumped to 180,000, and by 1960, doubled to 361,000. Traffic downtown started to snarl, and the air was growing thick with exhaust. It was clear that the time had come to plan, and, as in almost every other city, planning meant planning for automobiles.

Curitiba's official scheme called for widening the main streets of the city to add more lanes, which would have meant knocking down the turn-of-the-century buildings that lined the downtown, and for building an overpass that would link two of the city's main squares by going over the top of Rua Quinze de Novembro, the main shopping street.

But resistance to the plan was unexpectedly fierce. Opposition was centered in the architecture and planning departments of the local branch of the federal university, and the loudest voice belonged to Jaime Lerner.

Lerner, a native Curitiban who has been the mayor on and off for two decades, organized the drive against the overpass, out of what might almost be called nostalgia. "They were trying to throw away the story of the city," he recalls. And so the story of Curitiba begins with its central street, Rua Quinze—the one that the old plan wanted to obliterate with an overpass. Lerner insisted instead that it should become a pedestrian mall, an emblem of his drive for a human-scale city.

To prevent opposition, he planned carefully. "I told my staff, 'This is like war.' My secretary of public works said the job would take two months. I got him down to one month. 'Maybe one week,' he said, 'but that's final.' I said, 'Let's start Friday night, and we have to finish by Monday morning.' And they did, jackhammering the pavement, putting down cobblestones, erecting streetlights and kiosks, and putting in tens of thousands of flowers."

"It was a horrible risk, he could easily have been fired," said Oswaldo Alves, who helped with the work. But by midday Monday, the same storeowners who had been threatening legal action were petitioning the mayor to extend the mall. The next weekend, when offended members of the local automobile club threatened to reclaim the street by driving their cars down it, Lerner didn't call out the police. Instead, he had city workers lay down strips of paper the length of the mall. When the auto club arrived, its members found dozens of children sitting in the former street painting pictures. The transformation of Curitiba had begun.

But this was not some romantic revolution, a cultural protest of the sort so common in the wake of the '60s and so evanescent. Even this small victory was possible only because Lerner and his architect friends had thought so carefully about the future of the city. They had, among other things, carefully replotted the city's traffic flow, not only to make the downtown function without cars on its main street, but also to direct growth throughout the city. Instead of buying up buildings and tearing them down to widen streets, planners stared at the maps long enough to see that the existing streets would do just fine, as long as they were considered in groups of three parallel avenues. Traffic on the first avenue would flow one way, into town. The middle street would be devoted to buses, driving in dedicated lanes so they could move more quickly. A block over you'd find motorists heading out of town. And more important, once the planners had designated five of these structural axes leading out from the center of town like spokes in a wheel, they could begin to tinker with zoning. Along these main routes, high-density buildings were permitted—the apartments that would hold the commuters eager to ride the buses. Farther from the main roads, density decreases.

"Every city has its hidden designs, old roads, old streetcar ways," says Lerner. "You're not going to invent a new city. Instead, you're doing a strange archeology, trying to enhance the old, hidden design. You can't go wrong if the city is growing along the trail of memory and of transport. Memory is the identity of the city, and transport is the future."

Speedy buses and "space age pods"

Transport in the case of Curitiba means buses. Lerner and his team decided that buses needn't be stuck in traffic. They quickly designed a system of express lanes that sped travel to and from the downtown, and ridership began to take off. Sitting at a bus stop one day, [Lerner also] noticed that the biggest time drag on his fleet was how long it took passengers to climb the stairs and pay the fare. He sketched a plan for a glass "tube station," a bus shelter raised off the ground and with an attendant to collect fares. When the bus pulls in, its doors open like a subway's, and people walk right on. Amazingly, the city doesn't need to subsidize its bus service. The fleet is purchased and owned by private companies; the government assigns routes, sets fares, and pays each contractor by kilometer traveled. For about 30 cents, you can transfer as often as you want; and the whole network turns a profit.

Brilliance on the cheap

Cheapness is one of the three cardinal dictates of Curitiban planning. The city's parks provide the best example of brilliance on the cheap. When Lerner took office for the first time in 1971, the only park in Curitiba was smack downtown; the Passeio Publico, a cozy zoo and playground with a moat for paddleboats and a canopy of old and beautiful ipe trees, which blossom blue in the spring. "In that first term, we wanted to develop a lot of squares and plazas," recalls Alves. "We picked one plot, we built a lot of walls, and we planted a lot of trees. And then we realized this was very expensive."

At the same time, as luck would have it, most Brazilian cities were installing elaborate flood-control projects. Curitiba had federal money to "channelize" the five rivers flowing through town, putting them in concrete viaducts so that they wouldn't flood the city with every heavy summer rain and endanger the buildings starting to spring up in the floodplain.

"The bankers wanted all the rivers enclosed," says Alves; instead, city hall took the same loan and spent it on land. At a number of sites throughout the city, engineers built small dams and backed up the

> ## "[Many cities have] a lot of people who are specialists in proving change is not possible. What I try to explain to them when I go visit is that it takes the same energy to say why something can't be done as to figure out how to do it."
>
> **Jaime Lerner, mayor of Curitiba**

rivers into lakes. Each of these became the center of a park; and if the rains were heavy, the lake might rise a foot or two.

Mostly because of its flood-control scheme, in 20 years even as it tripled in population, the city went from two square feet of green area per inhabitant to more than 150 square feet per inhabitant. And green begets green; land values around the new parks have risen sharply, and with them tax revenues.

The industrial city
In a world of cities, states, and nations increasingly whipsawed by the demands of business, perhaps the best example of the value of Curitiba's independence is its Industrial City. [Instead of offering tax breaks to companies that promised jobs, Lerner] used eminent domain to purchase about 40 square kilometers of land seven miles downwind of downtown. The government put in streets and services, housing and schools, and linked the area solidly to the bus system, building a special workers' line that ran to the biggest poor neighborhood. It also enacted a series of regulations, stiff laws on air and water pollution and on the conservation of green space.

"What we've found is that regulation attracts good industries, the kind we want," says Oswaldo Alves. New businesses [and new jobs] continued to arrive throughout the 1980s, drawn as much by the quality of life for executives fleeing São Paolo as by the ease of doing business with nearby Argentina and Paraguay. By 1990 there were 346 factories in the Industrial City, generating 50,000 direct jobs and 150,000 indirect ones, and 17 percent of the entire state's tax revenue.

Houses with care built in
Though the population continues to grow steadily, it's indeed possible that Curitiba may have broken the back of its social problems. Since many of the people in the favelas have been evicted from their homes in the countryside, a house is an urgent need. Not just a shelter, a house they own, on a lot they own.

Until the mid-1980s, COHAB, Curitiba's public housing program, was fairly standard. But the main source of funding, the national housing bank, collapsed in 1985. At the same time, the demand for housing skyrocketed as the countryside poured into the favelas. The

city bought one of the few large plots of land left within its limits, a swath of farmland bounded by several rivers called Novo Bairro, or New Neighborhood.

We stood on a rise in Novo Bairro and watched as bulldozers scraped and contoured the hills. This cleared field would soon be home to 50,000 families, perhaps 200,000 people. The city was not building the homes, the new landowners were, sometimes with the aid of a city mortgage on a small pile of bricks and windows. And here is the moving part: With your plot of land comes not only a deed and a pair of trees (one fruitbearing and one ornamental), but also an hour downtown with an architect.

One of the first structures to go up at Novo Bairro was a glass tube bus station, linking this enclave to the rest of the city. "Integration" is a word one hears constantly from official Curitiba, another of its mantras. It means knitting together the entire city—rich, poor, and in-between—culturally and economically and physically. Hitoshi Nakamura is the city parks commissioner and one of Lerner's longtime collaborators. "We have to have communication with the people of the slums," he said one day. "If we don't, if they start to feel like favelados, then they will go against the city....If we give them attention, they don't feel abandoned. They feel like citizens."

A place for living
Creating that kind of identity, instilling whatever it is that keeps people from giving their lives over to gangs or to shopping malls, in a city that has tripled in size over two decades is far from easy.

I set out one day on the bike path that ran by my apartment, pushing my baby in her stroller, intent on compiling a sensory catalogue of a little of the urban pleasure Curitiba offered. Curitiba is a true place, a place full of serendipity. It is as alive as any urban district in the world: poems pasted on telephone poles, babies everywhere. The downtown, though a shopping district, is not a money-making machine. It is a habitat, a place for living—the exact and exciting opposite of a mall.

I had to remind myself, wandering through Curitiba, that without the planning and the risky gambles that created the conditions for it to evolve, its center would likely be dangerous and dying. There is one subtle reminder every Saturday morning. Municipal workers roll out huge sheets of paper down the pedestrian mall and set out pots of paint so that hundreds of kids can recreate the sit-in that drove away the cars and launched this pleasure-filled street at the beginning of Lerner's first term.

To learn from Curitiba, the rest of the world would have to break some long-standing habits. And the hardest habit to break, in fact, may be what Lerner calls the "syndrome of tragedy, of feeling like we're terminal patients." Many cities have "a lot of people who are specialists in proving change is not possible. What I try to explain to them when I go visit is that it takes the same energy to say why something can't be done as to figure out how to do it."

Excerpted from Hope, Human, and Wild *by Bill McKibben. © 1995 by Bill McKibben. Reprinted by permission of Little, Brown, and Company, Inc. All rights reserved.*

Selected Bibliography

Charles Abrams, *The Future of Housing*, New York: Harper & Brothers, 1946

Charles Abrams, *Man's Struggle for Shelter in an Urbanizing World*, Cambridge, Mass.: MIT Press, 1966

Acumen Fund, www.acumenfund.org

Aga Khan Award for Architecture, www.akdn.org

American Planning Association, "Individuals Who Influenced Planning Before 1978," www.planning.org/25anniversary/influentials.htm

Scott Anderson, *The Man Who Tried to Save the World*, New York: Random House, 2000

Architects/Designers/Planners for Social Responsibility, www.adpsr.org

Architectes de l'Urgence, www.archi-urgent.com/fr

Architects Without Frontiers, www.architectswithoutfrontiers.com.au

Archnet, www.archnet.org

Ashoka Foundation, www.ashoka.org/global/around_world.cfm

Association for Community Design, www.communitydesign.org

J. Baldwin, *Bucky Works: Buckminster Fuller's Ideas for Today*, New York: John Wiley & Sons, 1996

Barefoot Photographers, *Tilona: Where Tradition and Vision Meet*, New Delhi: Lustre Press, 2000

Anne Beamish, Reinhard Goethert, and Kristin Little, "Upgrading Urban Communities: A Resource for Professionals," School of Architecture and Planning, MIT: Special Interest Group in Urban Settlement, 1999–2001, www.mit.edu/urbanupgrading/upgrading

[unidentified director], *Before and After the Great Earthquake and Fire: Early Films of San Francisco, 1897–1916*, Library of Congress, www.loc.gov

Bryan Bell, ed., *Good Deeds, Good Design: Community Service Through Architecture*, New York: Princeton Architectural Press, 2004

Eugenia Bell, ed., *Shigeru Ban*, New York: Princeton Architectural Press, 2001

Robert Bennefield and Robert Bonnette, *Structural and Occupancy Characteristics of Housing: 2000*, Washington, DC: US Census Bureau, Nov. 2003, www.census.gov/prod/2003pubs/c2kbr-32.pdf

Builders Without Borders, www.builderswithoutborders.org

Building and Social Housing Foundation, www.bshf.org

Carol Burns, "Manufactured Housing: A Double Wide Analysis of Clockwork and Cloudwork," Cambridge, Mass.: Harvard Graduate School of Design, 1997

Carol Burns et al., "Manufactured Housing: A Double Wide Analysis," http://www.gsd.harvard.edu/studios/s97/burns/index.html

Eduardo Cadava and Aaron Levy, eds., *Cities Without Citizens*, Toronto: Coach House Books, 2003

Roberto Chavez, Julie Viloria, and Melanie Zipperer, *Interview with John F. C. Turner*, World Bank forum, Washington, DC, April 2–3, 2002, www.worldbank.org/urban/ forum2002/docs/turner-excerpt.pdf

Mary C. Comerio, *Disaster Hits Home: New Policy for Urban Housing Recovery*, Berkeley: University of California Press, 1998

Nathaniel Corum, *Building One House: A Handbook for Straw Bale Construction*, Bozeman, Mont.: Red Feather Development Group, 2004

Tom Corsellis and Antonella Vitale, "Transitional Settlement: Displaced Populations," 2005, www.shelterproject.org

Frederick Cuny, *Disasters and Development*, Dallas: Intertect Press, 1994

Frederick Cuny and Richard B. Hill, *Famine, Conflict and Response: A Basic Guide*, West Hartford, Conn.: Kumarian Press, 1999

Ian Davis, *Shelter After Disaster*, London: Oxford Polytechnic Press, 1978

Sam Davis, *Designing for the Homeless: Architecture That Works,* London: University of California Press, 2004

Design Corps, www.designcorps.org

Design Matters, www.artcenter.edu/designmatters

Jared Diamond, *Collapse: How Societies Choose to Fail or Succeed*, New York: Viking Penguin, 2005

Andres Duany, Robert Alminana, and Elizabeth Plater-Zyberk, *The New Civic Art: Elements of Town Planning*, New York: Rizzoli, 2003

Thomas A. Dutton and Lian Hurst Mann, *Reconstruction Architecture*, Minneapolis: University of Minnesota Press, 1996

Enterprise Foundation, www.enterprisefoundation.org

Hassan Fathy, *Architecture for the Poor: An Experiment in Rural Egypt*, Chicago: University of Chicago Press, 1973

Federal Emergency Management Agency, www.fema.gov

Philip L. Fradkin, *The Great Earthquake and Firestorms of 1906*, Berkeley: University of California Press, 2005

R. Buckminster Fuller, *Critical Path*, New York: St. Martin's Press, 1981

Belén Garcia, ed., *Earthquake Architecture: New Construction Techniques for Earthquake Disaster Prevention*, New York: Harper Collins, 2000

Thierry Garrel, dir., *Architectures*, 4-DVD series, Strasbourg: Arte, 2003

Sigfried Giedion, *Walter Gropius*, Mineola, NY: Dover Books, 1992

Nabeel Hamdi, *Housing Without Houses: Participation, Flexibility, Enablement*, London: Intermediate Technology Publications, 1995

Hecar Foundation, www.hecarfoundation.org

Jim Howard and Ron Spice, eds., *Plastic Sheeting: Its Use for Emergency Shelter and Other Purposes*, Oxford, England: Oxfam, 1988

Larry Huan, *How to Build a House*, Newtown, Conn.: Taunton Press, 2002

Intermediate Technology Development Group, www.itdg.org

Anthony Jackson, *A Place Called Home: A History of Low-Cost Housing in Manhattan*, Cambridge, Mass.: MIT Press, 1976

Jane Jacobs, *The Death and Life of Great American Cities*, New York: Random House, 1961

Dr. Ravi Jayakaran, *Participatory Poverty Alleviation & Development: A Comprehensive Manual for Development Professionals*, Monrovia, Calif.: World Vision, 2003

Sherry Jones, dir., "The Lost American," *Frontline*, PBS, Oct. 14, 1997, www.pbs.org

Walter Kälin et al., *The Face of Human Rights*, Baden, Switzerland: Lars Müller Publishers, 2004

Joseph F. Kennedy, *Building Without Borders: Sustainable Construction for the Global Village*, Gabriola Island, BC: New Society Publishers, 2004

Douglas Knerr, *Suburban Steel: The Magnificent Failure of the Lustron Corporation, 1945–1951*, Columbus: Ohio State University Press, 2004

Teresa Konechne, dir., *This Black Soil: A Story of Resistance and Rebirth*, Bayview, Va.: Working Hands, 2004

Spiro Kostoff, *The City Assembled: The Elements of Urban Form Through History*, Boston: Little, Brown, 1992

Shaun Robert Krenske, *Housing for Empowerment: More Than Just a Place to Eat, Sleep and Watch TV*, Muncie, Ind.: Ball State University, 2004

Robert Kronenburg, *Portable Architecture*, Burlington, Mass.: Elsevier/Architectural Press, 2003

Laboratorio de Creación Maldeojo, *No Waste*, Pentagram Papers 32, London: Pentagram Design, n.d.

Le Corbusier, *Towards a New Architecture*, Mineola, NY: Dover Books, 1986

Marc Lindenberg and Coralie Bryant, *Going Global: Transforming Relief and Development NGOs*, Bloomfield, Conn.: Kumarian Press, 2001

Donald MacDonald, *Democratic Architecture*, New York: Watson-Guptill, 1996

Rodolfo Machado, ed., *The Favela-Bairro Project: Jorge Mario Jáuregui Architects*, Cambridge, Mass.: Harvard University Graduate School of Design, 2003

Manhattan Institute, www.manhattan-institute.org

Andrew Maskrey, *Disaster Mitigation as a Crisis of Paradigms: Reconstructing After the Alto Mayo Earthquake, Peru*, London: Oxfam, 1989

Kenneth Maxwell, "Lisbon: The Earthquake of 1755 and Urban Recovery Under the Marques de Pombal," in Joan Ockman, ed., *Ground Zero: Case Studies in Urban Reinvention*. Munich: Prestel Verlag, 2002

David Moos and Gail Trechsel, eds., *Samuel Mockbee and the Rural Studio: Community Architecture*, Birmingham, Ala.: Birmingham Museum of Art, 2003

Robert Neuwirth, *Shadow Cities: A Billion Squatters, A New Urban World*, New York and London: Routledge, 2005

Oscar Newman, *Creating Defensible Space*, Washington, DC: US Dept. of Housing and Urban Development, Office of Policy Development and Research, 1996

Peter H. Oberlander and Eva Newbrun, *Houser: The Life and Work of Catherine Bauer*, Vancouver: University of British Columbia Press, 1999

Joan Ockman, ed., *Ground Zero: Case Studies in Urban Reinvention*, Munich: Prestel Verlag, 2002

Charles O'Connor et al., *San Francisco Relief Survey: The Organization and Methods of Relief Used After the Earthquake and Fire of April 18, 1906*, New York: Survey Associates, 1913

Paul Oliver, *Dwellings: The Vernacular House Worldwide*, New York: Phaidon Press, 2003

Philipp Oswalt, *Schrumpfende Städte: Band 1—Internationale Untersuchung*, Ostfildern, Germany: Hatje Cantz Verlag, 2004; English ed., *Shrinking Cities: Vol. 1—International Research*, Germany: Hatje Cantz Verlag, 2005

Sergio Palleroni and Christina Eichbaum Merkelbach, *Studio at Large: Architecture in Service of Global Communities*, Seattle: University of Washington Press, 2004

Martin Pawley, *Future Systems: The Story of Tomorrow*, London: Phaidon Press, 1993

John Peter, *The Oral History of Modern Architecture: Interviews with the Greatest Architects of the Twentieth Century*, New York: Harry N. Abrams, 1994

C. K. Prahalad, *The Fortune at the Bottom of the Pyramid*, Upper Saddle River, NJ: Wharton School Publishing, 2005

Phyllis Richardson, *XS: Big Ideas, Small Buildings*, New York: Universe, 2001

David Rieff, *A Bed for the Night: Humanitarianism in Crisis*, New York: Simon & Schuster, 2002

Sandra Rihs and Daniel Katell, "The Evolution of Slum Clearance Policies in London and Paris," United Nations Centre for Human Settlements (UN-HABITAT), vol. 7, no. 3, Sept. 2001

Robert Rubin, "Jean Prouvé," Yale School of Architecture, 2005, http://www.architecture.yale.edu/tropical_house/essay.htm

Bernard Rudofsky, *Architecture Without Architects*, New York: Museum of Modern Art, 1964

Helena Sandman, ed., *Jigeen Yi Mbooloo*, Helsinki: Finnish Ministry of Foreign Affairs, 2002

Jim Schwab et al., eds., *Planning for Post-Disaster Recovery and Reconstruction*, Chicago: American Planning Association, 1998

shelterproject, www.shelterproject.org

The Sphere Project, *Humanitarian Charter and Minimum Standards in Disaster Response*, Oxford, England: Oxfam, 2004

"The State of the World's Cities Report 2001," The United Nations Centre for Human Settlements (UN-HABITAT), Nairobi, 2002

Bill and Athena Steen and Komatsu Eiko, eds., *Built by Hand: Vernacular Buildings Around the World*, Layton, Ut.: Gibbs Smith, 2003

Robert William Stevens and Habitat for Humanity, eds., *Community Self-Help Housing Manual: Partnership in Action*, Croton-on-Hudson, NY: Intermediate Technology Development Group of North America, 1982

Richard N. Swett and Colleen M. Thornton, *Leadership by Design: Creating an Architecture of Trust*, Atlanta: Greenway Communications, 2005

Richard Sylves and Patricia Jones Kershaw, *Reducing Future Flood Losses: The Role of Human Actions*, Washington, DC: National Academies Press, 2004

"Technical Notes: Special Considerations for Programming in Unstable Situations," UNICEF Programme Division and Office of Emergency, New York, 2001

TreeHugger, www.treehugger.com

John F. C. Turner and Robert Fichter, *Freedom to Build: Dweller Control for the Housing Process*, New York: MacMillan, 1972

Kerry D. Vandell, "FHA Restructuring Proposals: Alternatives and Implications," *Housing Policy Debate*, Fannie Mae Foundation, vol. 6, issue 2, 1995

Agnes Varda, dir., *The Gleaners and I*, New York: Zeitgeist Films, 2000

Ann Varley, ed., *Disasters, Development and Environment*, New York: John Wiley & Sons, 1994

Volunteer Architects' Network, http://van.sfc.keio.ac.jp

David Von Drehle, *Triangle: The Fire That Changed America*, New York: Atlantic Monthly Press, 2003

Lester Walker, *The Tiny Book of Tiny Houses*, Woodstock, NY: Overlook Press, 1993

Peter M. Ward, *Self-Help Housing: A Critique*, London: Mansell, 1982

Col. Garland H. Williams, *Engineering Peace: The Military Role in Postconflict Resolution*, Washington, DC: United States Institute of Peace, 2005

Worldchanging, www.worldchanging.com

World Shelters, www.worldshelters.org

About the Contributors

Cameron Sinclair is the co-founder and executive director of Architecture for Humanity. Sinclair trained as an architect at the University of Westminster and at the Bartlett School of Architecture in London. During his studies Sinclair developed an interest in social, cultural, and humanitarian design. His postgraduate thesis focused on providing shelter to New York's homeless population through sustainable, transitional housing. After completing his studies he moved to New York, where he has worked as a designer and project architect.

Sinclair is a regular guest critic and lecturer at schools and colleges in the United States and abroad. Recently he served as a visiting professor at the Montana State University School of Architecture in Bozeman, and he is currently the Cass Gilbert Visiting Professor at the University of Minnesota College of Architecture and Landscape Architecture. He has spoken at a number of international business and design conferences on sustainable development and postdisaster reconstruction, including guest appearances on BBC World Service, CNN International, and National Public Radio.

In 2003 Sinclair was named a Nice Modernist by *Dwell* magazine. He is a recipient of the ASID Design for Humanity Award and the Lewis Mumford Award for Peace. In 2004 *Fortune* magazine named him as one of the Aspen Seven, seven people changing the world for the better. Most recently Sinclair was one of three winners of the 2006 TED Prize, which honors visionaries from any field who have shown they can "positively impact life on this planet."

Kate Stohr is the co-founder of Architecture for Humanity. She brings a background in daily news writing and an understanding of urban issues, planning, and infrastructure to the organization. As a freelance journalist she has written pieces for a number of national publications including the *New York Times*, *US News & World Report*, the *Christian Science Monitor*, *Dwell*, *Architectural Record*, and *Time Digital*. Her documentary production credits include *Biography* (A&E), *History Detectives* (PBS), *Escape from Death Row* (A&E), and *Night Court* (MSNBC).

Stohr received her bachelor's degree magna cum laude from New York University and her master's degree from the Columbia University Graduate School of Journalism.

Jason Andersen is completing his master's degree in architecture at Montana State University.

Peter Andrews, a recent graduate of Montana State University's masters program in architecture, is an aspiring designer working for Intrinsik Architecture of Bozeman, Montana. Andrews is originally from Bristol, Rhode Island; he received his bachelor's degree from Boston College in 1999 and via a volunteer program made his way out west, where he lives with his wife, Jennifer, and their dog, Fenway.

Cynthia Barton is an architect and writer based in New York, NY, who focuses on the intersection of architecture, the environment, and public health. Her humanitarian design work includes participating in Shigeru Ban's earthquake relief housing project in Gujarat, India. She holds a master's degree in architecture from Yale University, where her thesis focused on architecture for disaster relief operations.

Paul Berger is a British freelance journalist and writer based in Brooklyn, NY. His work has appeared in the *New York Times*, the *Washington Post*, the *New York Press*, the *Gotham Gazette*, *MovieMaker*, and Denmark's *Weekendavisen*. He writes a weblog under the pseudonym Englishman in New York at http://pdberger.com.

Laura Cole is a native of Memphis, Tennessee, and a graduate of the Memphis College of Art. She was an archivist for the photographer William Eggleston and has worked with urban outreach programs in her home city as part of art education programs. Cole sat on the board of directors of the South Main Arts Association and worked as gallery director for the Jack Robinson Gallery of Photography and Glasshouse 383.

Nathan Crane is completing his bachelor's degree in architecture at Montana State University. He is a snowboard instructor at Bridger Bowl.

Kathryn Meg Frankel, a student at the Quinnipiac University School of Law, is interested in the effects of domestic and international legal systems on the built environment, land-use planning, and economic development. She graduated from Cornell University with Distinction in 2005, after studying British history at the University College of London and studying in Spain.

Doug Halsey is a master's-degree candidate in architecture at Montana State University. He began this pursuit in 1987, but took a 12-year break to practice ski-bumming in Jackson Hole. He lives in Bozeman with his patient wife, Susan.

Justin Hollander, AICP, is a Ph.D. candidate in the Edward J. Bloustein School of Planning and Public Policy at Rutgers University. He also works as a community planner with the US General Services Administration. His research interests include shrinking cities, brownfields redevelopment, and the reuse of military bases.

Jennifer Lester attended the Harrington Institute of Interior Design in Chicago, and currently practices commercial interior design in Santa Monica, California. She leads the Santa Monica/Los Angeles Architecture for Humanity chapter.

Laurie Matthews earned her master's degree in architecture from Montana State University. She now lives in San Francisco, where she enjoys playing bluegrass on her fiddle, surfing, and practicing architecture.

Matthew Miller is an aspiring motivational speaker earning his master's degree in architecture at the Cranbrook Academy of Art. During the making of this book, he found himself in Bozeman living in an Airstream trailer down by the river.

Kreg Norgaard is completing his bachelor's degree in architecture at Montana State University. He is a Christian and an avid outdoor enthusiast. He is also a snowboard instructor at Big Sky Ski Resort.

Pages 2–3: photograph by Tal Adler, Yosefa Dresher
Pages 4–5: photograph by Jason Schmidt
Pages 6–7: photograph by Hollmén Reuter Sandman Architects

British Library Cataloguing-in-Publication Data
A catalogue record for this book is available from the British Library

ISBN-978-0-500-34219-0

Printed and bound in China

First published in the United Kingdom in 2006 by Thames & Hudson Ltd, 181A High Holborn, London WC1V 7QX

www.thamesandhudson.com

Reprinted 2007

First published in the United States of America in 2006 by Metropolis Books
Metropolis Books is a joint publishing program of D.A.P./Distributed Art Publishers, Inc.
155 Sixth Avenue, 2nd floor
New York NY 10013
www.artbook.com
and
Metropolis Magazine
61 West 23rd Street, 4th floor
New York NY 10010
www.metropolismag.com

Proceeds from the sale of this book will support the work of Architecture for Humanity.

METROPOLIS
BOOKS